Frankfurt School Perspectives on Globalization, Democracy, and the Law

Routledge Studies in Social and Political Thought

Frankfurt School Perspectives on Globalization, Democracy, and the Law

William E. Scheuerman

Routledge
Taylor & Francis Group
New York London

First published 2008
by Routledge
711 Third Avenue, New York, NY 10017

Simultaneously published in the UK
by Routledge
2 Park Square, Milton Park, Abingdon, Oxon OX14 4RN

Routledge is an imprint of the Taylor & Francis Group, an informa business

First issued in paperback 2012

© 2008 William E. Scheuerman

Typeset in Sabon by IBT Global

Library of Congress Cataloging in Publication Data
Scheuerman, William E., 1965–
Frankfurt school perspectives on globalization, democracy, and the law / by William E. Scheuerman.
p. cm. — (Routledge studies in social and political thought ; 55)
Includes bibliographical references and index.
ISBN 978-0-415-70183-9
1. Frankfurt school of sociology.   2. International economic integration.
3. Globalization.   4. Rule of law.   5. Neumann, Franz L. (Franz Leopold), 1900–1954.   6. Habermas, Jürgen.   I. Title.
HM467.S34 2008
301.0943—dc22   2007032565

ISBN13: 978-0-415-70183-9 (hbk)
ISBN13: 978-0-415-54129-9 (pbk)
ISBN13: 978-0-203-93237-7 (ebk)

Contents

Acknowledgments

While working on this manuscript, I was frequently reminded of two wonderful undergraduate teachers who introduced me to the tradition of Frankfurt-oriented critical theory. As an exchange student in Munich over twenty years ago, I was lucky enough to land in two seminars taught by Gerlinde Schwappach. Despite my bumbling German, much of what I learned there determined the intellectual path I have since taken. At Yale, my undergraduate advisor, the late George Schrader, encouraged me to write a senior thesis on the unfashionable topic of Karl Marx. The thesis was lousy, but the intellectual experience unforgettable.

As a graduate student still fishing around for a dissertation topic in the early 1990s, I was graciously invited by Jürgen Habermas to participate in his biweekly seminar on legal theory at the University of Frankfurt. The experience proved formative in ways that I never would have expected at the time. This volume directly grows out my participation in the seminar and the many things I learned there, especially from Ingeborg Maus and the late Bernhard Peters, a brilliant sociologist who recently died tragically of cancer.

Let me thank the following journals for allowing me to rework some previously published material included here: *Constellations, Political Theory, Praxis International, Ratio Juris,* and *Review of International Political Economy*. Sections of Chapters 5 and 7 appeared previously in books published by Blackwell's and Oxford University Press, respectively.

Introduction
Why the Frankfurt School?

Many books already describe myriad ways in which the ongoing process of globalization raises profound questions for democracy and the rule of law. The questions, of course, are both empirical and normative. How is globalization altering existing democratic practices and institutions, and what form should democracy take in response to globalization? What is the actual impact of globalization on those legal devices we associate with the ideal of the rule of law, and what type of rule of law should we try to achieve in the context of globalization? The attempt to tackle such questions has been at the very top of the scholarly agenda now for well over a decade.

What makes this book different? Despite the many criticisms leveled against its ideas below, the creative and wide-ranging contributions of the Frankfurt School tradition of critical theory proffer an unsurpassed starting point for making sense of the momentous political and legal transformations we are experiencing at the start of a new century. If we are to understand how globalization transforms existing political and legal institutions, and also successfully confront the difficult normative questions raised by such transformations, the Frankfurt School offers a veritable gold mine of intellectual resources.[1]

More specifically, the neglected writings of the first-generation Frankfurt School political and legal theorist, Franz L. Neumann, brilliantly illuminate many of the most surprising *legal* consequences of economic globalization. The greatest second-generation Frankfurt School critical theorist, Jürgen Habermas, offers a superb theoretical basis for rethinking *democratic politics* in our globalizing age. Part I critically but constructively engages with Neumann's legal theory in order to begin comprehending how globalization is presently affecting the rule of law. Part II then engages no less critically and constructively with Habermas' recent contributions to political and legal theory for the purpose of formulating a normatively as well as empirically sound political and legal response to globalization. In particular, the prospects of supranational democracy, conceived along Habermasian lines, are carefully considered.

In short, the first part of the book deals primarily with Neumann's usefulness as a basis for grappling with the globalization of law; the second part chiefly reflects on Habermas' theoretical prowess as a launching pad for making sense of globalization and democracy. Because democracy and the rule of law are mutually dependent and interrelated in crucial ways, however, inevitably there is some thematic and conceptual overlap between the two parts.

No easy answers to the tough normative and institutional questions posed by globalization are provided. Those readers who are looking for institutional blueprints will be disappointed. Many of my main claims are ultimately critical and negative in character. According to the argument developed below, Neumann was basically right to predict that some of the fundaments of the rule of law as classically conceived would be threatened with the prospect of decay and deterioration in the context of the massive social and economic transformations wrought by contemporary capitalism. Although I make some modest constructive suggestions, I am not always sure exactly what we should do about the more alarming implications of this trend.[2] As a first step, we need to allow that structural attributes of neo-liberal economic globalization, as Neumann would have predicted, engender deep impediments to the establishment of the rule of law, despite the fact that most scholars on both the left and right tend to expect otherwise. If we interpret the rule of law as requiring that state action should rest on norms that are relatively clear, general, public, and prospective, the emerging legal substructure of economic globalization suffers from a paucity of rule of law qualities. Neumann's heretical legal views, at the very least, force us to deal head-on with the tough questions that those of us committed to securing the rule of law must tackle.

Similarly, I admire Habermas' recent political and legal scholarship and believe, though I cannot fully defend this point here, it remains in many respects unequalled. If we are to revitalize democratic politics in a world where it too often seems fragile, we must turn to Habermas for illumination. Habermas and his followers formulate many powerful ideas about how and why we must work to deepen democracy beyond the contours of the existing nation-state. In the final analysis, however, I am ultimately skeptical of their efforts—including Habermas'—to build on his theory of deliberative democracy for the purposes of extending democracy to the supranational level.[3]

The following essays represent distinct but closely interconnected attempts to think *with* and sometimes *against* the Frankfurt School's two most significant political and legal theorists about the dilemmas posed by globalization to democracy and the rule of law. Even though their immediate implications may seem negative and unavoidably incomplete, I offer them as a stepping-stone to the systematic critical theory of globalization we very much need today.[4]

Most readers will not be surprised to learn that much of what follows constitutes a critical engagement with Habermas, perhaps the greatest representative of Frankfurt School critical theory in either its first or second generation and one of the leading intellectual figures on the planet today. Habermas, whose work has exerted an astonishing influence on a vast range of seemingly disparate intellectual fields, deservedly remains a widely respected and even somewhat fashionable figure in the academy. Even for those who disagree vehemently with him, Habermas' writings offer a challenge which any serious politically minded intellectual ignores at his or her risk. In contrast, some readers may be surprised and even startled by my recourse to Franz L. Neumann, the resident political and legal theorist of the early Frankfurt School, who never gained the same renown as Theodor Adorno, Erich Fromm, Max Horkheimer, or Herbert Marcuse, his colleagues at the Institute for Social Research in the 1930s and early 1940s.

Who was Franz L. Neumann? Neumann was born in Kattowitz in eastern Prussia in 1900 and died in Switzerland in 1954. His most important academic training took place at the University of Frankfurt under the tutelage of Weimar Germany's most famous labor lawyer, Hugo Sinzheimer. Following the completion of his studies at Frankfurt, in 1928 Neumann began a career in Berlin as a left-wing labor lawyer and political activist affiliated with the German Social Democratic Party. As a prominent socialist and as a Jew, Neumann was forced to leave Germany in 1933. He then spent a number of years at the London School of Economics with Harold Laski between 1933 and 1936, where he earned a second doctorate in the field of political theory, before making his way to the United States, garnering an affiliation with the Institute for Social Research (or "Frankfurt School," because it was originally based in Frankfurt, Germany before it was forced into exile by the Nazis). Along with Otto Kirchheimer, Neumann served as the Institute's political and legal theorist before joining the Office of Strategic Services in 1942 as coordinator for research on Germany and chief of research for the war crimes unit. In recent years, there has been a modest renaissance of interest in Neumann; some of the more engaging recent scholarship on the Frankfurt School implies that he played a greater role in its internal debates and squabbles than most scholars previously acknowledged.[5] In 1948, Neumann became a professor of public law and political theory at Columbia University.

Neumann's intellectual and professional career can be conveniently divided into three main periods. First, his early Weimar writings outlined a legalistic social democratic agenda for far-reaching political and economic reform. Interpreting Weimar as situated "between capitalism and socialism," Neumann, following Sinzheimer, relied on the progressive social reform clauses of the Weimar Constitution (Article 165, for example, called on workers and capital jointly to manage the economy) in order to defend the welfare state, advance the cause of labor, and prepare the way for a transition to democratic socialism. A central theme in his early writings was a preoccupation with the dangers of excessive judicial and administrative discretion: the Weimar judiciary and state bureaucracy remained firmly in the hands of antidemocratic and socially reactionary forces hostile to the labor movement. Following his mentor Sinzheimer, Neumann struggled to defend a novel and in many respects pathbreaking model of labor law, foreshadowing the ambitious visions of workplace democracy and legal self-regulation that European socialists and social democrats tried to advance after World War II. From the perspective of defenders of the Weimar social status quo, as well as from the standpoint of conservative jurists hostile to creative forms of state regulation, Neumann's ideas were always anathema. Yet his radical social and legal reformism was always wedded to a somewhat conventional brand of jurisprudence. In his view, the classical rule of law virtues of generality, clarity, publicity, prospectiveness, and stability represent universal accomplishments, which any acceptable left-wing alternative to the political and legal status quo must undertake to realize. Only norms of this type provide a minimum of security and predictability in legal decision making, help realize equality before the law, make power holders accountable, and promote the ideal of fair notice. They offer a necessary, albeit insufficient, contribution to both private and public liberty.[6] In Neumann's view, social democracy would have to maintain fidelity to the rule of law, even if it necessarily did so in a manner dramatically at odds with classical nineteenth-century liberalism.

While in exile in the 1930s and early 1940s, Neumann transformed this relatively narrow preoccupation with judicial and administrative discretion in the context of labor law into a broader argument about the decline of the rule of law in contemporary capitalism. Heavily influenced by Karl Marx, Max Weber, and Karl Renner, the central argument of *The Rule of Law: Political Theory and the Legal System in Modern Society* (1936),[7] *Behemoth: The Structure and Practice of National Socialism* (1944),[8] as well as many essays from the 1930s collected in the posthumous *Democratic and Authoritarian State* (1957),[9] was that the transition from competitive or classical liberal capitalism to contemporary monopoly or organized capitalism, in which large corporations gained a quasi-oligopolistic status and many traditional "free" market functions declined, inexorably undermined clarity, generality, publicity, and stability in the law. Rather than celebrating this legal trend, Neumann lamented it, arguing that the rule of law possessed an "ethical moment" transcending the sociological functions it had performed in classical capitalism.[10] Having experienced at close hand what the dismantlement of the rule of law typically meant (Neumann was detained by the Gestapo, and friends and family were murdered in Nazi death camps), he always maintained a refreshingly clear-headed assessment of its abiding strengths. Neumann thus broke decisively with orthodox Marxist critics of the rule of law who saw it as little more than a normatively superfluous legal "superstructure" for capitalism. In the final analysis, Neumann's own heavily Marxist ideas about the economic operations of contemporary capitalism are probably less original than the implications he drew from them for legal analysis. His Weimar writings had similarly remarked on the process by which vague and open-ended legal clauses, typically facilitating judicial and bureaucratic discretion, increasingly took on a prominent place within labor law. In the updated version of the argument, Neumann insisted in the 1930s and 1940s that the ongoing disintegration of general law, as observed by scholars on both the left and right since at least Max Weber, rested on a broader social and economic transition. As the social presuppositions of the modern rule of law in competitive capitalism decayed, large corporations increasingly tended to favor legal regulations having a vague and open-ended character. Given their power advantages vis-a-vis other social actors, vagueness and ambiguity in the law were best exploited by them, and loopholes in parliamentary legislation permitted privileged economic actors to subvert the intent of the lawmaker. Nazi Germany, which Neumann interpreted as embodying an especially virulent form of monopoly capitalism as well as the complete abandonment of the rule of law, was seen as representing a dire warning about the perils posed by contemporary capitalism to modern law's greatest accomplishments.

It is this second period in Neumann's career that has gained him the most attention, primarily from political and legal scholars on the left. For my purposes in this book, two of its features are especially valuable. First, Neumann's skepticism about the existence of a necessary fit or "elective affinity" between contemporary capitalism and the rule of law turns out to prove astonishingly prescient. A careful look at those forms of emerging legal regulation most closely related to economic globalization presents a surprising confirmation of Neumann's predictions. Even though academics, policymakers, and media pundits continue to envision the rule of law and capitalism as representing two sides of the same coin, Neumann was justified in his mistrust of the orthodox view—expressed with remarkable regularity in modern thought from John Locke to Friedrich Hayek—that capitalism typically requires a legal system based on clear, general, public, and stable norms. To be sure, globalizing capitalism is making use of a panoply of legal and law-like devices and institutions. However, many of them fail to instantiate a normatively sufficient dose of rule of law virtues: Economic globalization presupposes a legal substructure lacking in normatively desirable legal qualities.[11] Second, Neumann provides a refreshing corrective to a surprisingly widespread tendency on the contemporary academic left to discount the normative virtues of a traditional model of the rule of law. In sharp contrast to those who tend to see the rule of law as an impediment to realizing a more just and decent society, Neumann's perspective instead stresses the striking ways in which it is typically the politically and economically privileged who benefit most from the dismantlement of the rule of law. Of course, any decent society will need much more than the rudiments of the rule of law. Nonetheless, it remains hard to imagine how any society could achieve plentiful freedom or equality without them. Far too often, however, contemporary left-wing legal scholarship simply reproduces orthodox Marxism's kneejerk anti-legalism, even if it otherwise seems proudly post-Marxist: Marxist social and economic analysis goes out the window, but its instinctive hostility to the rule of law remains. Paradoxically perhaps, it was the Marxist-inspired Neumann who early on recognized the dangers of extreme varieties of anti-legalism.[12]

The final stage of Neumann's career is perhaps both the most interesting and least satisfying. After World War II, he remained true to his social democratic sympathies even as he distanced himself from classical Marxism. Throughout his career, Neumann had maintained a (for the Marxist tradition, quite unusual) faith in the virtues of the rule of law. In his late writings, as collected in *Democratic and Authoritarian State*, his sympathy for the tradition of liberal democratic political and legal thought took on even greater significance. Unfortunately, the mature Neumann's attempt to marry political liberalism with a critical view of contemporary social and economic trends was never consummated: His career was cut short by a fatal automobile accident in Switzerland. According to astute recent commentators, his late work was unfinished and politically defensive.[13]

Each of these three intellectual stages plays a decisive role in the main arguments developed in this volume. Let me explain why.

In my detailed exegesis and critical discussion of Jürgen Habermas' recent political and legal theory in Part II of this volume, I highlight its deep internal intellectual and political tensions. As I argue in Chapter 5, Habermas' brilliant magnum opus in political and legal theory, *Between Facts and Norms: Contributions Towards A Discourse Theory of Law and Democracy* (1992),[14] oscillates between a radical and a far more cautious and perhaps even institutionally conservative vision of democratic politics. Unfortunately, ambiguities at the heart of Habermas' project can be traced to a series of fundamental conceptual and analytic weaknesses. Chapter 6 then suggests that those tensions also bedevil his oftentimes fascinating proposals to update legal regulation in accord with contemporary social and economic exigencies, along the lines of what he has described as a "proceduralist" paradigm of law. Habermas is to be praised for thinking hard about legal reform. Yet the proceduralist model is ultimately less coherent than he recognizes. On one reading, it opens the door to useful reforms; on an equally plausible reading, it offers little more than a band-aid for the pathologies of contemporary law.

As his disciples have sought to apply Habermas' ideas to many of the challenges posed by globalization to democratic theory, Chapter 7 argues, they also inevitably find themselves hounded by similar conceptual and political tensions. Here again, we find a curious oscillation between radical (and probably unrealizable) models of transnational deliberative democracy and quite cautious models. The conceptual juxtaposition of deliberation to participation is overstated: democratic citizenship occasionally fades into the background in what at least purports to be a vision of radical democracy.

Perhaps no writer on globalization and democracy has garnered as much attention as David Held and his illuminating proposal, in part inspired by Habermas' political theory, to extend democracy to the supranational sphere by means of what he has dubbed "cosmopolitan democracy." However, Chapter 8 argues that Held and his intellectual allies would also do well to heed one of Neumann's insights: Social democracy without the rule of law is a misnomer at best, and at worst it is a recipe for illegitimate and potentially tyrannical power. In light of the awesome power that would necessarily accrue to any transnational or cosmopolitan state, we will need to make sure that experiments in transnational democracy realize far-reaching classical legal virtues. Held persuasively shows why democracy should be extended to the supranational level. Yet his model of what he describes as "democratic public law" rests on a highly problematic model of the rule of law, which threatens to undermine cosmopolitan democracy's admirable normative aspirations.

In Chapter 9, Habermas' own rapidly burgeoning body of recent writings on globalization and democracy is carefully examined. Although Habermas' ideas about the prospects of transnational democracy have undergone major innovations in recent years, and despite their undeniable advantages, they ultimately fail to resolve the internal analytic and political tensions from which both his recent work and that of his followers suffers.

But what does this have to do with Franz Neumann? Even though Neumann plays a seemingly insignificant role in Habermas' recent work in political and legal theory, it may be more than merely coincidental that similar tensions characterized his late or final stage. Like the mature Neumann, Habermas is now for many sound reasons deeply committed to deepening and revitalizing an identifiably liberal democratic political theory. Echoing the late Neumann, he has distanced himself from the more radical and overtly Marxist inclinations of his youth. Even more so than in the case of Neumann's final writings, the theoretical results are provocative and arresting. Nonetheless, it is hard to avoid the conclusion that Habermas' recent political theory, like Neumann's writings from the late 1940s and early 1950s, is politically and conceptually tension-ridden. An admirable quest to integrate the great achievements of political liberalism into critical theory results, as it did in Neumann's mature work, in an insufficiently critical analysis of contemporary society. To be sure, these tensions manifest themselves at a vastly more impressive theoretical level than in Neumann's more modest late writings. Yet they exist nonetheless.

Most of Part I is inspired by the second or crucial middle period in Neumann's intellectual career. Even though Neumann was obviously unfamiliar with many of the most striking features of globalization, Chapters 1 and 2 argue, his theoretical reflections from the 1930s and 1940s provide a commanding basis for examining the nexus between economic globalization and the rule of law. As Neumann would have predicted, classical rule of law virtues are less common than contemporary market ideologues tend to claim in precisely those arenas of economic life where globalization has been most intense. When we examine international business arbitration, the *Lex*

Mercatoria, regulation of the international banking and financial system, international corporate codes of conduct, the WTO, as well as many related areas of identifiably global economic regulation, we see that legal decision making suffers from substantial irregularity and unpredictability. The ongoing process of economic globalization sheds light on a number of the main inadequacies of Neumann's political and legal theory. Neumann's vision of the relationship between capitalism and law, for example, too often was overly mechanistic. Nonetheless, as Neumann's theory accurately predicted, antiformal trends in global economic regulation not only tend to benefit the most privileged segments of the business community, but there is also ample evidence that privileged economic interests often resist attempts to develop clear, public, and relatively general modes of legal regulation.

Of course, global business regulation is an immensely complex and relatively fluid field. My brief discussion in this volume can hardly be described as the final word. In addition, some evidence suggests that select legal arenas are undergoing a formalization of law along precisely those lines that the orthodox view of the necessary dependence of capitalism on the rule of law would have predicted.[15] Nonetheless, Neumann's contrarian position deserves a fair hearing: The empirical evidence in his favor is simply too strong. Even if his position turns out to be overstated, it still offers a useful corrective to naïve and deeply ideological views about a necessary fit or "elective affinity" between capitalism and the rule of law.

Chapter 4 deepens the discussion of Neumann's legal ideas, showing why Habermas, at least prior to the publication of his landmark *Between Facts and Norms*, posited claims about legal development and the rule of law vulnerable to Neumann's criticisms. In his writings on law in *Theory of Communicative Action* (1981)[16] and the *Tanner Lectures* he gave at Harvard in 1987, for example, he tended to misdiagnose the pathologies of recent legal development and simultaneously downplay the seriousness of some of the dilemmas generated by the lack of classical rule of law virtues in many spheres of law. Even though *Between Facts and Norms* goes some way towards correcting these weaknesses, his mature legal views—and especially his proposed proceduralist legal paradigm—still occasionally reproduce his earlier, somewhat dismissive view of classical formal law. Serving as a conceptual bridge to the discussion in Part II, Chapter 4 simultaneously stresses the relative strengths of Habermas' contributions to democratic theory.

Chapter 3 relates most closely to Neumann's early or Weimar-era intellectual stage as a practicing labor lawyer. As Neumann anticipated, antiformal trends are commonplace in that legal arena, labor regulation, where social conflict proves especially intense. For those of us committed to mitigating the harshest inequalities of present-day capitalism, perhaps no political goal is more pressing than the establishment of a regime of global labor regulation capable of effectively protecting labor rights beyond the increasingly cramped confines of the nation-state. Not surprisingly, left-oriented political activists and their allies are pushing for the creation of transnational labor standards. The evidence collected in Chapter 3, however, suggests that transnational labor standards are only likely to serve the interests of labor if they instantiate a substantial dose of traditional legal virtues. As in many other areas of existing global economic regulation, a paucity of classical legal virtues again plays directly into the hands of the most powerful political and economic interests. As Neumann similarly observed in the Weimar context, antiformal trends in labor regulation too often benefit socially privileged actors best situated to exploit ambiguous, private, and relatively informal legal mechanisms.

So why then the Frankfurt School? Its innovative theoretical insights, from both its first and second generation representatives, are essential to a critical theory of globalizing capitalism. Without the Frankfurt School, we simply cannot respond appropriately to the challenges of globalization.

Part I

Franz L. Neumann, Globalization, and the Rule of Law

1 Franz Neumann
Legal Theorist of Globalization?

Few facets of the Frankfurt School theorist Franz L. Neumann's political and legal theory are as unfashionable today as his neo-Marxist account of the decline of classical formal law. Even sympathetic commentators concede that Neumann relied on an idealized and probably unrealistic portrayal of classical liberal jurisprudence, as well as an excessively functionalist interpretation of legal development.[1] At times, Neumann indeed stressed the inexorable decay of modern law in a manner that obfuscates its key features at least as much as it helps make sense of them. Although Neumann sought to overcome the normative deficits of traditional left-wing legal theory by ascribing an "ethical function" to the rule of law, even this facet of his theory always remained underdeveloped. Neumann never fully liberated himself from a Weberian-Marxist intellectual background that ultimately minimizes law's immanent normative—and, more specifically, democratic—qualities.

Nonetheless, I would like to suggest that precisely those features of Neumann's thinking most criticized by contemporary commentators represent a surprisingly rich starting point for understanding key contemporary legal trends. My aim is not to resurrect Neumann's Marxism. It is striking, however, that Neumann's brilliant account of the economic origins of the "deformalization" of law anticipates core legal attributes of the ongoing process of globalization. Furthermore, Neumann's explanation for those trends seems prescient as well. Globalization provides substantial empirical support for Neumann's thesis that the altered context of contemporary economic activity tends to reduces capital's traditional reliance on relatively formalistic modes of law and legal reasoning. Neumann's emphasis on the manner in which the traditional "elective affinity" between capitalism and formal law no longer obtains within contemporary capitalism offers a useful corrective to contemporary neoliberal conceptions of globalization, according to which market-oriented economic reforms and liberal legal reform necessarily represent two sides of the same coin.[2] In contrast to the dominant neoliberal view, globalization suggests that Neumann was justified in suggesting that the relationship between capitalism and law was likely to be complicated by a limited interest among privileged business interests in achieving strict, clear, public, and prospective forms of general law.

I begin with an explanation for why I do not consider it implausible to interpret Neumann as having tackled issues presently grouped under the rubric of globalization. I then revisit his theory of the "functional transformation of law," before suggesting its virtues as a preliminary basis for interpreting ongoing trends in contemporary international economic law. In Chapters 2 and 3, additional evidence is adduced to support Neumann's counterintuitive insight that contemporary capitalism no longer relies as it once did on a panoply of legal institutions and devices long associated with the noble ideal of the "rule of law." Before providing this evidence, however, I suggest ways in which the legal structure of economic globalization shows how Neumann's analysis of legal development might be revised.

NEUMANN ON GLOBALIZATION

The present-day tendency to ignore the ways in which globalization represents a long-term historical process[3] may lead us to miss the fact that features of the ongoing debate about globalization were anticipated by a series of heated disputes about international law in the 1930s and 1940s. Neumann's main intellectual nemesis, and Germany's leading twentieth-century right-wing authoritarian theorist, Carl Schmitt, played a key role in those debates. Neumann's response to Schmitt represents a cautious attempt to grapple with what we nowadays describe as globalization.

Schmitt's infamous theory of the *Grossraum* [greater region] has rightly been criticized, not the least because of its unabashedly Nazi and anti-Semitic connotations.[4] However despicable his political aims, Schmitt's account of the *Grossraum* nonetheless succeeded in anticipating conspicuous features of the present-day debate about globalization. According to Schmitt's analysis, modern technology and contemporary forms of economic organization outstrip the legal and regulatory capacities of the nation-state; the increasingly supranational composition of such activity cries out for no less supranational forms of regionally based political and legal authority. Modern mass media allow political propaganda to reach the homes of foreigners living thousands of miles away at the blink of an eye; contemporary air warfare renders traditional national borders porous to an extent unfathomable to our nineteenth-century predecessors; markets and economic activity increasingly rest on complex cross-border networks. Existing nation-state borders consequently tend ever more to possess limited relevance given the economic and technological possibilities of a globe that seems to shrink in size daily, and the modern nation-state is destined to be jettisoned for a set of "greater regions" better attuned to the functional imperatives of the "space revolution" [*Raumrevolution*] presently revolutionizing the time and space horizons of crucial forms of human activity.[5] In this conceptual context, Schmitt not only viewed Nazi imperialism as a fitting answer to the political challenges of his time, but he also came to argue that a unified European continent (under German control, of course) might provide a better answer to the political and legal challenges at hand than its American and British competitors. Eerily echoing some contemporary right-wing critics of neoliberalism, Schmitt insisted on the need for extensive state intervention within contemporary capitalism and simultaneously insisted that indispensable forms of state coordination of the economy were destined to prove ineffective when undertaken on the global scale. In other words, a Nazi-dominated regionalized European *Grossraum* might succeed in negotiating the regulatory challenges of contemporary social and economic life, whereas the U.S. and British preference for a global free market—for Schmitt, nothing more than a specific form of imperialism derived from certain special traits of U.S. and British experience—risked stumbling on the instabilities of laissez-faire capitalism.[6]

If we bracket the unsightly facets of this account for just a moment, we can see that Schmitt managed to foretell at least three features of the contemporary debate on globalization. First, he rightly identified the nation-state's declining capacity for providing effective regulatory answers to a host of core—and especially economic—problems. Second, he no less accurately began to grapple seriously with dramatic ongoing changes in the space and time horizons of human activity, anticipating many facets of the present exchange among social theorists about the centrality of the process of "time and space compression" for understanding globalization. Well before Zygmunt Bauman, Anthony Giddens, and David Harvey, Schmitt rightly presaged that we could only make sense of the decline of the nation-state by focusing on the manner in which the heightened pace of human activity tends to minimize the significance of distance.[7] Third, he anticipated the increasingly widespread view that the best way to deal with the exigencies of globalization is by building regionally-based political and economic blocs able to protect its members from the vicissitudes of an unstable global neoliberalism under U.S. auspices. Of course, Schmitt would hardly have defended a *social democratic* European Union as a bulwark against the neoliberal "race to the bottom." Yet he might have recognized in the European Union an attempt to come to grips with some of his own worries about what he described as the irresponsible *Planfeindlichkeit* ["hostility to planning"] of Anglo-American models of market capitalism.

From his exile at the Institute for Social Research in New York City, Franz Neumann carefully followed the development of a distinct Nazi discourse on international law, and a substantial portion of his encyclopedic discussion of National Socialism, *Behemoth: The Structure and Practice of National Socialism*, is devoted to providing a detailed survey of it. Unlike contemporary Schmitt apologists, Neumann had no illusions either about Schmitt's significant role in that debate or the disturbing political implications of his reflections on the *Grossraum*. Although legitimately disgusted by Schmitt's manifest enthusiasm for the Nazis, Neumann conceded that the technical and economic facets of Schmitt's defense of the *Grossraum* raised difficult questions even for those hostile to Schmitt's normative and political preferences: "The decline of the state in domestic and international law is not mere ideology; it expresses a major practical trend."[8] In a wide-ranging discussion of Nazi imperialism, Neumann underscored the peculiarities of German development—in particular, Germany's status as a "late-comer" to industrialization—in order to explain the "efficiency and brutality" of Nazi imperialism.[9] In the context of a world divided among "powerful states, each of them committed to protect its own economy," free trade policies increasingly were unfeasible in interwar Europe.[10] Germany's far-reaching dependence on foreign trade thus meant that for Germany to integrate its neighbors' economies advantageously into its own, it could no longer rely on "mere economic exchange . . . [O]nly with the help of political domination that incorporates the states into Germany's currency system" could Germany hope "to trade successfully with them, that is, to transfer from them more labor for less labor."[11] Notwithstanding its distinct developmental traits, however, for Neumann there was no question that Nazi imperialism was integrally linked to structural components of organized (or, as he termed it, "monopoly") capitalism. According to the neo-Marxist argumentation at the core of *Behemoth*, Nazi expansionism represented the most barbaric manifestation of trends latent within contemporary capitalist development. To the extent that those trends were universal, the decline in the significance of national borders evinced by the case of Nazi imperialism suggested that the decay of the core institutions of the nation-state potentially constituted a universal phenomenon as well.

For Neumann, Schmitt's theory of the *Grossraum* offered a particularly onerous answer to the challenges of contemporary capitalist economic development, just as the emergence of Nazism represented a paradigmatic attempt to achieve political and legal forms suitable to the profound pathologies of monopoly capitalism. Neumann offered two responses to the Nazi theoreticians of the *Grossraum* of special interest for the present-day debate on globalization. First, he considered the claim that the achievement of a European *Grossraum* would allow for the unshackling of Germany from the pressures of the world economy wishful but misleading ideological talk. In contrast to a picture of the *Grossraum* as a protective shield against global capitalism, Neumann pointed out that a German-dominated Europe would probably remain dependent on foreign trade (in particular, for raw materials); Germany's real aim was to manipulate its hegemonic position within a regionalized European economic and political bloc in order to gain protection from some imports while using its enhanced powers to gain greater access to foreign markets.[12] Neumann thereby rightly intimated that the relationship between regional blocs and the global economy might take a variety of distinct forms. In the Nazi case (and in Schmitt's corresponding theory of the *Grossraum*), regionalization represented nothing more than an assault on the indispensable achievements of universalistic liberal international law. Its claim to immunize Germany from the global economy in reality constituted a mask for improving the competitive position of Germany's leading capitalist interests within the global economy at large. Neumann's warnings on this point remain relevant today.[13]

Second, Neumann seemed to interpret Schmitt's account of the decline of the nation-state as containing a kernel of truth but as overstated nonetheless. Perhaps he would have accused Schmitt of succumbing to what David Held more recently has aptly described as the "hyper-globalization thesis," according to which the traditional nation-state has now been stripped of any meaningful instruments for stemming the tide of globalization.[14] In any event, Neumann ultimately embraced an institutionally defensive position, according to which the gradual decline of the nation-state "expresses a major practical trend," while nonetheless continuing to insist on the lasting achievements of the Westphalian system of states in the face of the Nazi threat. For Neumann, the modern notion of the legal equality of states guarantees a modicum of predictability in international politics. Schmitt's quest to replace the traditional state system with a narrow set of *Grossräume*—each committed to developing a legal system appropriate to its "distinct" and particularistic ethnic and racial attributes—should remind us of the "progressive" functions of traditional notions of state sovereignty. The nation-state may be experiencing decay, but allowing it to be replaced by an international system that sheds the universalistic impulses of the modern state system would inevitably leave us with a system vastly more brutal than the existing one.[15]

Of course, whether Neumann would continue to insist on the progressive implications of state sovereignty in the context of contemporary attempts to develop liberal-democratic forms of regional authority (for example, the European Union) must remain an open question. At the very least, his skepticism forces those of us committed to developing new forms of transnational political and economic authority to make sure that they offer real gains in terms of self-government and the rule of law.[16]

The Decline of Formal Law

These introductory comments place Neumann's account of the deformalization of classical formal law in a fresh light. Neumann, of course, argued that the decline of classical law was ultimately generated by the economic structure of contemporary monopoly capitalism, and thus represented a more or less universal trend. In monopoly capitalism, Neumann posited, the classical entrepreneur tends to be replaced by cartels, syndicates, and massive bureaucratic firms of which he becomes little more than a functionary; capital and management functions diverge; the classical market declines and state intervention takes on unprecedented significance; many economic risks are eliminated for the largest firms. To the extent that "the antagonisms of capitalism are operating in Germany on a higher and, therefore, a more dangerous level," however, Nazi-dominated Europe provided a more unadulterated example of legal decay than the capitalist liberal democracies.[17] Since nonformal law chiefly serves privileged private interests, for Neumann it was no accident that the legal order most immediately subject to the interests of the oligarchic sectors of capitalism, Nazi Germany, would ultimately abandon classical formal law in a more radical manner than its rivals. The destruction of the rule of law was most complete under Nazism chiefly because of the virtually unchallenged hegemony there of the most privileged capitalist classes, in contrast to the situation in liberal democracy where political and legal devices function to limit the influence of monopoly capital.

I am not interested in defending every facet of Neumann's Marxist interpretation of Nazism here; its weaknesses have been widely documented. Nevertheless, it is telling that Neumann's interpretation of Nazi imperialism at least indirectly suggests a provocative view of the nexus between law and economic globalization. As we saw above, Neumann was well aware of the manner in which Nazi-dominated Europe constituted a developmental response to the nation-state's declining ability to grapple with the technical and economic imperatives of contemporary society: Visions of a Nazi *Grossraum* provided an ominous answer to the growing mismatch between the traditional nation-state and the transnational scope of key technical and economic activities. So Neumann's account of the relationship between the Nazi political economy and the decline of classical formal law, at least implicitly, amounts to suggesting that some features of what we presently describe as "globalization" are likely to exacerbate antiformal trends in the law.

We need not engage in tortured textual exegesis, however, in order to construct an account of the relationship between globalization and legal development on the basis of Neumann's ideas. His most well-known claim is that the transition from a relatively egalitarian mode of classical competitive capitalism to contemporary monopoly capitalism undermines the economic basis for a legal order resting on clear, prospective, and public general norms. These norms constituted the centerpiece of the traditional liberal ideal of the rule of law:

> If the sovereign is permitted to decree individual measures, to arrest this or that one, to confiscate this or that piece of property, then the independence of the judge is extinguished. The judge who has to execute such individual measures becomes a mere policeman. Real independence presupposes the rule of the state through general laws.[18]

In a competitive capitalist economy characterized by a rough equality among economic competitors, generality within the law was likely to be supported by a broad range of economic actors. General law was then not only legally advantageous but also economically sensible because individual legal interventions violated the principle of the equality of competition basic to a classical market economy.[19] In a mode of capitalism dominated by huge corporations possessing quasi-monopolistic status and numerous advantages vis-à-vis small entrepreneurs, general law becomes economically anachronistic:

> In a monopolistically organized system the general law cannot be supreme. If the state is confronted only by a monopoly, it is pointless to regulate this monopoly by general law. In such a case the individual measure is the only appropriate expression of the sovereign power.[20]

The key political question then becomes who possesses the authority to issue such individual measures, and whose interests are served by them. Neumann believed that the democratic welfare-state at least provided a forum in which the interests of subordinate social groups could gain recognition by nontraditional forms of lawmaking; his own commitment to Weimar labor law represented an attempt to establish new modes of post-classical law sensitive to the needs of the German working classes. But the collapse of Weimar indicated to him that such experiments were likely to prove fragile given the special position of monopoly capital within contemporary society. Privileged private interests would try to reduce the regulatory burdens placed on them in the democratic welfare state by pursuing a legal order better suited to their interests. They would tend to prefer legal forms in which their economic advantages might gain unmediated expression. For Neumann, the proliferation of vague, open-ended standards within contemporary law helped pave the way for the democratic welfare state. Nonformal legal forms might easily portend direct domination by large capitalist interests as well, however:

> Legal standards of conduct (blanket clauses) serve the monopolist . . . Not only is rational law unnecessary for him, it is often a fetter upon the full development of his productive forces . . . rational law, after all, serves also to protect the weak. The monopolist can dispense with the help of the courts since his power to command is a satisfactory substitute.[21]

Unless effectively hemmed in by liberal-democratic political institutions along with welfare state devices geared towards providing the working classes with some say in economic affairs, privileged economic interests are likely to make the most use of their de facto power advantages by minimizing meaningful legal constraints on their actions. Easily manipulated legal norms serve this purpose well, as do a host of related legal trends allowing the interests of large capitalists to avoid scrutiny by the ordinary courts of law. According to Neumann, precisely this had occurred within Nazi Germany, and thus Nazism represented a forceful warning to defenders of the rule of law everywhere about the dangers posed to it by contemporary capitalism.

Similarly, Neumann postulated that contract law was inevitably hollowed out by the transition from classical to contemporary capitalism. In early capitalism, the notion of a free contract rested on social as well as juridical postulates, as it presupposed a rough equality between economic competitors, and thus a real possibility that contractual relations might rest on a meaningful degree of reciprocity.[22] Contractual freedom, however, was soon reduced to its narrowly juridical features; even those contracts agreed to by manifestly unequal partners (between large and small businesses, for example) were deemed legitimate as long as a minimal set of formal-legal conditions were met. In this transformed view, contractual freedom was preserved even if the contract at hand managed to strengthen the position of a privileged monopolist. "Even when utilizing the form of the contract, his [that is, the monopolist's] economic power enables him to impose upon consumers and workers all those rules that he deems indispensable and that the other parties are forced to accept if they want to continue to exist."[23] Neumann worried that contemporary trends pointed to the demise of even those minimal protective functions performed by a narrowly juridical conception of contractual liberty, which at the very least guaranteed predictability in legal affairs by striving to provide a clear statement of the rights and obligations of parties to a transaction. For example, labor contracts always obscure structural inequalities between capital and labor. Yet fidelity to classical rule of law virtues (clarity, prospectiveness, and cogency) in labor agreements helps circumscribe capital's potentially awesome prerogatives. In Nazi Germany, Neumann hinted, monopoly capital found itself in the envious position of freeing itself from even such relatively minimal legal restraints. Contracts were increasingly jettisoned in favor of untrammeled forms of discretionary command suited to the preservation of the hegemonic position of key capitalist interests. Even where contracts manage to survive in contemporary society, however, they often rely on vague, open-ended, and moralistic phrases lacking a precisely definable justiciable meaning, thereby opening the door to their manipulation by economic interests in possession of the greatest de facto power.[24]

Now one surely could squabble with many features of this story. Nonetheless, for those familiar with the ongoing debate about globalization and the law, Neumann's diagnosis should seem remarkably prophetic. The most impressive study of global business regulation presently available notes that "the rule of law is not as influential in global regulatory regimes as it is in liberal nations . . . International regulation is not characterized by a rule of law which constrains."[25] The authors of the same study simultaneously point out that "the recurrently most effective actors" in global regulation are presently large corporations.[26] Those legal arenas pivotal to economic globalization are plagued by antiformal trends arguably as far-reaching as those that grabbed Neumann's attention over fifty years ago. Core features of international economic law remain, to a substantial degree, soft law lacking in key classical rule of law virtues. Moreover, substantial evidence suggests that the most privileged sectors of the global economy tend to benefit disproportionately from this scenario. In accordance with the spirit of Neumann's own reflections, let me briefly underscore some crucial antiformal trends in contemporary global economic law. In Chapters 2 and 3 we explore them in greater depth.

First, international business arbitration today is flourishing as a device for resolving disputes in the sphere of transnational transactions. Yet the legal structure of international business arbitration remains flexible and discretionary, characterized by a relative absence of the formal legal virtues of generality, publicity, clarity, and constancy. A vast legal literature now documents the manner in which arbitrators make use of the *Lex Mercatoria* and its indisputably vague clauses. Made up substantially of "general principles" ("usages of faith," "good faith"), the *Lex Mercatoria* provides surprising support for Neumann's prediction that in contemporary capitalism large business firms are likely to dispense with formal law.[27] Although international business arbitration appears to be undergoing a process in which its limited legalistic features have recently been fortified, it remains a system in which confidentiality is far-reaching and recourse to clearly focused legal rules (and standing precedent) circumscribed. Moreover, international business seems to be responding to evidence of a creeping legalization within international business arbitration by seeking alternative dispute resolution devices even more profoundly antiformal in character. Traditional forms of commercial arbitration now face a whole range of competitors (including variants of mediation and conciliation geared towards the business community) promising the speedy resolution of conflicts. A key selling point to global business for these modes of dispute resolution is their limited reliance on traditional formalistic legal devices. Many practitioners of international business arbitration worry that it has become too akin to traditional judicial settings, aggressively demanding a rollback of even the rather limited formalistic attributes of present-day international commercial arbitration.[28]

Similarly, existing forms of transnational regulation for multinational corporations (MNCs) and international finance are weak on traditional rule of law virtues.[29] Thus far, attempts at the transnational level to develop a clear set of strict guidelines for (MNCs) have generally been successfully subverted by large firms promising to develop their own voluntary "codes of conduct." But voluntary corporate codes of conduct are typically vague and open-ended, enforcement procedures are feeble or even nonexistent, and they rarely provide meaningful protection to those (especially employees) affected by them.[30] The dominant trend within transnational banking regulation is to move away from the model of imposing "strict, uniform, quantitative limits on the activities of the banks" in favor of outsourcing important elements of regulatory activity to the banks themselves.[31] Although much can be said in favor of this approach as a way of grappling with the dynamism of the financial sector, it not only raises difficult questions for defenders of the rule of law, but even those sympathetic to it worry about its high price in terms of democratic legitimacy.[32] Neumann's anxieties about the specter of nontraditional modes of law that ultimately represent an abandonment of liberal law's normative bases of legitimacy remain apposite to contemporary debates about self-regulation within global business.

What then of more ambitious intergovernmental attempts—most notably, the World Trade Organization (WTO)—to develop an effective transnational legal basis for the global economy? The WTO's dispute resolution devices hardly conform to traditional models of strict legality despite the WTO's self-advertised loyalty to the "rule of law." The WTO Agreement is "riddled with exceptions—grandfather clauses, waivers, balance-of-payment exceptions," along with vague and open-ended clauses, loopholes, and sectoral exemptions.[33] It provides substantial room for a highly discretionary process of adjudication; many of its decisions are likely to strike even those familiar with the complex norms making up the WTO legal system as controversial. WTO tribunals are confidential as well, and opinions expressed in the tribunal reports remain anonymous. This failing not only represents a violation of the modern ideal of the publicity of law, but it works in conjunction with the WTO's discretionary system of norms to raise the specter of an irregular system of adjudication whose only real commitment is to the core neoliberal beliefs presently driving WTO policy. The fact that WTO judges tend to share neoliberal assumptions hardly proves reassuring on this point either.[34]

The question of which social groups are best served by antiformal trends in present-day global economic law obviously is a complicated matter. But many commentators believe that so far they have proven especially opportune for privileged "global players" best able to exploit a soft legal structure porous to the influence of powerful economic groups.[35] International business arbitration is favored by transnational business in part precisely because it allows them to minimize the impact of other social constituencies on their activities; it represents an updated form of what Judith Shklar described as "arbitration under chamber of commerce auspices" whose very structure is geared towards maximizing the autonomy of businesses party to a dispute.[36] Multinational corporate codes of conduct too often provide a pseudo-legalistic window-dressing for the mistreatment of labor in poor countries; new modes of regulation within international finance arguably have helped rid the international financial system of its most blatant pathologies, yet consumers and others influenced by international finance have exercised little say over the emerging regulatory system. In any event, no one is plausibly arguing that existing global economic law is working to alleviate the injustices of contemporary capitalism or reducing the vast gap separating the rich from the poor on our ever more polarized planet.

The ongoing globalization of capitalism has also spawned a number of ambitious attempts to harmonize contract law in order to facilitate cross-border transactions. In this vein, the UN Commission on International Trade Law (UNICTRAL), International Institute for the Unification of

Private Law (Unidroit), and the Commission on European Contract Law have tried to reform of contract law so as to make it better suited to the dictates of a global economy. Transnational economic activity continues to require a network of enforceable contracts; Neumann's overstated Nazi-era expectation that contracts might disintegrate altogether remains unfulfilled. Nonetheless, substantial evidence confirms his prediction that fundamental changes in the nature of contemporary capitalism—in this case, the transition to an increasingly transnational economy—would likely contribute to the further deformalization of contract law.

In the legal literature on globalization and contract law, there is now a virtually universal consensus that transnational exchanges must be free of the excessively "static" as well as "inflexible and irrevocable legal remedies" presumably characteristic of earlier forms of contract law.[37] In this view, heightened possibilities for discretionary judicial activity are called for, and reliance on just those "general principles" whose implications Neumann considered so ambivalent is now identified as a central device for making discretion possible. Indeed, one object of Neumann's own anxieties, section 242 ("in good faith") of the German Civil Code, features strongly in the Unidroit *Principles of International Commercial Contracts* and the *Principles of European Contract Law* prepared by the European Commission on Contract Law.[38] A pervasive theme in the burgeoning legal literature on transnational contracts is the need for "dynamism" within contracts, along with growing skepticism concerning the virtues of traditional forms of codification, "many of us are becoming increasingly sensitive to the extent that codification of commercial law has not proven to be the most desirable goal."[39] Legal practitioners are no less unambiguous when describing the motivating force behind the general movement towards increased dependence on open-ended principles within transnational contracts: The changing contours of contract law are "primarily driven by business practice, not the grand theoretical structures of legal scholars" too often influenced by (allegedly) anachronistic and formalistic legal notions.[40] Commercial practice should directly shape contracts, and business practice in the global economy increasingly requires elasticity in the law:

> [i]f a contract appears insufficiently explicit to furnish a direct statement of the parties' rights, duties, powers, and liberties, then the arbitrators will construct it and fill the gaps in it by recourse to their own knowledge of how commerce works in practice, and how commercial men [sic] in the relevant field express themselves . . . What is important is the arbitrator should keep constantly in mind that he is concerned with international commerce, with all the breadth of horizon, flexibility, and practicality of approach which that demands.[41]

Of course, this trend hardly confirms Neumann's claim that antiformal trends in contract law are of greatest benefit to the most privileged segments of the capitalist economy. In fact, Neumann's own account of the transformation of competitive into monopoly capitalism fails to offer a sufficient conceptual framework for making sense of the process of economic globalization. The economic developments at hand are far more multifaceted and complex; some of Neumann's economic claims (for example, concerning the internal structure of the firm) are now badly in need of revision. If we keep in mind, however, that firms operating on the global level (and thus most likely to make use of the emerging contractual forms described here) more likely than not to belong to the most privileged sector of the capitalist economy, Neumann's claim that the largest and most powerful capitalist interests are likely to seek nonformal modes of law seems anything but outdated.

Law in High-Speed Capitalism

Neumann believed that powerful capitalist interests tried to escape the confines of Weimar's cautious quest to develop the outlines of the modern regulatory and welfare state by irresponsibly opting to support fascist dictatorship. As noted earlier, he considered the decline of classical formal law for the most part irreversible; which social interests could successfully harness antiformal legal trends hence became the key political question. In the Weimar Republic, socially subordinate groups possessed a real chance to influence legislation. The Nazis promised to eliminate that influence; key business interests thus were willing to take their chances with the Nazis.[42] Even though it would be manifestly absurd to equate fascist dictatorship with globalization, it might be useful to apply elements of Neumann's analysis to contemporary legal development. Economic globalization rests on a variety of distinct (technological, political, as well as immanently economic) sources. Nonetheless, it is striking that one of its more striking facets consists of the attempt to release key forms of legal decision-making authority (international arbitration, for example, or the WTO) from the direct oversight of the regulatory and welfare states that came to determine the contours of nationally based polities in significant segments of the developed world in the postwar era. Whatever its flaws, nation-state based liberal democracy provided relatively substantial possibilities for social groups historically excluded from the political process to shape both legislation and the administration of justice in accordance with their needs. From the perspective of Neumann's analysis, it should come as no surprise that privileged business interests ultimately sought to throw off the burdens of the postwar regulatory and welfare states; globalization, in part, represents one result of that backlash. David Harvey's fascinating analysis of the manner in which the economic crisis of the 1970s played a powerful role in initiating the economic changes that we now associate with globalization accords disturbingly well with elements of Neumann's own analysis of how the Great Depression generated new economic and political strategies within German industry. In both cases, a severe crisis not only forced key business groups into an increasingly hostile political stance vis-à-vis the achievements of the regulatory and welfare state, but also unleashed a series of economic innovations (Harvey talks of "post-fordism") ultimately subversive of those achievements as well.[43]

The precise nature of the relationship between traditional forms of national authority and the emerging modes of transnational business regulation described above is a complicated matter that would take us beyond the scope of this essay. Yet the ascent of international business arbitration, proliferation of soft law and self-regulation, and establishment of the WTO arguably constitute ambitious attempts to minimize the potential impact of the democratic nation-state over the supervision of globally operating businesses. Nonformal modes of law were obviously commonplace in the postwar welfare and regulatory states. Yet they were often overseen by political and legal bodies resting on liberal democratic procedures and committed to the ideals of the regulatory and welfare state. Whatever the legal ills of the regulatory and welfare state from the standpoint of traditional jurisprudence, they often represented a worthwhile trade-off in the quest to assure democratic legitimacy and social stability. The same cannot be said about most present-day forms of transnational business regulation. In order to free itself from what Carl Schmitt angrily described as the regulatory burdens of the "weak quantitative total state," business groups in the 1930s pursued a risky—and occasionally self-destructive—alliance with right-wing dictatorship. At the beginning of the twenty-first century, powerful economic interests may no longer need the help of a right-wing dictatorship in order to ward off challenges from below. Instead, they can preach the virtues of the "rule of law," while in fact establishing dispute resolution devices for the global economy that perpetrate their privileged position and make a mockery of traditional rule of law virtues. Where economic and technological innovations permit large-scale business to reduce the de facto and de jure significance of national regulation while simultaneously opting for an alternative supranational regulatory system lacking the minimal preconditions of formal legality (generality, clarity, prospectiveness, and publicity), we risk abandoning precisely those features of liberal democracy that allowed it to rein in privileged economic interests.

Many criticisms have rightly been directed at Neumann. My argument suggests two additional ones. First, like his colleagues in the Frankfurt School, Neumann was too quick to see the transition from liberal democracy to fascism as portending western civilization's general course of development. According to the argument developed here, he was right to worry about the "elective affinity" between contemporary capitalism and antiformal legal trends, even if many details of his account today must be considered misleading and even incorrect. But he was clearly wrong to imply that the elective affinity between contemporary capitalism and antiformal legal trends might only realize itself fully within fascist dictatorship; the present-day course of globalization suggests that alternative developmental paths cohere with the basic outlines of this trend as well. At the same time, even here Neumann still provides useful guidance. An immediate implication of his analysis is that one of the great political questions of our times is likely to concern the possibility of subjecting antiformal trends in international economic law to democratic and social purposes. Indeed, this is one of the key questions confronting participants in the ongoing debate about the prospects of transnational democracy and, on an even more immediate political level, the possibility of a democratic and socially sensitive European Union.

Second, Neumann's tendency to underscore the manner in which vague and open-ended legal clauses directly serve privileged economic interests means that his understanding of the nexus between capitalism and deformalized law too often took an overly mechanistic form. The legal literature on globalization hints at a more complex picture. To be sure, substantial evidence confirms Neumann's expectation that large firms often prefer antiformal law for reasons familiar to anyone who has spent time at the children's playground: When the rules of the game are vague or unclear, it is often the biggest boys (and sometimes girls) who succeed in enforcing their interpretation on the other players. This is only the tip of the iceberg, however. Transnational economic processes are characterized by high levels of simultaneity and instantaneousness, chiefly because new technologies (rapid-fire computerized economic transactions, for example) are playing a pivotal role in the global economy. The globalization of financial markets would be unimaginable without the dramatic recent developments in information technology, as would numerous parallel developments among major "global players." Subcontracting, outsourcing, "small batch" and short production runs, and "just in time" inventory flows and delivery systems: each of these innovations can be interpreted as manifestations of a larger trend towards accelerating production and consumption, and each has been facilitated by technological changes allowing transnational enterprises to minimize the significance of distance and duration while maximizing the economic opportunities provided by new possibilities for instantaneousness and simultaneity. To be sure, modern capitalism has always operated to revolutionize the time and space horizons of economic activity. As Harvey reminds us, capitalism is a

> revolutionary mode of production, always searching out new organizational forms, new technologies, new lifestyles, new modalities of production and exploitation and, therefore, new object social definitions of . . . time. The capacity to measure and divide time has been [constantly] revolutionized, first through production and the diffusion of increasingly accurate time pieces and subsequently through close attention to the speed and coordinating mechanisms of production (automation, robotization) and the speed and movement of goods, people, information, messages, and the like.[44]

Nevertheless, when high-speed forms of informational technology make it possible for firms to produce distinct components of a single commodity in dozens of different countries, or when internet stock brokers in Hong Kong can communicate instantaneously with their peers in Toronto, it becomes difficult to deny that the time and space horizons of contemporary economic activity are experiencing especially far-reaching changes in our day and age. Although always essential to capitalism, the "compression of space and time" is now taking particularly dramatic forms, as evinced by a variety of economic innovations deriving from new technologically based possibilities for instantaneousness and simultaneity.

Neumann's legal theory never adequately thematizes this feature of capitalist development, notwithstanding its obvious centrality to Karl Marx's own account.[45] Yet its implications are profound for legal development. The literature on globalization includes numerous suggestions that traditional formalistic legal procedures too often are rapidly rendered anachronistic given the dynamic character of contemporary economic change and high speed pace of innovation: The "half-life" of many forms of traditional legal regulation indeed appears to be undergoing a dramatic decline. The legal sociologist Boaventura de Sousa Santos adeptly captures the enigma at hand at when he points out that the "speed and social acceleration" of contemporary social and economic processes means that "law will be easily trapped in the dilemma: either to remain static and be ignored, or to keep up with social dynamics and be devalued as a normative reference."[46] Unidroit justifies its own reliance on "soft" law by underscoring the necessity of contractual law able "to take account of the constantly changing circumstances brought about by the technological and economic developments affecting cross-border trade practice."[47] In a discussion of corporate codes of conduct, the political scientist Kathryn Sikkink has suggested that large transnational corporations (TNCs) are often hostile even to relatively modest forms of strict, codified regulations because "[f]lexibility in export and marketing strategies is one of the essential requirements of a corporation, and . . . detailed, specific marketing regulations . . . could seriously hamper the TNC's ability to organize its activities globally."[48] In the same vein, a prominent international business lawyer observes that large transnational firms are now oftentimes hostile to "hard" transnational regulation because "[a]dvanced technology and organizational techniques permit MNCs to transmit information, shift production, alter marketing strategy, and otherwise adapt to changing business conditions on a scale and a pace unthinkable only a decade or two earlier."[49] The altered time and space horizons of crucial forms of transnational economic activity means that strict uniforms norms are likely to constrain large firms so as to reduce unduly their capacity for dealing with the breathtaking pace of change in the global economy.

On one level, this diagnosis merely confirms Neumann's prescient observations from the 1930s and 1940s: Contemporary capitalism offers a surprising challenge to traditional conceptions of the rule of law as resting on strict, clear, prospective, general norms. But it also raises the ante for those of us sympathetic to a relatively traditional concept of the rule of law. To the extent that the deformalization of law seems integrally related to the *dynamism* of contemporary economic development, how can we preserve that dynamism while simultaneously guaranteeing a reasonable measure of rule of law virtues? Must we choose between the rule of law and a system of production driven incessantly to accelerate the pace of economic life? Or might it be possible to preserve what is worthwhile about the dynamism of contemporary economic life—*and* achieve both greater social justice *and* the rule of law?

The intellectual legacy of Franz Neumann offers no easy answers to these questions. But Neumann's much-maligned legal theory provides an excellent starting point for helping us formulate them.

2 Economic Globalization and the Rule of Law

Faith that the ongoing globalization of the capitalist economy is destined to strengthen the rule of law is virtually universal today. Most mainstream political rhetoric marries economic liberalism to the rule of law: The loaded phrase "market democracy" is repeated with depressing regularity in order to express the purported verity that the worldwide pursuit of neoliberal economics, representative democracy, and the rule of law are all pieces of the same pie. Within the scholarly community, Friedrich Hayek is only the most influential recent intellectual to insist that the intensification and integration of international capitalism is conducive towards augmenting the rule of law both at home and abroad.[1] Yet free market thinkers are hardly alone in their embrace of this position. A host of centrist and even left-wing students of economic globalization similarly exhibit a knee-jerk belief in an "elective affinity" between capitalism and the rule of law.[2] Left and right diagnoses of globalization and legal development often concur. The major difference is that the free market right celebrates globalizing capitalism and the emergence of complementary international legal structures, whereas the left often remains skeptical of globalization and emerging forms of transnational legal coordination.

As I suggested in Chapter 1, however, the commonplace assumption of an "elective affinity" between economic globalization and the rule of law may be misleading. Some evidence does suggest that economic globalization is generating a unification of basic technical standards within a wide array of economic sectors.[3] Nonetheless, a careful examination of novel forms of legal decision making most closely connected to economic globalization shows that they exhibit only a limited dose of those legal virtues typically associated with the traditional ideal of the rule of law. Economic globalization relies on ad hoc, discretionary, closed, and nontransparent legal forms fundamentally inconsistent with a minimally defensible conception of the rule of law. Furthermore, I argue that what the Frankfurt School theorist Franz L. Neumann would probably have described as the pervasive *Situationsjurisprudenz* [situational jurisprudence] of contemporary capitalism, *pace* neoliberal claims to the contrary, cannot be described as an atavistic leftover from the dark ages that predates the victorious ascent of free market ideology on the global scale in the 1980s.[4] The rule of law often remains incomplete because the economic giants who have gained the most from globalization benefit unambiguously from discretionary, informal, and situation-specific forms of legal activity. In a political and economic climate characterized by fervent competition between states driven to attract and cultivate economic investment, nation-states have undertaken little action to counter international capital's preference for porous, open-ended law.

I then suggest that the experience of contemporary economic globalization raises fundamental questions for both traditional and contemporary legal theory. The widely accepted view that capitalism presupposes a substantial amount of legal predictability may be overstated in an era in which the ongoing "compression of space and time" provides economic actors with the ability to conduct economic transactions at a lightning pace.

LAW IN A GLOBAL AGE

Let me begin by defining two central concepts. First, I follow intellectual convention by defining the rule of law as requiring that state action rests on legal norms (a) general in character, (b) relatively clear, (c) public, (d) prospective, and (e) stable. According to the mainstream of liberal jurisprudence, only laws of this type can help provide legal equality, assure fair notice, and guarantee the accountability of power holders. Generality protects against arbitrariness by demanding that like cases are treated in a like manner. Clarity means that the activities of those who apply or enforce the law can be held to relatively coherent standards and thus potentially controlled by those subject to the law. Publicity demands that citizens have fair notice of when and how those with power will intervene. Similarly, laws must exist at the time an act is committed in order to furnish fair notice. Secret and retroactive laws make it impossible for citizens to know how power holders are permitted to act. Stability within law not only facilitates fair notice but also helps bind officials to legal norms and minimizes potentially unwanted exercises of discretion. Rapid or confusing changes within law exacerbate the possibility of unaccountability and potentially allow power holders to usurp powers that may not properly belong to them. In the traditional view, only a system of legal norms of this type can hope to assure a minimum of predictability and determinacy within legal decision making. In this vein, we might easily accept the gist of Hayek's famous quip that "stripped of all technicalities this [that is, the rule of law] means that government in all its actions is bound by rules fixed and announced beforehand—rules which make it possible to foresee with fair certainty how the authority will use its coercive powers in given circumstances, and to plan one's individual affairs on the basis of this knowledge."[5] For the sake of argument, it is probably best to downplay other conditions that one justifiably might include in a full-fledged definition of the rule of law—for example, the existence of independent courts outfitted with effective review powers. The reason for this is that both judicial and enforcement mechanisms remain notoriously underdeveloped in international private law; this is true of most of the legal arenas to be discussed here as well. Yet it would be trivial to claim that they thus lack a legal character simply because their enforcement mechanisms are weak, just as it would be unfair to claim that the United Nations lacks any legal significance whatsoever because its enforcement instruments remain inadequate. Far more interesting here is the question of whether we can detect evidence of a move towards a minimum of legality (that is, generality, clarity, publicity, prospectiveness, and stability in rules), a basic presupposition of the rule of the law in any more ambitious sense of the term, in novel forms of international economic coordination. The problem at hand is elucidated somewhat by means of James Rosenau's helpful conceptual distinction between "governance" and "government," where governance refers both to international organizations (for example, the World Trade Organization or International Monetary Fund) backed by formal political authority deriving from the combined power of member nation-states, as well as nongovernmental mechanisms based on shared goals that may or may not exercise police powers. Governance is a broader category than government. The distinction is helpful for us because the former term includes both explicit intergovernmental institutions and a variety of emerging international decision-making structures whose relationship to the formal authority of existing nation-states remains ambivalent. For our purposes, the legal character of nongovernmental bodies in the international political economy is just as important as the familiar question of whether formal organizations (for example, WTO) possess some of the minimal features of the rule of law.[6]

The ambivalent term "economic globalization" also requires clarification. We need to guard against the dangers of an overstated model of globalization, in which market openness and capital mobility are exaggerated, and the fact that economic integration today primarily takes the form of regional triadization, is simply ignored. Too often, sloppy usage of the term economic globalization unfairly cripples those who hope to make legitimate use of both nation-state and emerging regional political devices in order to grapple with the pathologies of neoliberal globalization. Nation-states still do have an important role to play in the regulation of markets, multinational corporations (MNCs) remain home-based in many meaningful ways, trade and exchange are not fully global in the literal sense of the term (in part because substantial sections of the international economy have simply been ignored by most foreign investors), and not all present-day trends towards market openness are historically unprecedented. At the same time, the term economic globalization remains helpful to the extent that it captures the (a) internationalization of capital and financial markets, (b) increases in the volume of trade in semimanufactured and manufactured goods between the industrialized economies, (c) growing importance of MNCs in the world economy, and (d) near universal movement towards regional economic and political blocs (NAFTA, ASEAN, EU).[7] It is also helpful if (e) conceived as including what Susan Strange and John Stopford have described as the "new pragmatism" between capital and individual nation-states.[8] Neoliberalism is now so hegemonic that even the poorest members of the international political community today generally accept the dogma that states should do all they can to attract and support both national and international capital. The result is a fierce intensification among (and within) nation-states for capital that takes a variety of both old and new forms: increased government-supported research and education outlays for "national champions" and foreign firms considered economically useful, tax breaks, and a multiplicity of direct and indirect subsidies. Although it remains true that global business has turned a cold shoulder to Africa and some other parts of the world, an aggressive quest to attract and cultivate foreign investment, in some contrast to the situation in the 1970s when MNCs often met with skepticism and even hostility, has become truly global in character.[9] Collaboration between government and the relatively oligopolistic firms prominent internationally has become the rule and not the exception to an extent that probably would have surprised even political moderates just twenty years ago.[10]

Towards a Global State of Exception?

By means of a survey of four legal areas (international business arbitration, business taxation, finance and banking regulations, and GATT) pivotal to economic globalization, I want to begin to show how this "new pragmatism" has paved the way for a number of alarming legal trends. Although neoliberals still harp on the need for more ambitious international legal reforms in order to strengthen market competition, the international legal system has already responded quite effectively to the legal preferences of a substantial segment of the international business community. Unfortunately, little evidence suggests that a defensible version of an international rule of law is resulting. On the contrary, globalization appears to be deepening trends towards private, discretionary, and ad hoc forms of rule. Such trends have long been evident on the domestic scene.[11] But their appearance on the international scene suggests that they threaten to take on even greater significance in the future.

International Arbitration and the *Lex Mercatoria*

One of the most popular methods of dispute resolution now employed by large firms operating abroad is arbitration.[12] On the surface, the reasons for the arbitration boom seem straightforward. As a growing number of businesses extend overseas operations, the familiar problem of "hometown justice" takes on fresh significance. A popular how-to book with the catchy title *How to Make Global Deals* rightly observes that foreign capital long faced hostile courts and bureaucracies, especially in the developing world.[13] Even today, a German firm contracted with a Brazilian company, for example, is likely to prefer that conflicts be resolved in a German court, whereas the Brazilian firm is likely to favor recourse to Brazilian law. Within this context, international business arbitration seems a fair compromise to both parties. Contracts between firms based in different legal systems now typically include clauses assuring that conflicts are to be resolved by "neutral" forms of international arbitration (provided by private services such as the International Court of Arbitration and International Chamber of Commerce), and the popular business literature for aspiring global players enthusiastically heralds the advantages of arbitration for those hoping to avoid unfair treatment by foreign partners. The practice of allowing foreign businesses to "outsource" the regulation of legal conflicts has now been accepted by most countries as a legitimate way to facilitate international trade and exchange.[14] Not surprisingly, many countries initially resisted attempts by foreign investors to attenuate the direct role of nationally based courts and legal norms.[15] But faced with fierce global competition for foreign capital, even those legal systems resistant to arbitration have now pretty much abandoned their traditional reservations.

The legal status of international business arbitration remains controversial in the burgeoning scholarly literature on the topic. For good reason, legal traditionalists question whether its practices deserve to be described as a form of law in the first place, and a growing number of enthusiasts see arbitration as paving the way for a global system of economic law. Despite these controversies, consensus exists on at least two points. First, international business arbitration is highly discretionary and probably ad hoc in character. Second, international business arbitration tends to resemble a system of private self-regulation, in which conflicts between private firms are resolved, in a confidential manner, by arbitrators attuned to the practical and ideological needs and preferences of the international firms most likely to employ arbitration services. Arbitration's enthusiasts see both features as crucial to its alleged success.[16]

A main legal basis for international business arbitration is the *Lex Mercatoria*, the customary law of merchants and traders operating abroad. Although its roots are premodern, the *Lex Mercatoria* has enjoyed something of a renaissance in recent years, as both practitioners and scholars have tried to rescue it in order to outfit international business arbitration with some legal justification.[17] Here as well, specialists continue to debate the strengths and weaknesses of the *Lex Mercatoria*. Yet no one disputes that its basic norms tend to be vague and open-ended. The *Lex Mercatoria* consists to a great extent of common sense business standards (e.g., contracts should be negotiated in "good faith"; unforeseen difficulties should be overcome in "good faith"; the "usages of trade" are to be relied on in order to resolve conflicts). Arbitrators are encouraged to make use of such open-ended terms when resolving business disputes. Predictably, the result tends to be a system of justice fundamentally antiformalistic in character. Arbitrators also advertise their services by promising secrecy. With great success, they remind the business community of the bad publicity that often accompanies court battles, especially those in foreign countries. Would not Exxon's image have been tarnished somewhat less after its recent environmental mishaps if it could have solved its dispute with the residents of Alaska by means of private arbitration? Adamant proponents of the *Lex Mercatoria* go so far as to suggest that it constitutes a general model for the reform of international law as a whole.[18]

It is easy to see why arbitration has become so popular within the international business world. Everywhere the well-to-do are withdrawing from public institutions by moving to wealthy suburbs, purchasing expensive private security, schooling, and even sanitation services.[19] International business arbitration constitutes another example of this universal tendency to secede from public institutions, an international legal complement to the "gated communities" presently popping up throughout the United States. The confidentiality of arbitration means that businesses can keep their dirty laundry out of the public eye. Although even its proponents occasionally worry about the discretionary character of the *Lex Mercatoria*, most claim that the impressive power granted arbitrators allows them to provide justice to a degree allegedly missing from traditional judicial and administrative devices. From the perspective of a growing number of international firms, discretionary jurisprudence is unproblematic, as long as arbitration firms are chosen by the affected firms and those who negotiate conflicts are well-schooled in the special business practices of the parties to a conflict.

Just as important, arbitrators share a fundamental commitment to the "commercial ethic" of economic liberalism.[20] Revealingly, the how-to literature underlines the alleged "arbitrariness" of national legal systems: Traditional legal formalism, it seems, is the main source of irregular power, not informal justice. Of course, this blatantly ideological view—foreign business clearly fears traditional courts and administrators more concerned with the public interest than corporate profit—masks a valuable half-truth. At least on occasion, relatively formalistic domestic laws have been "biased" against international capital, and time-consuming legal formalities occasionally have countered the flexibility sought by economic actors struggling to master the ever-changing situational imperatives of the global marketplace. Arbitration potentially provides international firms with a welcome escape from such problems.

As one academic defender of the *Lex Mercatoria* notes, "[f]ormalistic facades are not necessary to achieve the sensible results dictated by a commercial ethic."[21] As long as it is run by and for international business, informal justice suits the needs of global players just fine.

Multinational Corporations and Business Taxation.

Notwithstanding their growing importance within the international economy, multinational corporations remain notoriously undertaxed. Even

Ronald Reagan reportedly was shocked to learn in 1983 that General Electric and fifty-seven other huge American corporations paid less in taxes than his personal secretary. But the problem is by no means specific to the United States. In Germany, BMW, Siemens, and Daimler-Benz have cleverly manipulated the German tax code so as to avoid paying any taxes whatsoever.[22] Multinational corporations everywhere have managed to reduce dramatically their financial contributions to the coffers of both home and guest countries. In 1950, 26.5% of the federal government receipts of the United States were financed out of corporate taxes. Reagan seems to have quickly overcome his initial state of shock: An immediate result of his tax cuts was that corporate contributions amounted to a measly 6.2% by the mid-1980s.[23]

This impressive achievement stems from the success of MNCs in warding off even modest attempts to establish international legal codes capable of effectively regulating their activities. A powerful political alliance of MNCs and the wealthy countries of the North (in which most MNCs are based) decimated attempts within the United Nations to develop a minimal code of conduct for MNCs. Even attempts by the International Chamber of Commerce and OECD—neither particularly hostile to the MNCS—thus far have resulted in little more than a series of political proclamations possessing mere symbolic significance. International private law affecting multinational capital remains at best "soft" law, and important sectors of the international business community and their powerful political allies have done all they possibly can to keep it that way.[24]

The example of international business taxation is particularly revealing. The international tax system is uneven, porous, and deformalized; a confusing body of bilateral tax treaties represents the main source of law here. Even modest attempts to codify international tax law, in part by replacing highly discretionary standards with rules exhibiting some clarity and generality, have faced fierce resistance from the business community. This has proven a smart move: MNCs evade taxes chiefly by taking advantage of loopholes stemming from existing discrepancies among and between national tax codes. In addition, national tax systems have simply been outgunned when forced to grapple with the enormous and ever-growing problem of intrafirm transfers within large international firms: How is one to effectively tax internal transactions within firms involving massive movements of goods and services, particularly when firms have an obvious interest in underestimating the real economic value of the exchanges? Some research suggests that large corporations today prefer the status quo, in which the amount of taxes to be paid by MNCs in such cases is determined by ad hoc, closed-door negotiations conducted by corporate tax lawyers and government officials.[25]

Of course, the open-ended legal norms that provide the legal basis for such negotiations could hypothetically serve as one, albeit limited, instrument for making sure that international capital pays its fair share of the tax load. Yet given the fact that nation-states everywhere now compete aggressively to keep and attract capital, many large corporations have had little to fear from ad hoc negotiations with governmental officials. MNCs can close their operations, throw thousands out of work, and move elsewhere. A presidential personal secretary can quit her job and maybe even change her national residency, but her threat to do so is unlikely to lead tax officials to try to entice her to stay with a lucrative package of tax benefits.

Some trends towards private self-regulation are evident in this legal arena as well. Prominent voices demanding reforms of the status quo have argued that multinationals need to be more effectively regulated by the World Trade Organization. They insist, however, that the WTO is only likely to respect good economic sense, if multinationals are granted rights within the WTO hitherto limited to nation-states.[26] In this spirit, the recent *Multilateral Agreement on Investment* (MAI) draft of a code regulating foreign investment, sponsored by the Organization for Economic Cooperation and Development (OECD), aspired to outfit MNCs with the right to force their host countries to appear before international arbitration bodies in the case of a conflict. Fortunately, a complex political coalition, in which global activists played a decisive role, prevented promulgation of the MAI. Yet it remains a revealing example of a more general tendency in international business regulation which, alas, has not been consistently averted. If the MAI had been passed, host countries, as well as other interested constituencies (e.g., labor unions and environmental groups) would have been denied the same right in relation to the MNCs. Not only would MNCs have been outfitted with powers akin to those of individual nation-states, but MNCs would have possessed legal authority in some ways superior to those of their host countries. Mesmerized by the neoliberal faith in the harmonious market, the rich and powerful countries which pushed unsuccessfully for this reform showed little anxiety about the possibility that their "own" MNCs might someday employ such clauses against the very countries that are now pushing aggressively for it.

Even minimal reforms in this direction would potentially result in a dramatic transformation of traditional international private law. Though many MNCs possess economic muscle far superior to that of small and medium states, mainstream jurisprudence thus far rightly has refused to put MNCs on the same legal plane as the traditional subjects of international law, conceived as legally equal, independent sovereign states.[27] In effect, neoliberalism is now demanding that contemporary international law finally "catch up" with the realities of an international political economy that looks quite different from the relatively egalitarian, small-scale capitalism presupposed in much of classical liberal jurisprudence. Albeit unwittingly, neoliberalism thereby tends to advocate a worrisome reduction of normativity to facticity. To the extent that IBM and Philips possess greater economic significance on the world scene than Togo or even Denmark, why not adjust international law to accord with this state of affairs? If economic efficiency or growth are the only values that matter, all the better: From the perspective of a narrow model of economic rationality, many MNCs are probably more deserving of legal autonomy than most of the traditional subjects of international law.

Proposals of this type bode poorly for the future of international law. Rather than supplanting the problematic international status quo with a superior democratic world-federation, we would merely have jettisoned one of the more ambivalent features of traditional international law. In exchange, we would have gained an inferior alternative in which the economic mammoths that already roam the globe gain unmediated legal and political authority to match their awesome economic resources.

Why not take a step further and grant voting powers in the United Nations to British Air or General Motors?

International Banking and Banking

Finance and banking not only constitutes the most intensely globalized sector of the world economy, but its legal infrastructure is surprisingly informal, ad hoc, and relatively private as well. Although a growing chorus of voices, led by none other than George Soros, demands stricter state-based regulation of international money flows, the main site for the regulation of international banking probably remains a set of Basel-based institutions (including the Bank for International Settlements and the Committee of Banking Supervisors) established by the wealthy countries of the North in the mid-1970s. Decision making in these bodies is not only dominated by central banks and representatives of commercial companies active in banking and finance, but the Basel institutions generally shy away from rigid regulations and clear, formal rules in favor of flexible, open-ended guidelines and recommendations. The informality of the Committee's recommended "best practices" is one reason why a vast number of banks worldwide have endorsed them.[28] Although providing some minimum of common standards, they fail to interfere with the more free-wheeling and speculative forms of behavior endemic to the "casino capitalism" practiced today in the financial sector.[29] Like those in the business community who advocate private arbitration and the *Lex Mercatoria*, international bankers prefer a system of highly discretionary private self-administration over government-backed forms of classical law.

Similar legal trends can be identified in the closely related realms of international insurance and accounting, as well in the credit ratings system that has taken on enormous importance to the financial community within the last decade.[30] Private investors as well as political entities depend on "good grades" from private credit-rating systems such as Moody's and Standard and Poor; a bad debt security rating can doom either an aspiring politician or corporate leader. Yet here as well, discretionary private self-government is the rule and not the exception. Credit ratings are made by committees whose composition and deliberations remain confidential. In part because the ratings committee is encouraged to pursue information from competitors and disgruntled employees, the rating systems is relatively subjective. Although a dissatisfied firm or political unit can appeal an unacceptable rating, no governmental regulation assures that a rating can be overturned. Within the United States, ratings have been classified as legitimate expressions of opinion and thus protected as a form of free speech.[31]

Notwithstanding its obvious democratic deficits, the International Monetary Fund (IMF) can hardly be described as private self-regulation in the sense that I have used this term thus far.[32] The IMF is an intergovernmental body whose rules are well-enforced by powerful member-states who long have seen the IMF as central to economic liberalization. Nonetheless, here as well, economic globalization seems to have been accompanied by important examples of legal deformalization. Although the original Articles of Agreement of the International Monetary Fund was hardly a model of legal clarity, the Agreement has since been further watered down in a number of crucial areas. The abandonment in the 1970s of the Bretton Woods system of fixed exchange rates for the contemporary "non-system" of floating exchange rates was only made possible by Amendments to the original Articles of Agreement which constitute "soft law and softer law than the provisions of the original Articles."[33] Even a former General Counsel and Director of the Law Department of the IMF publicly suggested that increased legal amorphousness in the IMF Agreement threatens to undermine the IMF's official commitment to legal uniformity and evenhandedness.[34]

Representatives of debtor nations are unlikely to be surprised by this revealing concession. The IMF continues to resist attempts to establish a set of clear general rules for dealing with debtors and potential deadbeats. Whenever the specter of default on an IMF-backed loan looms large, negotiations are conducted on an ad hoc basis. The reasons for this preference are obvious enough. Legal uncertainty is a useful tool in the hands of creditors (most important, banks and the governments allied with them within the IMF) hoping to maximize concessions from those countries which have failed to live by the harsh commercial ethic of contemporary economic liberalism. Depending on the economic and political importance of a country and the character and prospects of its government, individual justice is parceled out by the IMF either with severity or generosity.[35] Here as well, legal formality would simply represent an inconvenient impediment to the most privileged economic interests on the international scene.

The G-5, G-7, and now G-8 meetings and summits, the most important attempt by the wealthy (and mostly) western countries to grapple with the instability of money markets and exchange rates after the demise of Bretton Woods, for the most part have also remained informal and ad hoc in character.[36] Even the minimal endeavor to agree to a set of formalized economic indicators as a common starting point for expanding multilateral economic surveillance have proven controversial.[37] Revealingly, the lesson drawn by the historian Harold James is that the limited success of the meetings in part is to be attributed to excessive transparency and public scrutiny, notwithstanding the fact that political leaders long have praised the summits precisely because they allow elected officials, financial ministers, and central banks to undertake international economic coordination, as Helmut Schmidt appreciatively commented, "hidden from the public."[38] Yet from the perspective of those close to the IMF, high-level participation by elected officials is problematic because it threatens to "politicize" international economic coordination. For these voices, "concentration by more technocratic policymakers on policy fundamentals" alone can assure successful international monetary cooperation.[39]

The General Agreement on Tariffs and Trade (GATT) and World Trade Organization (WTO)

At first glance, WTO, as well as its predecessor, GATT, offer a neoliberal success story at odds with much of the evidence provided here. Dedicated to establishing an open trade regime based on the principles of nondiscrimination and unconditional reciprocity, GATT succeeded in reducing impediments to foreign trade over the course of fifty years. Its successor, the WTO, is probably the closest thing we have today to an international "constitutionalism of neoliberalism."[40] The WTO arguably rests on the classical rule of law preference for a relatively coherent legal code, and its enforcement mechanisms have undoubtedly been strengthened in recent years. The WTO seems to entail a crucial step towards fulfilling the expectation that economic globalization is ultimately destined to generate an ever more effective system of cogent, prospective legal rules.[41]

A closer look immediately suggests the problematic character of this common picture of it. In its final rendition, the GATT Agreement numbered 22,000 pages and weighed 424 pounds; it bore little resemblance to the relatively accessible legal codes sought by traditional liberal jurists. One instead is reminded of the legal "Egyptian hieroglyphics" which so worried the formalist jurist Jeremy Bentham.[42] A central source of its complexity—which, by the way, plagues the WTO as well—was that it remains "riddled with exceptions—grandfather clauses, waivers, balance-of-payment exceptions," alongside vague clauses, loopholes, and sectoral exemptions for a host of important industries and products.[43] Of course, neoliberal defenders of the WTO are well aware of its legal weaknesses. Yet here as well, their narrative at best captures peripheral facets of the enigma at hand. According to economic liberalism, exceptions to the principle of nondiscrimination in trade generally stem from irrational state actors, beholden to "special interests," who wrongly believe that local industries unlikely to survive the harsh climate of international competition deserve special protection. From this perspective, the legal weaknesses of the WTO derive from an economically irrational hostility to market competition and a concomitant paternalistic interest in defending likely economic "losers" (for example, European agriculture). As far as the WTO's failure to regulate a host of nontariff subsidies

is concerned, economic liberals here as well tend to write off such concessions to an atavistic and irrational hostility to free markets. Once recalci-
trant elected officials finally acknowledge the virtues of market competition,
the argument goes, they are sure to embrace the extension of the WTO to
many new forms of subsidies presently tolerated within the global market
economy. From this perspective, the achievement of a Brave New World of
international free trade and a corresponding international rule of law are
just a matter of time.

This interpretation suffers from an obvious flaw. As an empirical point,
the main threat to the WTO commitment to legal generality does not always
come from economic "losers" located in parts of the world that have yet
to pursue neoliberal reforms but instead arguably from the rich countries
(including the United States) which historically have relied on legally problematic clauses to nurture and support technology-intensive industry."[44]
Ties between governments and technologically advanced industries have
become especially intimate in recent years, as individual nation-states fight
to make sure that large firms based within their countries are able to compete successfully in the emerging global marketplace of the twenty-first
century. In the context of heightened international economic competition,
states are driven to engage in the cultivation and support of those industries (e.g., that of semiconductors) widely seen as essential to economic
success in the next century. Even within the narrow intellectual confines
of economic liberalism, it remains unclear why such forms of economic
husbandry are necessarily irrational. With neither hidden nor open forms
of state support for such industries, it is unlikely that many of the economic leaders in these fields—recall the pivotal role of defense spending
in the emergence of the American computer industry—would have gained
their positions in the first place. A growing number of states simply have
internalized the rules of the international marketplace and thus have joined
hands with select industries in order to arm themselves for international
economic competition. The universal acceptance of core features of economic liberalism turns out to be one reason why many states seek exceptions to the principle of universal free trade and thus undermine the legal
integrity of international economic agreements.

Pace neoliberal ideology, the international economic environment
remains characterized by oligopolistic tendencies, and much recent evidence suggests that globalization has simply strengthened these trends. In
a context of less-than-perfect market competition, it is hardly self-evident
that states are acting irrationally by fighting to make sure that "their"
multinational firms gain access to a share of the world market, even if
this requires abrogating the principle of nondiscrimination in trade. By
pursuing exceptions for the sake of defending strategic industries, political
officials oftentimes reveal a more realistic sense of the actual structure of
the global economy than do the liberal ideologues whose rhetoric masks
the reality of economic globalization.

The left-wing international lawyer David Kennedy is thus in part right when he notes that the emerging international trade regime rests on an "archaic distinction between [the] normal and abnormal."[45] Exceptions to WTO and similar treaties are justified typically by reference to a model of economic "normalcy" in which trade is perfectly unconditional and reciprocal. Yet "abnormal" exceptions never vanish. New products and industries requiring cultivation in order to prepare them for international competition inevitably appear.[46] In light of the fact that there are always likely to be more players in the international economic marketplace who potentially benefit from either hidden or open state support than those who can do without such support altogether, WTO may be destined to remain an agreement in which the exception is more important than the rule.[47]

LEGAL SECURITY AND THE COMPRESSION OF SPACE AND TIME

Whether it takes the form of private self-regulation or enforceable economic agreements backed by powerful member-states, the legal substructure of economic globalization is characterized by highly discretionary modes of decision making. Not only is there little evidence that the globalizing of capitalism is strengthening classical rule of law virtues, but instead a great deal of evidence suggests the existence of an "elective affinity" between globalizing capitalism and informality within law. To a surprising and arguably alarming extent, Franz L. Neumann's dissenting view that modern capitalism would decreasingly rely on crucial attributes of the classical rule of law is supported by significant empirical evidence.

Indeed, preliminary evidence suggests that similar legal trends are also at work within nation-states.[48] The deleterious side effects of neoliberal globalization are in essence "thrown back" at existing nation-states which then struggle to grapple with them; the erosion of basic legal protections often results. Two examples have to suffice for now. Dramatic increases in capital mobility have been accompanied by equally awesome movements of people across borders. "The scale and diversity of today's migrations are beyond any previous experience."[49] In particular, growing inequality between poor and rich countries, exacerbated in part by neoliberal policy, drives many to flee economic misery for a better life in the rich countries. Legal systems in recipient countries then respond with immigration and asylum codes that are not only more repressive than previous codes but entail vast increases in the discretionary powers of immigration authorities, border police, and the internal security apparatus. A pervasive "normlessness" within this area of the law is increasingly common even in those countries officially committed to the humane United Nations agreements on the rights of refugees and immigrants.[50] Similar trends can be identified within the criminal law. As criminal syndicates go international, individual states respond by weakening the legal integrity of criminal codes. According to some accounts, deformalization has been a marked trend within the criminal law over the course of the past decade as well.[51]

These legal trends raise obvious problems for both right- and left-wing authors who still accept the traditional assumption (endorsed by classical theorists as diverse as Karl Marx and Max Weber) that capitalism necessarily requires substantial legal security and thus clear, prospective, general legal norms and relatively formalistic, determinate modes of legal decision making. They also suggest problems for influential currents within contemporary left-wing legal theory that celebrate legal indeterminacy while downplaying the empirical fact that the main beneficiaries of indeterminacy within international private law today often are privileged global players. Although Critical Legal Studies (CLS) contributions occasionally underline some of the real limits of traditional liberal forms of international law, the CLS embrace of legal indeterminacy provides a poor starting point for making sense of the perils posed by global capital's exploitation of open-ended, indeterminate law. CLS scholarship on international law offers a vivid example of the profound intellectual confusions common among the left in the American legal academy today: Purportedly critical writers inadvertently endorse precisely those legal trends which are likely to exacerbate social and economic inequality on the global scale.[52]

In a similar spirit, the German legal theorist Gunther Teubner argues that we should not worry too much about antiformal trends within global economic law. In his view, "the determinacy of rules is a misleading criterion. The existence of an elaborate body of rules is not decisive. What matters is a self-organizing process of mutual constitution of legal acts and legal structures."[53] But the fact that the "mutual constitution of legal acts" within international economic law is presently dominated by MNCs and policy wonks sympathetic to their interests should at least make us somewhat cautious before tossing traditional liberal conceptions of law to the wayside. Of course, there are places within every legal system where formal rules and traditional decision-making forms are indeed of limited value.[54] But I doubt that they legitimately include those emerging legal structures that presently give privileged economic interests vast and arguably unprecedented influence over the fate of large segments of humanity.

Are we then to discard the traditional view that capitalism requires substantial legal security and stability altogether? Let me try to offer two possible answers to this question. Although basically different in structure, the answers may be compatible with one other. Empirical evidence can be found for both claims, and it is possible that both may coexist, however uneasily, in the contemporary legal universe.

Recall our discussion of international arbitration and the *Lex Mercatoria*. Although its legal structure suggests substantial discretionary power, legal security in an important sense *is* guaranteed here. As noted above, arbitration is both sympathetic to business interests and familiar with the "usages of trade" relevant to the economic sectors at hand. The *Lex Mercatoria* potentially represents an eminently bourgeois mode of emerging global customary law in which legal stability is guaranteed not by formal legal devices but by the relative homogeneity of legal decision makers and the fact that arbitrators and international business share relatively similar social interests and ideological views. Although the legal materials constitutive of the *Lex Mercatoria* provide extensive freedom for arbitrators, the fact of the matter is that a certain amount of regularity and even predictability may result in international arbitration as a result of the social and ideological background of those outfitted with discretionary authority. At the very least, its ad hoc character is mitigated by the fact that "likeminded" arbitrators guarantee some element of the traditional legalistic ideal of "like decisions for like cases."[55]

Only additional research in legal sociology can determine if this interpretation helps us make sense of the legal trends at hand. But I should note that the recent literature on international economic law does provide at least some empirical support for this possibility. This literatures describes how a selective "Americanization" of some forms of legal practice, precisely where legal decision making is most closely tied to globalization, seems to be taking place.[56] The structure of American corporate law firms are imitated by their foreign competitors, American credit and arbitration services are in hot demand worldwide, and aspiring lawyers and bankers flock to the United States for legal training, where they are likely to be exposed to the economic liberalism of the enormously influential Law & Economics movement.[57] A Swiss legal scholar has even suggested that the American impact on legal thinking and practice today rivals that of Roman law within medieval Europe.[58] In this manner, economic globalization arguably *is* accompanied by a "globalization of (some features of American-style) law," in which an increasingly homogeneous set of legal methods and concepts functions to guarantee some measure of legal regularity.

A second, more surprising interpretation of the relationship between globalization and the rule of law is conceivable as well. References to the "compression of space and time" are commonplace in the literature on cultural globalization. At a minimum, this expression is meant to capture a striking shift in the time and space horizons of everyday experience that has taken place in our century. In the crudest terms: modern technology and communications "shrink" space and "shorten" time. If villagers in rural Canada can experience the same thing at the same time (for example, a financial transaction) as city dwellers in Vienna, then "they in effect live in the same place, space has been annihilated by time compression."[59] When a Swede can watch, via television, as Chinese police fire at student protestors, a synchronization of time and space occurs. Space is typically measured in time. As the time it takes to link disparate geographical points shortens, space is compressed: The world of the high-speed jet is smaller than that of the stagecoach. Of course, neither space nor time has literally been condensed.

But in an age of air travel, e-mail, and instantaneous computerized financial transactions, "there" seems less distant from "here" than it once was, and the "future" always seems posed to collapse into the "present."

To the extent that this diagnosis is accurate, it impacts directly on the experience of legal security. Legal security is clearly a timebound concept: It is primarily a demand that relevant features of the future remain relatively predictable and thus manageable. The compression of space and time thus potentially revolutionizes the phenomenological relationship between the economic actor and legal security. When economic transactions can take place across continents at a dazzling pace, the perception of the role of legal security and stability is transformed. Of course, capitalism always necessarily requires an indispensable minimum of secure legal institutions (most obviously, certain legal guarantees of private property). But beyond that minimum, the compression of time and space probably reduces the economic actor's sense of dependence on an extensive set of relatively stable general legal norms.

Let me try to illustrate this abstruse claim with a simple example. It is 1749 in the colonial backwaters of North America. A merchant engaging in trade with representatives of the First Nations is likely to prefer significant legal continuity and stability within the colonial legal code. His business requires long, time-consuming, and risky trips. From the perspective of the trader, one way to minimize unnecessary risks is to try to make sure that laws affecting him remain unchanged by the time he completes his journey and returns to the coast from the North American hinterlands. It clearly makes good economic sense to seek a relatively stable system of contracts, a tax code unlikely to change during the course of his journey, and many other predictable legal norms and practices. Rapid shifts in the code—for example, confusing new taxes on the sale of furs—are best avoided. In turn, the clarity and transparency of legal norms facilitates the merchant's understanding of the code and helps contribute to the reduction of unnecessary uncertainty. And its generality means that he is not disadvantaged in relation to other similarly situated merchants and traders.[60]

Now let us return to the present. A financial trader sits in front of a computer terminal in London. She presses a few keys on a computer. Enormous quantities of foreign currency are instantaneously swapped. The transaction is completed within a few brief moments.

Does our London trader experience exactly the same need for legal stability as her predecessor in colonial America? Perhaps not. For the colonial trader, legal stability in part was a tool for counteracting uncertainties resulting from the distance and duration of his business. But the technologically induced compression of space and time means that both sources of uncertainty have already been reduced for our modern financial broker. In a sense, modern technology seems to take care of some of the functions performed for the colonial merchant by a stable legal code. Even when modern legislatures initiate rapid changes in the legal code, our financial trader, operating at lightning speed, is likely to have more than enough time to adjust her practices accordingly. Rapid-fire transactions are unlikely to be disrupted by changes in law because many market transactions are computerized whereas legislative changes, thus far, are not. The merchant in the city is likely to find even relatively frequent changes within the law less threatening than her colonial predecessor.

But the point is not just that our modern capitalist may experience less of an immediate need to counteract certain forms of uncertainty by legal means. It may even be the case that a relatively discretionary, open-ended system of law actually suits the immediate economic self-interest of our modern financial trader to an extent that would have shocked her predecessor. In a world in which economic success requires speedy reactions to complex, ever-changing movements of vast quantities of goods and services, a system of legal coordination providing substantial room for discretionary decision making might be exactly what the financial trader in the city prefers. Her economic transactions take place at a fast pace; quick changes in market conditions require enormous flexibility and equally quick reactions on her part. In this context, legal forms that allow for flexible, situation-specific decision making potentially mean that legal actors can adjust nimbly to the changing dynamics of the marketplace. In contrast, stable general norms may come to seem an impediment to the rapid adjustments required by the latest dictates of the globalizing marketplace. A "static" set of laws may interfere with the "dynamic" requirements of the marketplace. Codified law appears "dead" and "life-less," an odd leftover from the past and fundamentally unsuited to the latest dictates of the marketplace.

This second interpretation need not dispute the obvious fact that globalization is generating novel forms of uncertainty and insecurity. Nor should we exaggerate the importance of this "ideal type" of contemporary financial trader to the overall economic scheme of things: Whereas the financial markets have been revolutionized by the compression of space and time, this is clearly not so on the same scale in other areas of the economy. My point here is merely that certain immanent features of contemporary capitalism potentially help explain why so many business people today are willing to embrace informal, situation-specific forms of law.

Despite virtually universal claims to the contrary, neoliberal economic globalization is unlikely to make a significant contribution towards strengthening of the rule of law. Yet clear, prospective, public, general legal norms remain valuable if we are to tame arbitrary power deriving from political and economic inequality. The guarantee of a minimum of personal security remains basic to any worthwhile democratic polity. Democratic citizens need a robust rule of law, even if international business may not.

If I am not mistaken, the battle for the rule of law entails a battle against the pathologies of neoliberal globalization. For starters, we need to strengthen the social and environmental standards and their enforcement mechanisms, which have already been included in some transnational economic and political agreements (in particular, NAFTA and the EU). We also need to make sure that other international economic agreements (especially the WTO) finally include such clauses.[61] In order for these standards to prove effective, they are going to have to take a relatively cogent legal form. Given the enormous power advantages enjoyed virtually everywhere by business in relation to organized labor and environmentalists, we have to assume that the business community generally is best poised to exploit legal ambiguities within these treaties. As we repeatedly see in the context of negotiations about regulating climate change, the biggest polluters typically prefer open-ended, empty environmental law. Within the global economy, the biggest exploiters are similarly likely to favor vague forms of private law and toothless social and environmental regulations.

Unfortunately, recent attempts to develop effective global social regulations have met with little success. For anyone committed to at least mitigating economic inequality, the struggle for labor rights necessarily deserves a central role. However, global labor regulation continues to founder in part because of the same pathologies diagnosed in this chapter: Its legally porous character renders it vulnerable to easy manipulation by the most powerful political and economic actors on the global political economy. Once again, we find a troubling confirmation of Franz Neumann's worry that the economically privileged too often tend to benefit from the demise of classical rule of law virtues.

3 Transnational Labor Standards
The U.S. Experience

With Democrats again in control of the Congress, and with the real possibility of a Democratic President in the White House, U.S. citizens are likely to see a push to implement transnational labor protections, according to which basic workplace standards (including health and safety regulations, minimum wage laws, bans on child labor), and fundamental union rights (for example, free association and the right to organize) must be institutionalized transnationally so as to better accord with the realities of a global economy. In sharp contrast to his Republican successor, who amassed the most ferocious antilabor record of any modern U.S. president, Bill Clinton periodically made a point of announcing his fidelity to the idea of enforceable cross-border protections for labor. In particular, he was an outspoken defender of the one type of transnational labor standard (so-called corporate "codes of conduct") popular in the board rooms of large multinational corporations; his longstanding support for extending trading privileges to China was accompanied by an official promise to encourage U.S. businesses operating there to respect a coterie of voluntary labor standards.[1] The North American Free Trade Agreement (NAFTA) only made its way successfully through Congress in 1993 because of the simultaneous ratification of a labor "side-agreement" with Mexico and Canada, the North American Agreement on Labor Cooperation (NAALC), which was similarly predicated on achieving cross-border protections for labor. Within the World Trade Organization (WTO), under the last Democratic Administration, the United States was the most influential member-state demanding that global free trade be tied to a proposed "labor clause" requiring respect for core labor rights and workplace standards. In this area of policy, as in so many others, Clinton in fact built on the legacy of his immediate predecessors: Throughout the 1980s and early 1990s, the United States made the extension of trading privileges conditional on the acceptance of "internationally recognized worker rights," and a substantial range of decisive trade laws still on the books—for example, the Generalized System of Preferences (GSP), which helped open the American market to developing countries—includes express legislative commitments to the maintenance of minimal workplace standards and labor rights in those countries with which the

United States conducts business. With the demise of the most right-wing government in modern U.S. history, Americans can expect to see a renewed push at the national level to build on this legacy.

In short, one attribute of what passes for mainstream Democratic and liberal politics in the United States has been the oft-repeated assurance that "going global" need not generate a "race-to-the-bottom." Transnational labor protections constitute an important device for responding to increasingly widespread popular anxiety at home about the deleterious side effects of globalization. Of course, it is easy to understand why transnational labor protections have proven so appealing to important political constituencies. Transnational labor protections indeed seem well-suited as a remedy for some of the pathologies of globalization, and it is no surprise that U.S. labor unions and their political allies time and again have endorsed transnational labor protections. Neoliberal globalization poses a direct challenge to nationally based labor rights and workplace standards, one of the core achievements of working class movements since the nineteenth century. Even in the United States, whose enormous domestic economy leaves it relatively well-positioned to navigate the waters of economic globalization, basic labor protections have suffered substantial setbacks as a result of globalization. For example, only in 1965 was organized labor able to gain meaningful legal protections against "runaway shops" in the domestic setting: In *Textile Workers v. Darlington Mfg. Co.*, the Supreme Court suggested that businesses that closed unionized facilities and then moved production to facilities in nonunionized areas of the country violated the backbone of modern U.S. labor law, the National Labor Relations Act. Unfortunately, the recent shift of production to low-wage and nonunionized facilities abroad undermines the significance of *Darlington*'s protections against domestic "runaway shops." American labor law has also long included guarantees against coercive or threatening actions undertaken by employers aimed at preventing workers from joining or participating in labor unions. Yet considerable evidence suggests that traditional protections against coercive employer activity are proving fragile in light of capital's heightened capacity to shift or outsource production overseas if employees refuse to kowtow to employer demands. Organized labor's weapon of last resort, the right to strike, is weakened if business finds it feasible to move operations abroad to low-wage and nonunionized settings, or simply wait out a strike and rely on production from alternative productive sites located abroad.[2]

Notwithstanding the understandable appeal of transnational labor standards, this chapter argues that the existing American system of transnational labor protections thus far represents a false humanitarianism which has born few fruits for labor either in the United States or abroad. In particular, I focus on the legal structure of U. S. transnational labor protections in order to explain their flaws. By means of a survey of the key versions of transnational labor protections presently supported by American legislators and some important U.S. business interests, I argue that their internal legal weaknesses render them at best ineffective and at worst an instrument for problematic attempts to assure the political and economic hegemony of the United States, especially in those parts of the world in which the United States traditionally plays a dominant role. In a concluding section, I consider possible lessons of recent U.S. experience with transnational labor standards for recent debates about a WTO labor clause. According to the argument developed here, the inefficacy of existing U.S. transnational labor protections derives in part from their failure to institutionalize minimal rudiments of modern formal legality (generality, publicity, clarity, prospectiveness, and stability). Although it is now fashionable on the left in the legal academy to downplay the value of the classical demand for a system of general, public, prospective, and relatively clear and stable legal norms, I believe that this enmity constitutes a political and intellectual stumbling block for those of us intent on constructing a transnational legal order capable of protecting the rights of working people around the globe.

Inspired by the neglected work of Franz L. Neumann, the early Frankfurt School's main jurist, I argue that the abandonment of traditional attributes of modern legality is beset with ambiguity; in certain contexts, it chiefly serves privileged political and economic groups. When the rules of the game are vague or unclear, or when they fail to provide "fair warning" by allowing for a multitude of inconsistent interpretations, oftentimes it is those possessing the greatest de facto economic and political power who gain.[3] Of course, as Neumann frequently pointed out, if a particular statute exhibits the classical virtues of modern legality, this hardly ensures its socially progressive character; a vast range of (potentially conflicting) political and economic goals are consistent with the notion that law should take a general, public, prospective, and relatively clear and stable form. However, it is hardly an accident that precisely in those settings in which key American political and economic elites are willing to accept legal standards having potentially progressive policy implications, the resulting norms often lack the minimal preconditions of an effective system of formal rules. The classical attributes of modern legality make up indispensable prerequisites for the successful operation of any system of enforceable norms: Inconsistent and vague rules, open to a variety of constantly changing interpretations and thus unable to guide let alone bind power holders effectively, are unlikely to achieve any coherent or consistent policy aims. The legal theorist Lon Fuller once relied on a wonderful metaphor to make this simple yet crucial point: The "art" of legality, like carpentry, can serve either good or bad purposes; clear, prospective, stable, general norms can advance either immoral or moral policies, just as a carpenter can use his skills to build either an orphans' asylum or a racially exclusionary country club. "But it still remains true that it takes a carpenter . . . to build an orphans' asylum, and that it will be a better asylum if he is a skilled craftsman equipped with tools that have been used with care and kept in proper condition."[4] Similarly, the effective pursuit of progressive public policy typically necessitates substantial reliance on the classical attributes of legality. The paucity of such legal virtues within U.S. transnational labor norms helps explain their inefficacy: the resulting pliability inevitably undermines their humanitarian and progressive goals.

My account here does not rely on an idealized contrast between an over-stylized and potentially misleading model of nationally based formal labor law and emerging antiformal transnational labor protections. To be sure, in few developed countries have domestic labor protections represented para-gons of traditional legal virtues. Yet even if we concede that much domestic labor law always represents "a chaotic amalgam of conceptualism and real-ism, rule-boundedness and ad hoc balancing, [and] deference to non-judi-cial sources of law and unhesitating faith in the superiority of the judicial mind," its fidelity to the legal virtues of generality, clarity, stability, and prospectiveness is markedly superior to what we find in recent U.S. transna-tional labor protections.[5]

Transnational labor standards constitute an increasingly pivotal con-tested terrain in which a panoply of competing social and political interests struggle to grapple with globalization in ways consistent with their (often-times contradictory) social interests. From this perspective, it is hardly sur-prising that their legal form is complex and ambivalent as well. Nonetheless, the evidence collected here suggests that any effective attempt to challenge the political and economic status quo so as to better serve the interests of labor both in the United States and abroad would do well to fight for stan-dards which embody crucial attributes of formal legality.

RECENT U.S. ADVOCACY OF
TRANSNATIONAL LABOR STANDARDS

Corporate Codes of Conduct

The last two decades have witnessed the proliferation of voluntary business "codes of conduct" detailing safe and healthy work conditions, grievance procedures, antidiscrimination norms, and bans on child labor and substan-dard wages.[6] Many "global players" now consider it indispensable to good public relations to endorse and advertise their support for codes of conduct: The OECD has identified 182 codes of this type (most of which became effective after 1995), and the International Labor Organization (ILO) reports that American-owned multinationals are leading the way in intro-ducing and pushing for them; they seem increasingly widespread among U.S.-based firms (for example, Starbucks, Levi Strauss & Co., and Reebock) whose marketing depends on brand name and the successful projection of a sense of "goodwill" among consumers.[7] Typically promulgated by large multinational enterprises or on an industry-wide or sectoral basis, the codes represent paradigmatic forms of business "self-regulation," and some of the most powerful nation-states are publicly advocating them as innovative attempts to come to grips with the substantial regulatory problems posed by globalization. The United States has been a particularly enthusiastic partisan for multinational codes of conduct; former President Clinton combined his strong support for "free trade" policies with endorsements for voluntary codes of conduct for American firms operating abroad.

It is easy to understand how present-day political and economic trends are driving the growth of voluntary codes of conduct. Business self-regulation accords well with the reigning neoliberal mood: Voluntary codes allow large economic actors to acknowledge widespread public anxieties about globalization, while meshing harmoniously with a pervasive hostility to traditional forms of state-backed economic regulation. Government support for such codes similarly means that politicians can exhibit concern for the deleterious social consequences of globalization without invoking the hostility of prospective private investors sensitized to even the slightest evidence of a "hostile business climate." No wonder that Clinton was so enamored of voluntary codes: Here, at last, seems to be concrete evidence for the possibility of a "third way" beyond the "rigidities" of the traditional interventionist state as well as the extreme free market policies of Thatcher or Reagan. The trend also comports with the view among many academics and policy experts that conventional forms of state activity in the economy too often are likely to prove inflexible and hence ineffective given the dynamic and fast-paced character of contemporary economic life. According to this position, regulatory activity in contemporary capitalism needs to deal seriously with both the complexity and fluidity of economic relations, and thus new forms of interventionist activity would do well to delegate substantial powers of policymaking to nonstate actors possessing "better information, knowledge, and understanding of increasingly complex, technology-driven, and fast-changing public policy issues" than their peers in the legislature or state bureaucracy.[8] Encouraging individual corporations to devise their own situation-specific codes of conduct thus would seem a natural way to begin institutionalizing an alternative to the purported inflexibility of the traditional interventionist state. Large multinationals have made much of this theme as well, as they resist demands for extending traditional forms of state-backed economic regulation into the global economy by insisting that "crude" old-fashioned general law often hinders business more than buttress it.

A careful examination of the codes of conduct endorsed by many multinationals, however, places corporate hostility to traditional forms of state-backed legal regulation in a different light. Notwithstanding repeated calls to acknowledge the centrality of complexity and diversity in contemporary economic life, the codes in fact include a large number of striking commonalities. Rarely do they include clear or effective procedures for dealing with violations, and only a tiny minority of them provides room for independent monitoring or third party enforcement. According to an ILO survey, those potentially affected by the codes—especially managers and workers in foreign plants operated by multinationals—many times are unaware of the existence of the codes in the first place; multinationals presently seem more interested in publicizing the codes to consumers (in the rich countries) than at sites of production in underdeveloped countries.[9] According to the ILO, the voluntary codes are also characterized by a real paucity of references to the basic rights of organized labor (the right to association and collective bargaining), and some are expressly anti-union.[10] They are vague and imprecise, typically consisting of little more than open-ended hortatory declarations (promising "fair and adequate compensation," "just and fair wages," and "good and safe conditions of work") but weak on specifics or the details of implementation. At times, it is difficult to avoid the conclusion that they merely constitute a ploy to ward off legitimate public criticism. For example: despite a sorry record of labor abuse that has generated significant public attention, U.S. apparel producers and retailers operating abroad piously announce their "commitment to the betterment of wages" and "ethically based business practices" (without even beginning to specify what form "ethical" business takes). The American retailer GAP—according to labor activists, a heinous exploiter of sweatshop labor—declares that overtime should be compensated according to "a level that ensures humane and productive work conditions," while the antiunion garment firm Sarah Lee promises "competitive wages" and "superior" work conditions. In short, the codes are often filled with pretty-sounding but oftentimes meaningless language, and they provide no reliable mechanism for rendering their humanitarian goals practically effective.[11] No wonder that the ILO concluded in its 1998 report on voluntary codes of conduct that "the current lack of standardized principles and procedures hinders" quality implementation of their stated goals.[12]

The flexible character of the voluntary codes indeed serves global players well. It remains difficult to understand exactly why such flexibility is necessitated by recent economic innovations (for example, new information technology), however, and not just the old-fashioned quest to improve one's competitive position by means of a more effective exploitation of labor. The scarcity of classical legal virtues within the codes plays an important role in making sure that they typically amount to little but a cosmetic front for the mistreatment of labor in many parts of the world. The fact that the codes are typically unclear and poorly publicized to those potentially affected by them, for example, undermines their efficacy: A vague declaration of "sound and safe working conditions" hardly can provide even a minimum of certainty and predictability to employees, and it is unclear how one might effectively enforce norms of this type in the first place. Although the codes initially seem to mimic traditional forms of state-backed legality, they in fact represent a system of pseudo-legality ill-equipped to achieve the humanitarian goals which corporate public relations officers emphasize when bragging about them.

Revealingly, one important recent attempt to transform voluntary corporate codes into an effective protective device for labor has simultaneously generated a dramatic improvement in their classical legal virtues. Facing a series of lawsuits in which labor activists and the Union of Needletrades, Industrial and Textile Employees (UNITE) brought public attention to appalling labor practices commonplace within the garment industry on the U.S. Pacific Ocean territory of Saipan. By 2003, twenty-seven garment retailers (including J. Crew, Dress Barn, Nordstrom's, Polo Ralph Lauren, Sears, Roebuck & Co.) agreed to accept a code of conduct that represented a major improvement over previous ones. First, the code is a detailed document, including highly precise norms covering a vast range of activities of concern to garment workers in Saipan: The code consists of strict rules guaranteeing the publicity of its standards to workers in affected plants. Second, the retailers accepted a legitimate system of independent monitoring. Its legalistic attributes suggest a real chance of employing the code as an effective check on corporate abuse; labor activists continue to describe it as a victory.[13]

From the perspective of recent debates about globalization and the prospects of transnational labor regulation, the Saipan agreement is significant from another angle as well. The code contains detailed norms challenging paternalistic practices (for example, bans on nighttime visitors in living quarters) to which workers in Saipan have typically been subjected. One reason that the agreement is so precise and detailed is precisely because it zeroes in on the specific problems of poorly paid (mostly Asian) garment workers on the periphery of the American economy. The Saipan agreement thus might be taken as buttressing the view that corporate codes of conduct represent a potential site for meaningful political contestation.[14] In addition, the agreement lends initial support to the view that effective economic regulation today needs to rely less on "blunt" forms of centralized state lawmaking and more on delegations of decision-making authority to nonstate actors (in this case, labor unions and the garment industry). Nonetheless, two caveats should probably be kept in mind by those who take the Saipan agreement as evidence that effective forms of global legal regulation necessitate handing over substantial decision-making authority to nonstate actors. First, traditional state institutions still do play a decisive role in the Saipan agreement: A lawsuit filed in American courts generated the present agreement, and a central feature of the new code of conduct is the assurance that existing U.S. labor and workplace standards will finally gain effective and consistent enforcement in Saipan. Even if some delegation of authority to nonstate actors is required by the complexities of the contemporary global economy, state institutions will need to oversee that authority. In addition, this authority will need to institutionalize core features of modern legality. Second, codes of this type are likely to remain the exception to the norm, chiefly because large firms—even within the garment industry in Saipan, most of whose representatives have refused to accept the agreement thus far—are likely to prove more successful in many other settings in warding off similar pressures to codify the semantically mushy and ineffective codes of conduct preferred by them. In the case of Saipan, activists and labor unionists were able to counteract the power imbalance between business and labor by appealing to the existence of domestic U.S. labor laws poorly enforced within Saipan despite its status as a U.S. territory. In the time-honored tradition of relying on the courts to advance social reform within the United States, labor activists smartly complemented their grassroots activity by turning to the judicial system to challenge an injustice taking place on American soil; the fact that "peonage" was still practiced in the United States played an important role as well in the labor movement's successful public relations campaign. Alas, this is a special condition unlikely to obtain when American multinationals engage in similarly exploitive practices outside the traditional jurisdiction of the American legal system. Then it is unlikely to suffice for labor activists to appeal to domestic courts or domestic public opinion in order to achieve basic labor protections.[15]

American "Aggressive Unilateralism"

It is no accident that some American multinationals have been leading the way in promoting voluntary labor codes of conduct. Beginning especially in the 1980s, substantial political pressure on Congress to grapple with the consequences of capital mobility has generated a variety of legislative undertakings aimed at guaranteeing that countries trading with the United States respect basic labor rights and standards. An immediate incentive for U.S.-based multinationals to initiate their own voluntary codes of conduct is the perception that American legislators increasingly are receptive to the idea of trying to improve the labor protections guaranteed by U.S. trading partners by means of what effectively amounts to unilateral action in the international political arena. Unsurprisingly, in light of the growing reliance on cheap foreign labor, key segments of the corporate community in the United States have proven anything but enthusiastic about this trend, and large U.S.-based firms obviously are trying to undermine the raison d'etre of legislative action by preemptively generating their own (allegedly superior) voluntary codes. Nonetheless, within the last twenty years Congress has approved a variety of laws making the extension of trading benefits to foreign countries dependent on the acceptance of minimal labor rights and workplace standards. Widely touted by Congressional Democrats sympathetic to the AFL-CIO as a puissant tool for countering the uglier consequences of globalization for American workers, a number of key pieces of trade legislation (including the latest version of the Generalized System of Preferences [GSP], Omnibus Trade and Competitiveness Act, and U.S.-Caribbean Trade Partnership Act) now include labor-conditionality clauses. The most important consequence of this legislation has probably been its impact on developing countries, which in many cases can only hope to gain trading privileges from the United States if they agree to have their labor practices scrutinized by the executive branch of the American government and, in particular, the United States Trade Representative.[16]

At first glance, this legislative trend seems to constitute an unambiguous victory for both American workers threatened by cheap imports from low-wage countries in the Caribbean, Latin America, and Southeast Asia, with which the United States conducts so much trade. The most powerful nation-state on earth is now on record as acknowledging that globalization necessarily must be linked to a conscious political effort to improve the position of workers long subject to brutal political repression and harrowing abuse; understandably, the labor movement and its legislative allies were optimistic when Congress first started to pass legislation of this type in the mid-1980s during the dreariest days of the Reagan presidency.[17] Nonetheless, few who have looked carefully at the details of Congress' attempts to encourage American trading partners to exhibit a commitment to basic labor rights and workplace standards still share this optimism today, in light of an overwhelming body of evidence suggesting the ineffectiveness of Congress' foray into the realm of transnational labor protections. In contrast to voluntary codes of conduct, congressional lawmaking at least would seem to place the impressive weight of American political authorities on the side of labor in many parts of the world. But to a significant extent, due to a paucity of even the most basic attributes of legality, such legislation has not only failed to serve its original purposes but has on occasion functioned as a convenient legal front for perpetrating great power Realpolitik in precisely those parts of the world in which the United States has long treated other members of the international community as second-class citizens.

An impressive body of research by labor and human rights lawyers convincingly attributes the failure of congressional legislation in this arena to its embarrassingly vague, open-ended character: "unacceptably vague language . . . has allowed successive Presidents to undermine its enforcement."[18] As the human rights lawyer Philip Alston notes, "the form in which the standards are stated is so bald and inadequate as to have the effect of providing a carte blanche to the relevant U.S. government agencies, thereby enabling them to opt for whatever standards they choose to set in a given situation."[19] The GSP declares that trading partners must "take steps" to guarantee "internationally recognized worker rights," without specifying which "steps" the lawmaker has in mind. The reference to "internationally recognized worker rights" (which plays a key role in related congressional legislation as well) is not only sketched out inadequately in the legislation, but it also stands in a murky relationship to ILO conventions on basic labor rights and standards. Some observers have simply taken this clause as a reference to the ILO's detailed and oftentimes impressive attempts to codify minimal labor protections, but since the legislation fails to refer to the ILO, and the United States has yet to ratify most of the relevant ILO conventions, this reading conveniently ignores the impressive interpretative problems at hand. Too often, the vagueness of U.S. "international worker rights" legislation works to transform it into a cover for broad exercises of executive prerogative inconsistent with the interests of workers either in the United States or abroad, in part because "the procedures established for the implementation of the worker rights legislation appears to ignore, in an almost studied fashion, the various ways in which [relatively cogent] ILO norms could be taken into account."[20] Thus, Administration officials in 1989 and 1990 cynically declared that death squad attacks on labor union leaders in El Salvador were consistent with their determination that El Salvador had successfully recognized international worker rights (and thus was deserving of U.S. trading privileges) since "worker rights" are supposedly unrelated to basic political rights or even the right of association; labor organizers were pursuing "political" goals, and thus their activities supposedly failed to fall under the rubric of "internationally recognized worker rights." In effect, because labor activists in El Salvador rejected a narrowly economistic model of "business unionism," they were deemed undeserving of the protections promised by U.S. labor conditionality legislation. In contrast, the ILO has long made it clear that its minimal labor standards necessarily include the right of association and therefore preclude violence committed against labor leaders.[21]

Alongside its amorphous wording, trade legislation containing labor-conditionality clauses also suffers from the decision to leave its application and enforcement chiefly in the hands of the executive, thereby transforming international labor standards into a convenient foreign policy football, but hardly an instrument for improving labor conditions in those developing countries with which the United States does business. The determination of whether or not a trading partner respects basic labor rights is a top-heavy process in which the United States Trade Representative, and ultimately the President, is given the final authority to concretize the vague imperative to respect "internationally recognized worker rights."[22] In accordance with a long tradition of relaxing rule of law standards in foreign policy areas, the courts have been hesitant to allow for challenges to the executive's determinations, notwithstanding their frequent disregard for ILO standards. Far too often, U.S. courts have simply ruled that the executive's sizable discretion in this area represents a legitimate form of prerogative power indispensable to foreign policy success.[23] In practical terms, this permits and even encourages the executive to subject labor standards to global strategic considerations, as both Republican and Democratic administrations have demonstrated time and again. Republican Administrations have regularly provided stamps of approval to the horrible labor practices of regimes such as those in El Salvador, Guatemala, Haiti, Malaysia, Singapore, Suriname, and Guinea for obvious ideological and strategic reasons; they go so far as to claim that even those states in which forced labor and the most egregious violations of basic union rights were commonplace successfully acknowledged "internationally recognized worker rights" or at least were "taking steps" to do so.[24] Notwithstanding President Clinton's lip service to the importance of achieving transnational labor standards, this basic pattern repeated itself under his administration as well. Clinton aggressively supported extending trading privileges to China despite its widely documented labor abuses, and broader strategic political and economic concerns played an important role in determining his interpretation of U.S. international labor rights legislation. In a telling case, in 1994, Clinton ordered a suspension of an ongoing U.S. investigation of Indonesia's labor practices immediately prior to an important visit he had planned there and which *The Wall Street Journal* described as motivated by the United States' search for Asian allies in the context of heightened United States-Japan trade tensions.[25]

Problems of this type have encouraged legal scholars sympathetic to the idea of transnational labor protections to call for greater legal integrity in domestic legislation concerning foreign labor practices. According to this view, only a substantial clarification of the exact purpose and scope of the legislation at hand, along with an attempt to tighten legislative controls on executive prerogative in its application, have a chance of succeeding in overcoming the evident pathologies of the U.S. legislative status quo, which allows presidents to get away with describing outrageous abuses of labor rights as consistent with internationally recognized worker rights.[26] Otherwise, the present system of what Alston accurately describes as "aggressive unilateralism," in which the United States imposes its own interpretation of conveniently flexible labor standards on would-be trading partners, is likely to remain unchallenged. In short: substantial evidence suggests, as in the case of corporate codes of conduct, that the struggle to improve the status of working people ultimately needs to rely on some minimal yet indispensable features of formal legality.

Albeit unrealistic in light of the present political climate in the United States, much can be said in favor of this view. Congressional legislation in this area undoubtedly suffers from a lack of legal virtues, and American progressives undoubtedly would do well to try to overcome this lacuna. At the same time, critics of the existing worker rights legislation are right to focus attention on the extent to which the legal flaws described above are structurally related to the unilateral character of the American attempt to enforce labor standards on a global scale. Historically, liberal great powers have always subscribed to the notion of a humanitarian system of universal international law, while simultaneously making sure that the international legal system provides adequate mechanisms guaranteeing that the norms of international law are unlikely to be effectively enforced against their political and economic interests. In this spirit, the United States often delights in labeling the actions of its rivals on the international political scene "illegal" and even "criminal," while simultaneously relying on its enormous power advantages to guarantee that many of its own equally dubious actions are rarely effectively prosecuted: One need only recall the ineffectiveness of international courts in trying to punish the United States for its illegal mining of Nicaragua's harbors or the present-day American opposition to the establishment of a standing international criminal court. In short, even multilateral forms of international legal coordination often suffer from a "subjective" application of norms as a result of the profound political and economic inequalities characteristic of the contemporary international arena. The risk of such subjectivity is heightened when a great power is effectively able to undertake unilateral action in its dealings with states that are economically dependent on it. Particularly in relation to developing countries desperate to attract American investors or gain access to American markets, vague and open-ended unilateral labor standards allow the United States to act in an ad hoc manner, at times functioning as a billy club to be wielded against those out of favor with Washington policymakers, while at other junctures providing a way to reward those exhibiting the proper docility in relation to the rules of the global political economy as defined by Washington and its allies. The flawed legal structure of the norms at hand conveniently serves the interests of a great power for whom flexibility in their application is of supreme importance for strategic political and economic reasons. Of course, there are many pressing reasons why developing countries such as El Salvador, Guatemala, and Indonesia are likely to seek trading privileges with the United States. By making free trade dependent on the acceptance of "internationally recognized worker rights" as defined exclusively by the United States (and, more specifically, the U.S. executive), the United States can of course appear to be endorsing humanitarian transnational forms of labor regulation while, in actuality, interpreting and applying those norms in a highly discretionary manner so as to serve a coterie of political and economic purposes unrelated to the struggle to protect working people from the vicissitudes of globalization. How else can we explain why those applying U.S. international labor rights legislation have been able to get away with providing trading privileges to some of the most repressive labor regimes on the planet?

From this perspective, the vagueness plaguing U.S. labor-conditionality clauses in trade law is inextricably tied to a broader problem, namely the United States' occasional preference for "going it alone" in international politics, especially in its dealings with those countries in the Caribbean, Latin America, and Southeast Asia that traditionally compose its political and economic "sphere or influence." As long as transnational labor regulation is limited chiefly to the unilateral discretionary decisions of an economic and political superpower, it would be a mistake to expect too much from it. Transnational labor protections are unlikely to gain consistent application unless supported by an effective system of multilateral political coordination.

The North American Free Trade Agreement

The emergence of regional political and economic blocs (NAFTA, EU, and ASEAN) suggests the possibility of a path beyond the pathologies of vague labor protections unilaterally interpreted and applied in accordance with the dictates of superpower Realpolitik. In the face of some empirical evidence suggesting that ongoing changes in contemporary capitalism primarily fall under the rubric of economic triadization or regionalization, the emergence of regional forms of governance would seem to provide a natural playing field for those hoping to develop effective transnational strategies in order to counteract the erosion of labor standards and rights. And not only does NAFTA represent a multilateral body dedicated to the advancement of regional economic integration, but it is also at least formally committed to minimizing "social dumping" by developing a shared framework of labor standards and rights.

Unfortunately, NAFTA has yet to make much headway in halting the "rush-to-the-bottom" in labor protections, as evinced by a continuing pattern of labor abuse in precisely those areas of the North American economy—for example, the low-wage Maquiladoras region at the U.S.-Mexican border—now booming in part as a consequence of NAFTA.[27] Revealingly, both Ralph Nader and the conservatives at the *Wall Street Journal* agree that the supervisory system established by the North American Agreement on Labor Cooperation (NAALC) has proven ineffective.[28] Even when those dispute resolution devices (most important, the NAO, or National Administrative Office) established in each of NAFTA's three member-states for the purpose of enforcing the labor side-agreement finally get around to acknowledging possible illegalities, effective sanctions are unlikely to be enforced: Workers who successfully file complaints are typically left with nothing but a piece of paper acknowledging the justice of their cause, and even after a favorable ruling on their behalf, their jobs are unlikely to be reinstated or their labor union recognized.[29] The most severe sanction thus far seems to be a piddling $9,000 fine leveled against a Hyundai subsidiary in Tijuana for violations of basic health and safety rules; the U.S. government cannot even confirm that Mexico ever actually received payment from Hyundai. Some initial evidence suggests that the possibility of gaining redress for a violation of labor standards by means of NAALC is functioning as a useful organizing tool for labor activists struggling to focus public attention on dire workplace conditions found within increasingly broad sectors of the North American economy.[30] To be sure, it would be dogmatic to preclude a priori the possibility of transforming the NAALC mechanisms into a more effective tool for labor than it presently is; indeed, part of that process of transformation might very well rely on making use of NAALC precisely in order to show how its existing institutional form clashes with its own more ambitious stated goals. But as it stands today, NAALC is chiefly providing a humanitarian window dressing for the ongoing reorganization of the North American economy along fundamentally neoliberal lines. Just as American multinationals love to deflect criticism by advertising their (ineffective) corporate codes of conduct, so too does NAALC provide North American politicians and officials with a convenient device for obscuring NAFTA's real-life impact on workers.

Here as well, the legal structure of NAALC helps explain its inefficacy. First of all, NAALC presupposes the existence of three distinct national systems of labor law, and it does nothing to promote the harmonization of labor law among NAFTA's members.[31] As a result, it necessarily fails to discourage mobile capital from "shopping" for locations—for example, the southern side of the Rio Grande—with excellent access to lucrative markets but weak records of protecting labor rights and standards. The notion of the generality of law is a complex one, since the demand for like rules for like cases begs the question of what constitutes a "like case" in the first place. Nonetheless, it is striking that NAALC is predicated on the right of businesses operating within North America to treat employees in an inconsistent and highly differentiated matter for the sake of maximizing profits. Mexican employees at a Hyundai subsidiary in Mexico are likely to be subject to a different set of labor rules than those in Canada or the United States., and employees doing the same job for the same firm in three different parts of the North American "common market" hypothetically could be subject to three very different labor law regimes.[32] The much-touted legal integration of the North American economy, it seems, is consistent with a highly differentiated and arguably inconsistent set of labor protections. From a business perspective, a harmonization of standards in accordance with the lowest common denominator would probably prove most advantageous. In light of the improbability of realizing this preference in the immediate future, however, the maintenance of three distinct systems of labor norms has much to be said on its behalf from the perspective of capital: NAFTA makes it easier for firms to outsource or shift production to areas with lax labor laws, or at least plausibly threaten to do so, thereby at the very least improving capital's bargaining position in relation to labor where labor rights and standards are likely to be most generous.

NAALC mainly requires of each member that it "ensure that its [own] labor laws and regulations provide for high labor standards"(Article 2) without specifying how labor systems as different as those within North America can simultaneously provide "high" standards.[33] The fact of the matter is that Mexican labor law, though impressive on paper, is poorly and inconsistently enforced, while U.S. labor law is lacking as well when compared to its more generous Canadian sister. NAALC also calls for each of its member-states to enforce its own system of labor law. Yet even this demand is probably a paper tiger. Although NAALC calls for an extensive system of trilateral consultation and information sharing on a broad range of labor-related topics, it specifies that its dispute resolution mechanism ultimately only applies to three specific areas: occupational safety and health, child labor, and minimum wage issues, and even then only in the case of a "persistent pattern" of abuse (Article 27). NAALC effectively excludes from the outset the possibility that its trilateral dispute mechanisms might ever actively intervene in matters concerning labor union rights in such a way as to generate an arbitral decision and financial penalty; in order to avoid any ambiguity on this matter, the architects of NAALC expressly relegated crucial labor rights to an agreement annex as a way of emphasizing their limited significance for the dispute resolution system. In case labor activists nonetheless still try to employ the meager possibilities provided by NAALC, the agreement also includes a crucial escape clause: Article 49 expressly states that inaction in enforcing health and safety standards, child labor laws, or the minimum wage is legal when it "reflects a reasonable exercise" of the member-state's "discretion with respect to investigatory, prosecutorial, regulatory or compliance matters," or when it "results from bona fide decisions to allocate resources to enforcement in respect of other labor matters determined to have higher priorities." In (only slightly more) blunt terms: NAALC probably need not be enforced if any of its member-states willy-nilly determines not to do so.[34]

In addition to its circumscribed scope, the NAALC system of dispute resolution is complicated and opaque, and it is likely to take years and enormous energy (as well as resources) in order to see a complaint through to the end. Grievances wind their way through a complex process involving consultations between national representatives (at the NAO),

> ministerial consultations, through [to] an evaluation by a committee of experts, to a draft and final evaluation report, to party-to-party consultation, to an arbitration panel [chosen by NAFTA's three members], through an initial and final report by the arbitration panel, to the possible reconvening of the panel, to a second possible reconvening of the panel, to the imposition of a 'monetary enforcement assessment,' to the possible reconvening of the Arbitration panel, to a final report to the parties in dispute.[35]

No wonder that labor activists have found NAALC so frustrating: its Kafkaesque legal attributes prevent it from serving as an effective instrument for supervising even the limited arena of labor-related issues with which it is concerned. A revealing double standard is at work as well. As one labor advocate has rightly noted, "[t]he procedure established here contrasts sharply with other forms of dispute resolution" established for business, which is provided with relatively efficient and speedy devices. Capital, it seems, is deserving of the chief accouterments of an effective system of justice, whereas labor is not.[36] For example, NAALC's enforcement procedures are controlled by its three member-states; labor obviously can influence this process, but the pursuit of a complaint ultimately rests in the hands of political authorities. In contrast, NAFTA gives business comparatively unmediated power to force the resolution of a conflict. For example, Chapter 11(B) allows private firms to submit certain complaints against member states to a three-person tribunal, one of whose members is chosen by the affected member-state, another by the firm, and a third jointly by the two parties;

NAFTA thereby effectively grants states and corporations equal authority in some crucial decision-making matters. In contrast, the procedures making up NAALC seem to have been rigged so as to hinder the protection of even basic labor rights and standards. In a similar vein, investors and holders of intellectual property rights are granted direct access by NAFTA to the courts of any of its member-states, but NAALC (Article 42) denies this same right of access to labor.

Many critics have persuasively argued that NAALC can only serve labor interests by overcoming its manifest legal ills, and others have gone even further to demand that a progressive reform of NAFTA must pursue an "upward harmonization of labor standards and rights"—that is, movement beyond the present acceptance of a differentiated and inconsistent system of labor rights and standards.[37] Efforts in this direction are surely deserving of applause. Nonetheless, one should have no illusions about the imposing hurdles facing this strategy. Here as well, a paucity of rule of law virtues is tied to the existence of awesome real-life power inequalities; the admirable quest to enhance the legal integrity of NAALC implies a serious challenge to those inequalities. As we saw above, the vague and open-ended character of unilateral labor standards makes them a useful instrument of American Realpolitik. Although the trilateral character of NAFTA at least potentially serves as a check on the traditional U.S. preference to "go it alone" in matters affecting its North American "backyard," NAFTA's escape clause (Article 49) provides possibilities for member-states to disregard NAALC's stated aspiration to achieve "high" labor standards throughout North America. Of course, one can imagine any of NAFTA's three members making use of this exception clause; in particular, it seems well-suited as a loophole for Mexican elites trying to ward off legitimate criticism of corruption within the Mexican labor movement. Nevertheless, it is worth noting that legal vagaries of this type ultimately tend to privilege interests possessing the most impressive de facto economic and political power: When the rules of a game on the playground are unclear, it is most likely the biggest and strongest kids who will succeed in enforcing their particular interpretation. Similarly, Article 49 provides an obvious instrument not only for North America's biggest economy and greatest political force to escape from obligations potentially imposed on it by NAALC, but its interpretation is most likely to favor the United States, given its enormous factual power advantages vis-à-vis Mexico and Canada.

This prospect raises fundamental questions about the limits of regional political and economic blocs in situations where one member-state is obviously so much more powerful than its peers.[38] Although the multilateral character of NAFTA anticipates the possibility of counteracting the United States' preference for politically pliable unilateral labor standards, NAFTA will probably never fully succeed at this task.[39] Only a broader multilateral system of political and legal coordination, predicated on a real possibility of neutralizing the United States' tremendous de facto economic and political advantages, possesses a superior chance of guaranteeing a consistent system of genuinely humanitarian transnational labor standards.[40]

LABOR STANDARDS AND THE WTO

Under the Clinton Administration, the United States' apparent willingness to rely on the World Trade Organization (WTO) in order to enforce core labor rights and minimal labor standards seemed to present an exciting potential resolution to the enigmas described above.[41] The WTO is an authentically multilateral organization, in which decision making by consensus is the norm, thus arguably offering better prospects for exercising an effective check on great power Realpolitik than NAFTA or even the IMF and World Bank, whose weighted voting devices unambiguously privilege the United States and other major powers. In addition, the WTO's dispute resolution devices contain some legalistic attributes, at least when compared to many other forms of international economic regulation, and a number of important rulings have already been decided against the most powerful capitalist states (including the United States). For this reason as well, there seems to be solid testimony that the inclusion of a "labor clause" in the WTO not only might stand a chance of gaining effective enforcement but that its application could take a relatively consistent and universal form.

The United States' recent support for revising the WTO indeed seemed surprising in light of the leading role played by the United States in aggressively advocating neoliberal policies worldwide. It also generated an unusual constellation of political forces, in which U.S. officials at least briefly appeared to stand alongside the Nordic countries, the international labor movement, and progressive activists defending a "labor clause" as an instrument for reforming the WTO in order to counteract the ugliest consequences of economic globalization. U.S. support for amending the WTO also pitted the United States against developing countries which see even the most minimal forms of transnational labor regulation as constituting protectionist devices aimed at thwarting legitimate competition from low-wage countries now finally beginning to challenge Western Europe, Japan, and the United States on the global market.[42] In a surprising twist of events, precisely those countries which twenty-five years ago complained so vehemently about the imperialistic intentions of (mostly American-owned) multinationals, now found themselves aggressively denouncing even the most pallid transnational labor protections as dangerous attempts to buttress western economic hegemony.[43] To be sure, there was something disingenuous about the recent rediscovery of crude free-market arguments against minimal labor protections among political elites in China, India, Indonesia, Egypt, and Malaysia. It is hardly self-evident that restrictions on the use of child or prison labor express a particularistic western cultural arrogance inconsistent with non-Western forms of cultural identity. Furthermore, many of these same countries have long publicly endorsed ILO conventions covering basic labor rights and standards; from the perspective of international law, they already are at least formally obliged to respect models of labor rights and standards far more ambitious than anything likely to emerge out of the WTO.[44] Legitimate worries about the cultural insensitivity of the rich countries of the West, mixed in with a heavy dose of understandable but ultimately misguided populism, are being cynically employed by elites in the developing world in order to justify some of the nastiest facets of authoritarian capitalism.

Nonetheless, there are good reasons for worrying that a reformed WTO might serve as an instrument for perpetuating the privileged position of the United States within the global political economy. However disingenuous, there is a grain of truth to criticisms emanating from the developing world. On the one hand, activists and labor unionists are right to try to modify the WTO so as to assure transnational labor rights and standards. The WTO is not only here to stay, but it is likely to continue to play a significant role in global economic life, and thus it would be irresponsible for the left to abandon it as a site of political struggle. On the other hand, it is probably no accident that the United States was willing to support a WTO labor clause. The evidence examined in the first section of this essay underscores the likelihood that certain key representatives of the American political and corporate classes have come to understand that seemingly humanitarian labor clauses in trade agreements hardly need impinge on neoliberal policy, as long as the relevant clauses lack minimal attributes of modern formal legality. Although the left is obviously justified in thematizing WTO insensitivity to the side effects of globalization, it will need to fight hard to minimize the possibility that any revision of the WTO reproduces the legal perils discussed above. Otherwise the international labor movement may find itself hoodwinked by the appealing rhetoric—but unattractive reality— of pseudohumanitarian labor standards, just as their allies in the AFL-CIO have seen their high hopes shattered by the cynical record of U.S. domestic legislation concerning "internationally recognized worker rights."

How then might a WTO labor clause be vulnerable to the pathologies of discretionary legal application and enforcement according to the dictates of great power Realpolitik? Notwithstanding WTO's promotion of its decision-making procedures as a paragon of consensus-oriented multilateral global democracy,[45] in fact the insistence on consensus "actually operates as a sort of weighted-voting provision, given that the larger powers will undoubtedly always have a presence at any important decision-making opportunity." A consensus only needs to be achieved among members actually present at meetings when decisions are made, which in practical terms means that countries which "find it financially or politically difficult to have adequate representation at the WTO may find decisions made that they do not want."[46] If strictly applied, the norm of consensus would indeed provide every member with veto authority. But in part by failing to formalize a right of veto for those members not in attendance, the most powerful member-states are likely to gain "an even larger share of the power than policy or equity might dictate."[47] In short, the much-touted informality of the consensus-oriented decision-making structure of the WTO risks playing into the hands of the richest and most powerful countries arguably no less than do the weighted-voting devices operative within the IMF or World Bank.

Nor do the WTO's dispute resolution devices neatly conform to traditional models of legality, despite the WTO's self-advertised fidelity to the idea of the "rule of law." The WTO Agreement is filled with exceptional clauses and vague loopholes. It bears little resemblance to the relatively clear and cogent legal codes sought by advocates of modern conceptions of legality, instead providing vast scope for a highly discretionary process of adjudication. In addition, deliberations of WTO tribunals are confidential, and opinions expressed in the tribunal reports remain anonymous.[48] Not only does this failing represent a blatant abrogation of the modern ideal of the publicity of law and legal proceedings, but it works alongside the WTO's discretionary system of norms to raise the specter of an irregular mode of adjudication whose only real commitment is to the core neoliberal beliefs presently driving WTO policy. The fact that WTO judges tend to share "an institutionally derived [neoliberal] philosophy about international commerce" only exacerbates this problem.[49] In short, there are legitimate reasons for worrying that the WTO dispute resolution mechanisms provide ample possibilities for powerful interests in the global political economy to undermine the classical principle of treating like cases in a like way.[50]

The prospect that a labor clause within the WTO might take the form of one of the "general exceptions" to free trade already accepted as part and parcel of the WTO legal system should raise some eyebrows. The International Metalworkers' Federation has long argued that escape clauses allowing countries temporarily to restrict low-price imports which seriously disrupt domestic production should be expanded so as to apply to imports whose low price has been influenced by a failure to respect basic labor protections, while others have suggested that the numerous escape clauses outlined in Article XX (which already refer to public health and environmental matters) should be amended to cover labor issues.[51] In light of the argument developed above, it should be clear why this approach may prove ill-suited to the interests of labor; it should also be clear why a great power like the United States is likely to benefit from it. A general escape clause "implies unilateral measures and does not envisage the desired multilateral negotiations," thereby providing individual WTO member-states with possibilities for reneging on trade commitments when a particular condition (allegedly) has not been satisfied.[52] As one prominent trade law expert has pointed out, the language of these escape clauses "is so general and ambiguous . . . that nations" have often claimed to fulfill their prerequisites "in many plausible but marginal circumstances," and escape clauses have been abused on many occasions during the history of GATT and the WTO.[53] Here as well, it becomes easy to conceive of a labor clause—particularly if allowed to take a relatively open-ended form, as do most of the existing escape clauses in WTO—serving as legal front for crude power politics. Even if every WTO member were formally outfitted with the authority to make use of an escape clause of this type, the possibility of unilaterally freeing oneself from legal obligations ultimately is most likely to serve the interests of those in possession of the greatest de facto economic and political influence. It is difficult to imagine a scenario in which a developing country might renege on its free trade obligations with the United States by legitimately appealing to evidence of labor abuse in the United States. An "uppity" attitude of this type simply does not pay given the present-day distribution of power in the global political economy, where many developing countries desperately need American investment or at least access to the American market. At the same time, the United States—as we have seen—now has a long history of using labor clauses within its traditional sphere of influence in order to mask its exercise of political and economic pressure with humanitarian rhetoric. Little imagination is required to see the United States similarly making use of a WTO labor escape clause for the sake of pursuing, on the global scale, its economic and political interests. The historical record suggests that the United States is most likely to threaten to employ a labor clause of this type in order to gain concessions (e.g., the breakup of Korean *chaebols* or the privatization of public property in India) where labor abuses may indeed be rampant, while simultaneously ignoring similar records of abuse in countries more willing to toe the line of the "Washington Consensus." Unfortunately, it is improbable that the United States will be serious about challenging the mistreatment of labor even in those countries subject to its unilateral application of a labor escape clause: Experience with existing U.S. transnational labor standards suggests that countries are likely to receive the necessary stamp of approval as soon as cosmetic reforms are made and the desired political and economic concessions to the United States are forthcoming.

A skeptical assessment of the U.S. endorsement of a WTO labor clause is justified for another reason as well. As many commentators have pointed out, recent American enthusiasm for a WTO labor clause initially seems odd in light of the fact that the International Labor Organization already functions, albeit inadequately, as the main multilateral institution committed to developing a network of transnational labor protections. Despite the widely acknowledged weaknesses of the ILO system of enforcement, the organization does have a long history of grappling with the difficult problems faced by advocates of transnational labor rights and standards: Most important for our purposes here, the ILO has thought long and hard about how to develop a system of norms that acknowledges the real economic and cultural complexities of the task at hand (for example, the fact that a minimum wage today surely must take a different form in Great Britain or Switzerland than in India), while nonetheless striving to achieve legal integrity and efficacy.[54] And the ILO possesses an impressive administrative apparatus (including a well-trained staff of researchers and experts on labor issues and labor law), as well as relatively close ties to the labor movement and activists sympathetic to it. So if the United States is genuinely concerned about developing effective transnational labor protections, why does it not simply ratify the numerous ILO norms which it thus far has failed to endorse and join forces with the many labor unions long committed to undergirding the nascent ILO-based system of transnational labor standards? Labor unions have long struggled to strengthen the ILO's presently insufficient enforcement mechanisms, but they increasingly have faced fierce resistance from employers and many ILO member-states.[55] Surely, the United States could help play a role in turning the tide within the ILO in favor of labor.

The question is easily answered. Whatever its faults, the ILO is not only a multilateral organization but one that takes seriously the notion that great powers should be subject to the same rules and standards as lesser powers: The ILO has long been committed to the principle that transnational labor protections must rest on fair and consistent procedures having a real chance of being employed effectively against all member-states, not on open-ended legal loopholes or escape clauses vulnerable to unilateral application and gross manipulation. American ambivalence towards the ILO points to "a major discrepancy between the United States' refusal to submit itself to multilateral accountability (through the ILO), and its preparedness to subject others to a form of accountability in which the United States acts as the sole legislator, judge, jury, and enforcement authority."[56] The United States is ultimately uninterested in genuinely strengthening the ILO because unlike the WTO, an enhanced ILO would offer a more effective forum for those hoping to pose a political challenge to neoliberalism and U.S. unilateralism: The ILO is a relatively democratic organization committed to advancing the cause of both an international "rule of law" *and* social reform. The ILO's unusual decision-making structure—in which organized labor possesses the same number of votes as business representatives[57]—meshes poorly with the direction of contemporary U.S. policy. Neoliberalism has successfully suggested to political and elites virtually everywhere that they now can get their way without granting a meaningful say in economic affairs to organized labor. Not surprisingly, the United States—the main political force supporting neoliberalism on the global scale—is uninterested in strengthening an organization that increasingly looks like a throwback to the days when labor unions were seen as having a legitimate role to play within the capitalist economy.

In short, the disturbing legacy of U.S. transnational labor standards raises difficult questions for those of us committed to taming globalization by means of assuring effective global legal protections. The U.S. experience suggests that labor activists enthusiastic about the prospect of including social and labor standards within the WTO would do well to pay close attention to the pathologies of the U.S. experience; from the perspective developed here, a (dramatically) reformed ILO is probably a better starting point for making sure that transnational labor standards ultimately realize the interconnected tasks of protecting basic rule of law virtues and challenging the increasingly shocking inequities of the global capitalist economy. My aim here has not been to cast equal doubt on all policy options, notwithstanding my critical comments regarding many different types of present-day transnational labor standards. But those of us committed to supporting a viable worker rights strategy would do well to recognize the nature of the difficulties at hand. I do this not for the sake of deflating the dream of a global economy both respectful of worker rights and the rule of law, but rather because we can only move towards that ideal if we remain brutally honest about the complexities of the political tasks at hand.

4 Neumann Versus Habermas
The Frankfurt School and the
Case of the Rule of Law

At a historical junction when fascism was well on its way to becoming Europe's dominant political force, the Institute for Social Research's resident political and legal theorist, Franz Neumann, came to see a variety of modern legal ideals as enduring contributions to democratic politics. Fascism's abandonment of them represented nothing less than liberal bourgeois society's rejection of its greatest achievements. For Neumann, a defense of a rather traditional conception of the rule of law played a key role in this project. While Max Horkheimer and Theodor Adorno were using Max Weber to offer a traumatic and somewhat one-sided portrayal of Western development, Neumann instead relied on Weber to salvage the emancipatory universalistic features of the modern legal tradition, in his eyes embodied most clearly in the ideal of the rule of law and its emphasis on clearly formulated general legal norms which do "not mention particular cases or individually nominated persons, but which [are] issued in advance to apply to all cases and all persons in the abstract." [1]

Throughout his illustrious career, Jürgen Habermas has tended to criticize precisely this position.[2] In arguing against Weber and Weberian analyses, which stress the importance of the systematic and coherent semantic form of law for understanding what is specifically "modern" about it, Habermas worries that it leads too many authors, as it did Weber, to an unjustifiably hostile assessment of nonformal modes of law seemingly essential to the democratic welfare state, where vague legal standards, indefinite blanket clauses, and other legal acts arguably incompatible with classical conceptions of the rule of law are widespread. By means of a comparison of Neumann and Habermas' respective restatements of the Weberian story of legal rationalization, I accept the basic soundness of Habermas' concerns. Yet I also reformulate Neumann's argument and show why the anxieties about nonclassical modes of law underlying it, despite Habermas' occasional claims to the contrary, need to be taken seriously. Neumann's admittedly old-fashioned defense of a classical conception of the rule of law is more vital to Habermas' own project than he cares to admit. I also respond to criticisms which Habermas potentially might raise against my project of synthesizing traditional concerns about the structure of the legal norm with a critical theory of law and democracy.

NEUMANN ON LEGAL RATIONALIZATION

In *The Theory of Communicative Action,* the programmatic contours of Habermas' legal thinking in many ways strikingly parallel Franz Neumann's during the late 1930s and early 1940s. Neumann also undertook to recast Weber's groundbreaking analysis of the rationalization of law in *Economy and Society* in an explicitly democratic and anticapitalist fashion, and his mammoth 1936 *Governance of The Rule of Law* examined "the process of the divorce of positive from natural law, by which positive law became self-sufficient and autonomous . . . a process which, from the analogy of Max Weber's famous generalization of the 'disenchantment of the world,' we may call a 'disenchantment of law'."[3] With its overtly Weberian contours later deemphasized, the argument then formed the basis for Neumann's famous articles in the *Zeitschrift für Sozialforschung*[4] and the theoretical core of the 1942 *Behemoth: The Structure and Practice of National Socialism.*

Ambitiously synthesizing social history, a critical sociology of ideas, and an examination of political and legal theory extending from Aquinas to Hegel, Neumann's study traces the transformation of universalistic natural law into a system of codified positive general legal norms like that which Weber had described as modern rational legality.[5] Like Weber, he highlights the centrality of the increasing systematization and precision of law. In his gloss on this thesis, legal development in the West is essentially the story of the struggle to rid it of vague standards (e.g., "emergency," "necessity," "prerogative") which provide easy openings for poorly restrained, irregular, situation-specific forms of raison d'etat-type state action; hence, Neumann's description of western legal development as an epic battle between sovereignty and law. Yet in anticipation of Habermas and in contradistinction to Weber, Neumann argues that praiseworthy trends towards a fully rational-legal order are destined to remain unfinished within the confines of a bourgeois social and economic order. Contra Weber (as well as Marx), "bourgeois" formal law is not, in reality, merely bourgeois. Though complementing capitalism at some historical junctures, general law ultimately conflicts with it. If the rule of law is to be preserved, capitalism will have to be challenged. In my reading of the complex and multisided *The Governance of the Rule of Law,* Neumann advances this highly provocative argument most directly by means of pointing to four competing paths of legal development, each of which offers a separate answer to the normative and practical problems posed by the disintegration of natural law as well as distinct and more or less secularized versions of the modern rule of law. If we are to appreciate both the merits of Neumann's own gloss on the problem of legal rationalization as well its differences vis-à-vis Habermas' more recent reconstruction of Weber, we will have to take a closer look at them.

Neumann first describes a "classical liberal" path allegedly implied by the Lockean rule of law and then more fully worked out by Blackstone and Dicey as well as English political practice in the eighteenth and nineteenth centuries. Here natural law was eventually abandoned and replaced by (a) the idea of parliament as absolutely sovereign and (b) the belief that parliament can only issue law general in nature. Appearances to the contrary, Neumann argues, these tenets were not contradictory given a particular social configuration presupposed by them. General norms were essential to guaranteeing economic calculability in early capitalism, and a close fit between a classical liberal legal order based on them and a competitive bourgeois economy consisting of relatively equal small and medium entrepreneurs obtained: The early liberal state did "not intervene by individual measures because such an intervention would violate the principle of the equality of competitors" so sacred to early bourgeois economic ideology.[6] Conveniently, parliamentary institutions sympathetic to bourgeois development, like those found in Britain during the period in question, typically limited themselves to issuing general norms.

Emphasizing this version of the rule of law's role in disguising the hegemony of privileged bourgeois strata, Neumann is quick to point to its limitations. Political participation was limited to a narrow group of property owners; the general legal norm did little more than preserve early capitalist economic calculability and conceal the concrete power claims of an emerging bourgeois power elite: "In paying reverence to the 'law,' one can conceal the fact that the 'law' is made by man."[7] Neumann complements this view that the classical liberal model provided little legal security to the lower classes with an innovative analysis of common law, building on Weber's similar analysis in *Economy and Society* but going beyond it in a number of ways: The common law remained irregular and traditional precisely in those areas where its systematization might have generated real security for broad masses of the population. According to this view, general law was discarded whenever the basic imperatives of the bourgeois order were threatened or when it came to justifying colonialism. Sovereignty never vanished here: Lockean prerogative "coincides with the sphere of competence of the federative power"—that is, with foreign policy, and Locke's own willingness to trade in the rule of law for lawless state action on the theoretical level was all too representative of real-life English colonial practice.[8]

Although Neumann's discussion of this developmental path focuses on debunking it by pointing to its ugly bourgeois underside, the structure of his critique depends on taking the classical liberal legal norm seriously. Crucially, the problem here is not the legal general norm per se, but instead the failure and even impossibility of extending its advantages to all classes in a highly antagonistic social setting: Only this explains why Neumann tries to identify some redeeming qualities even in this basically bourgeois rendition of rule of law, and why even here he tells us that classical law "has in the first place the function of establishing equality"—albeit an equality primarily among the propertied.[9] At least as far the well-off are concerned, general law provided legal security and contributed to personal liberty. Insofar as it fit and thereby helped perpetuate a developing capitalist economy characterized by a relatively wide dispersion of economic resources, it secured some measure of real economic equality as well. Even in its most explicitly bourgeois form, formal law was always more than mere ideology; even in classical liberalism there were intimations of what Neumann describes as its historically "transcendent" "ethical function." When the legislator need not act according to general norms—if he "can issue individual commands, if he can arrest this or that man, if he can confiscate this or that property"—the most basic measure of legal security is badly undermined.[10]

In a second "authoritarian legalist" path, whose theoretical outlines Neumann locates in Kant's jurisprudence, natural law has similarly vanished, but only a dreary form of authoritarianism has replaced it. With the nineteenth-century Prussian *Rechtsstaat* in mind, Neumann describes the familiar story of the failed and defensive German middle classes, "politically in a state of subjection and . . . content with making money," who traded off the right to control parliament for the mere promise that legal security is to be guaranteed by clear, public, general law.[11] Arguing against Weber and many others who have underplayed the significance of law's genesis for determining its legitimacy, Neumann thinks that this path demonstrates that the replacement of natural law with the mere demand for coherent systematized formal law is likely to be a dreadful recipe for authoritarianism, albeit an authoritarianism predictable in character. The general lesson here is that the universalistic legacy of natural law optimally should culminate both in the demand for "equality before the law" (and the generality of law) *and* decision making resting on universal participation. Though Weber insists that modern rational law necessarily lacks any real normative basis, Neumann, anticipating Habermas, believes that the rule of law should not burn its bridges to classical natural law: A democratic version of the rule of law will have to restate that legacy's lasting insights in a sufficiently modern form. According to Neumann's reading of Kant, the Enlightenment philosopher failed to tie his ethical theory adequately to his legal and political philosophy; this failure constituted a crucial source of the democratic inadequacies of Kant's thought as well as an exemplary case of the ills of nineteenth-century Germany. Specifically, Kant's distinction between "external" (legal) acts and duties from "internal" (moral) not only foreshadowed the emergence of legal positivism, but in fact it already represented a positivist position: The mistaken and politically troublesome quest to separate an analysis of law from the question of democratic legitimacy was already implied here. Kant's formalistic moral theory and the vision of the social contract resulting from it either must hide implicit substantive assumptions sanctifying private property, in which case its formalism is a fraud, or, alternatively, the Kantian social contract has to be interpreted in such a formal manner that it is capable of being used to justify pretty much anything. If the latter is the case, it suggests why Kant's theory was ultimately impotent in the face of the exercise of state sovereignty. Able to legitimize virtually anything, its well-known compromises with the Prussian status quo were more than coincidental. In this reading, the Kantian social contract is merely a "transcendental idea," an abstract and exceedingly formalistic standard which need not result in political democracy and is incapable of undermining irrational authoritarianism: "The natural law has disappeared with it; but with it, democracy also."[12]

Neumann's description of a third and as of yet unrealized path, based on a sympathetic exegesis of Rousseau, intends to show how we might overcome the weaknesses of its historical competitors. Neumann also clearly thinks that this model should orient left-wing political practice. "At the frontier of bourgeois thought," its outstanding characteristic lies in the anticipation of an egalitarian post-capitalist order which the author believes might finally allow us to complete the liberation of the legal order from nongeneral raison d'etat-type law. Here, the general legal norm takes on "an entirely ethical function": as Rousseau's theory implies, general legal norms embody a democratic general will only given far-reaching social and economic equality. Amidst inequality, it may well be for the common good to undertake legislative actions nongeneral or situation-specific in structure. "If the state is confronted by a monopoly, it is pointless to regulate this monopoly by general law. In such a case, the individual measure is the only appropriate expression of the sovereign power."[13] This indeed is why Weber's view that formal law complements capitalism only obtains for small-scale competitive capitalism—and even there, as noted, only to a limited extent. Neumann seems to believe that given the nonegalitarian structure of contemporary capitalism, nongeneral law becomes a necessary evil, something that conscientious legislators cognizant of the virtues of the legal security provided by classical general law should struggle to avoid but that is, at times, inescapable. In any case, only in an alternative postcapitalist world—or so Neumann's surprising social democratic revamping of Rousseau posits—does the French philosopher's argument obtain: Only then does general law express a genuinely democratic "general will," and only then would there no longer be any need for nongeneral state action (directed, for example, at a particular corporation). General law could finally be universalized, its virtues accrue to everyone, and the rule of (general) law finally made perfect. Neumann himself depicts this possibility in even more dramatic colors: "The sovereign power then ceases to be sovereign, it is no longer an external power confronting the subjects. It is rather society which governs and administers itself"; "Rousseau's theory is, in fact, an interpretation of the Marxian theory of the withering away of the state; of the emergence of a society free from external rule."[14] On this as of yet unrealized path to rational legality, state power itself has finally been tamed and the epic struggle between sovereignty and law resolved. In a world of democratic republics, substantial economic equality, and a legal order limited to clearly formulated general norms, unregulated exercises of state authority would become both unnecessary and impossible. The state would nominally maintain its monopoly on coercion, but what would this really amount to?

Now, there are undoubtedly a number of genuine problems with this account. However, let me focus on what I take to be most relevant for our comparison to Habermas. Notwithstanding Neumann's claim that this third path presupposes a democratic political setting, he revealingly says remarkably little about this feature. Beyond praising Rousseau for seeing the social contract as "an ideal to be realized in history" and making odd references to some undefined vision of a decentralized "organic democracy" (in contrast to "atomistic constructions of democracy"), we are told nothing of any substance.[15] This is hardly accidental. Here, "the individual will and general will coincide"; Rousseau's "theory resembles that of Marx ... Marx has filled in Rousseau's logical structure with history," and as in Marx's rather antipolitical and antipluralist utopia, Neumann likely believes that a particular mode of social and economic organization guarantees this coincidence without political conflict and exchange, like that essential to a genuinely democratic mode of politics, having to play much of a role.[16] As in the case of Rousseau himself, general law is ultimately conceptualized as expressing a substantive "general will" directly extant in social and economic life. Like Habermas, and in contradistinction to Weber, Neumann has no qualms about locating an "ethical moment" in the rule of law. Yet he identifies this ethical feature directly with the generality of the legal norm. In the final analysis, democracy ultimately appears to be little more than a presupposition, though a crucial one, which helps legal generality manifest an ethical quality which is seen as being implicit in it.

From Habermas' perspective, this is all very revealing. The second-generation Frankfurt critical theorist has famously criticized Weber for relying upon a truncated conception of rationality that exaggerates the significance of the systematic and coherent semantic structure of law, while obscuring the centrality of the rational argumentation underlying a broader complex of practices and institutions that generate democratic legitimacy.[17] In his view, legality does require legitimacy, but this legitimacy can only be conceptualized in terms of formal procedures supportive of the uncoerced exchange of opinions: Law's reasonableness stems from the (universal) debate and exchange which generate it and not its semantic form. This was never grasped by Weber because he doubted the possibility of institutionalizing a modern, disenchanted procedural morality. Those who continue to emphasize the general structure of the legal norm risk reproducing Weber's error: They focus on law's semantic generality and tend to underplay the democratic process' "procedural universalism" of (universal) participatory and communicative rights and procedures essential to the "types of deliberation and decision making that take equally into consideration all relevant aspects of an issue and all interests involved."[18]

Despite its advances vis-à-vis Weber, Neumann's argument would seem to confirm Habermas' anxieties. Neumann continually suggests the importance of law's (general) democratic genesis, but in his obsessive Weberian focus on law's semantic form, he is never able to adequately work out this insight. Although Habermas can locate the sources of modern legitimacy in a theory of democracy, this path seems barred to Neumann, who uncritically accepts too many of Weber's basic assumptions—not the least of which was Weber's cramped conceptualization of rationality.[19]

Interestingly, *The Governance of The Rule of Law* opens with a refreshingly appreciative assessment of the social contract tradition in Western political thought, with Neumann telling the reader that "even if . . . no state ever was established by contract, the category of the Social Contract might be a methodological principle necessary for the justification of the state or freedom from it."[20] The idea of the social contract, he tentatively observes in the work's opening pages, could offer the starting point for a rational theory of political legitimacy. Unfortunately, this insight is never fully developed. Instead Neumann accepts a set of typically Hegelian criticisms of the social contract tradition, and then in the closely related "Types of Natural Law" (1940), he reduces the significance of the social contract to a question of philosophical anthropology: "Every social contract reduces the will of the state to the wills of the individuals and must thus have a definite view of man's character prior to the conclusion of the social contract."[21] Alternative visions of political legitimacy (based on the social contract), it seems, are to be evaluated according to the conceptions of human nature from which they are derived. Again, Neumann's relationship to Weber is illuminating here. Recall that in Weber's own gloss on the process of legal development, he had analogously argued that a perfectly formal or value-free social contract freed from any substantive natural law elements is illusory. In Weber's view, such a view of the social contract would have to depend upon a system of natural law consisting "entirely of general legal concepts devoid of any content."[22] The idea of a perfectly formal contract would have to be based on presuppositions so abstract in nature that they could only generate the most trivial conclusions. Both Neumann and Weber point to a real conceptual dilemma here; the idea of a truly formal reading of the social contract rightly remains controversial.[23] But the immediate consequences of this position for both authors nonetheless remain problematic. In the case of Weber, it is in part responsible for the well-known democratic deficiencies of his theory. Convinced of the impossibility of freeing the idea of the social contract from traditional moral presuppositions, he ultimately is less interested in its underlying insight—the fact that it posits a mode of (implicitly democratic) decision making between truly free and equal persons—than that it contains substantive moral assumptions no longer universally tenable in a morally disenchanted universe. Neumann becomes similarly obsessed with the substantive presuppositions of the social contract ideal, and, like Weber, obscures its core intuition that political legitimacy derives from a set of procedures securing the free and equal participation of all.

In contrast, while acknowledging the dangers of traditional models of the social contract, Habermas rightly does justice to its basic intuition that "only those regulations can come about that have the uncoerced agreement of all" and sees in it a "post-traditional" concept of procedural morality basic to conceptualizing democracy.[24] The social contract anticipates a pluralistic mode of politics based on a genuinely free exchange of opinions, the aspiration to consider all interests in the formulation of policy, and the hope that only the most defensible arguments will guide state action. State action can be rationalized not by subordinating it to "general" legal norms but instead by means of the generality of a genuinely inclusive brand of freewheeling deliberative politics.

NEUMANN VERSUS HABERMAS?

But perhaps we can turn the tables a bit. Even Neumann does not deny that law at times needs to take a nonclassical form. When he practiced labor law in Weimar Germany, he eloquently defended a novel conception of legal regulation, in which "self-administration" via new modes of labor participation and specialized labor law courts supplemented traditional parliamentary and constitutional lawmaking. Formulating a vision of libertarian social democracy, Neumann posited that direct state regulation of every facet of the economy would not only prove ineffective but would also engender a troublesome statization of social relations inconsistent with autonomous political and economic action. In other words, he defended a post-traditional interpretation of the rule of law in many respects at odds with classical liberal models of legislation and adjudication. Nonetheless, Neumann simultaneously insisted on the necessity of preserving classical rule of law virtues. He apparently saw no reason to exclude the possibility of embodying them in new forms of regulation.

What ultimately distinguishes him from Habermas is a more supple argument than may at first be apparent. His argument need not, in short, be read as a nostalgic defense of classical liberal law. He not only forcefully criticized classical liberal legal models in *Governance of the Rule of Law*, but his own activities as a social democratic activist and labor lawyer highlight his own deep reservations about a dogmatic fidelity to orthodox modes of lawmaking.

Inspired by the modern legal tradition's fascination with the proper (e.g., clear, general, public, prospective) structure of the legal norm, Neumann reminds us of a familiar yet decisive reality of modern political and economic life. One way, of course, by which power can be effectively regulated is by means of the legal norm. Law is the language of state authority, and if its use of this language is confused and unclear, its authority potentially will be exercised by public and private bodies—administrators, judges, or in the case of the *Lex Mercatoria*, privileged "global players"—in a correspondingly irregular fashion. If government bureaucracies are permitted to act inconsistently, if the judiciary is left to make sense of blanket clauses which can be interpreted to mean almost anything, and if private groups are outfitted with broad and ill-defined grants of authority, new forms of poorly harnessed power are likely to emerge: The possibility of autonomous social and political action most certainly will be undermined. To be sure, even the most precise legal terminology is open to alternative interpretations; nor does legal precision guarantee that the substance of a legal norm is just. Still, this should not lead us to miss the significance of the qualitative leap into discretionary decision making which the proliferation of antiformal trends in the law and post-classical legal clauses ("in good faith," "just" and "reasonable," "unconscionable," or "in the public interest") make possible. Even if we should criticize Neumann's democratic theoretical deficiencies, he was right to worry about the dangers of discretionary law.[25]

To be sure, democracy needs more than formal law. By the same token, it is hard to conceive of the possibility of a political order with energetic publics, vigorous debate, and a responsive set of institutions when poorly regulated state and new forms of public/private authority are insufficiently regulated by legal means. Ineffectively constrained decision-making bodies—at either the national or transnational level—threaten to drain the wellsprings of political and social autonomy.[26] At the very least, classical rule of law virtues provide an important way by which their activities can be carefully channeled. As part of a broader theory of democracy, the rule of law has a necessary place.

Admittedly, it has oftentimes been the political right which has pointed to the dangers of antiformal trends in the law precisely because it hoped to undermine post-liberal forms of regulation essential to the modern welfare state.[27] In contrast, political progressives like Habermas have rushed to defend them—in order to fight off right-wing attacks on the welfare state and to defend its undeniable achievements. But perhaps it is time to recognize the limitations of this division and the blindfolds it has burdened us with. Neumann, who believed that we could have both social equality and the virtues of classical law, radical social and economic reform as well as legal security, new experiments in legal regulation along with a healthy dose of classical legal virtues, can help us see why.

The immediate source of this rather old-fashioned faith in classical law probably lies in his analysis of a fourth "fascist" answer to the crisis of legal disenchantment, whose broad outlines Neumann found implicit in the legal thought of Carl Schmitt. According to this view, just as the core of Schmitt's project during the Weimar Republic's final years amounted to an argument for a mass-based plebiscitary dictatorship freed from the restraints of what he disdainfully called the "normativistic" rule of law, essential to Nazi law is its disposal of even the most minimal remnants of the universalism of the Western political and legal tradition. Despite its similarly authoritarian and bourgeois character, even authoritarian legalism à la nineteenth-century Prussia remained loyal to the classical ideal of the general legal norm. In contrast, the totalitarian Nazi Behemoth-like "rule of lawlessness" failed even on this score. In Nazi Germany, antiformal trends in the law ran amok; vague legal standards and blanket clauses predominated: "Having formerly been stepchildren of law, they now are become its darlings."[28] If the great unfinished task of legal rationalization is to rid law of imprecise terms that provide a front for unrestrained state sovereignty, Nazi law instead represented a horrific quest to subordinate the entire legal order to such principles and thus a historical regression of unheard of proportions. Whereas Schmitt's theory insisted on the primordiality of the "norm-less decision" along with the centrality of the emergency situation, Neumann provocatively argues that Nazi law gave something disturbingly akin to this seemingly abstract idea a very real and concrete form. Amorphous legal standards (most infamously, "the racial feelings of the folk") provided a perfect legal basis for a system where every one of the Nazi power elite's "decisions," regardless of its content or form, was to be legitimized. In other words, Schmitt's "norm-less" legal decisions became the legal order's guiding principle, and the state of emergency, in fact, was made into an everyday affair. Appropriately, fascist legal ideologues—Schmitt prominent among them—proceeded to exert an inordinate amount of energy in developing a so-called "institutionalist" theory of law allegedly suitable to the particular needs of the German "folk community" and the requirements of an epoch supposedly in need of equally particularistic, flexible, situation-specific forms of state regulation; this, they now argue, alone provided a "modern"(!) alternative to the "static," "lifeless" liberal rule of law and its allegedly anachronistic insistence on the generality of state action.[29]

Although it would be manifestly ridiculous to associate terroristic fascist law with contemporary antiformal legal trends, in earlier chapters of this volume I have suggested that the legal substructure of the ongoing process of economic globalization nonetheless exhibits some real dangers. Neumann's theory proffers a useful starting point for apprehending the dangers at hand. Despite its many competing virtues, this may not be the case for Habermas. Throughout his career, Habermas has arguably failed to appreciate the pivotal role formal law should play in taming economic privilege. Both in his "Tanner Lectures" and the important essay "Popular Sovereignty as Procedure: A Normative Concept of the Public Sphere," for example, he criticizes Enlightenment thinkers, such as Rousseau and Kant, for arguing that general law automatically allows the political community to express its common interests, insisting that they, like many more recent authors, confuse law's semantic generality with the broader and more basic "universality" of democratic politics.[30] For Habermas, the consequences of this criticism and the related ones mentioned above seem to be as follows:

Although correctly arguing for a richer conceptualization of democratic politics than that offered by those who tend to defend a more conventional view of the rule of law, Habermas, more problematically, does not seem especially concerned about the increased importance of vague and often-times oddly moralistic legal standards ("in good faith") and administrative discretion in the law. In contrast to thinkers as diverse as Locke, Montesquieu, Rousseau, Kant, and Hegel, for whom the generality of the legal norm itself constitutes an important condition for the exercise of legitimate political power, Habermas here tends to eliminate classical legal virtues from his list of those procedures essential to democratic decision making.

Yet this interpretation of writers such as Rousseau and Kant ignores a pivotal source of the modern tradition's preoccupation with general law. Perhaps more clearly in the case of theorists Locke and Montesquieu than Rousseau or Kant, the structure of the legal norm is seen as significant because it helps restrain state action by forcing governmental bodies to act in a manner which is predictable and calculable. This, in turn, is seen as essential for political and social freedom and as constituting a check on absolutist political tendencies. The problem with Habermas' highly selective interpretation here is that it allows him to forget that the structure of the legal norm may continue to serve as a possible instrument for regulating and channeling the exercise of state authority. Like none other, Habermas' vision of democracy places great weight on the idea of autonomous publics as part of a discursive civil society free from the "system imperatives" of the state administration. Especially a model as ambitious as this one needs to give an important place to the belief that every conceivable tool for effectively regulating state action should be employed. Classical legal virtues make up one crucial component of that "combination of power and intelligent self-restraint" he rightly believes state action needs to take.[31]

Just as Habermas' reconstruction of Kantian moral theory has shifted emphasis away from the (general) semantic structure of the moral command to the process of universalization which generates it, so too does he tend to downplay the form of law while stressing the broader processes that produce it. But we need to ask if this is altogether satisfying. In distinction from the moral sphere, political decisions are, of course, backed up by the state and its rather impressive arsenal of coercive instruments. This is one reason that institutionalized rights are essential to democratic politics: They help protect the citizen against potential abuses of state authority and thus buttress discursive processes in society. But this is also at least implicitly why classical liberalism focused on the virtues of clearly formulated general legal norms. In demanding that state action be prevented from taking forms which they saw as incompatible with autonomy, the great critics of political absolutism correctly saw the legal norm as one way by which state power could be tamed. Particularly in an era where new forms of poorly regulated and undemocratic public and private power are flourishing at the global level, the perils of irregularly exercised authority seem especially apparent.

HABERMASIAN REJOINDERS

Two possible counterarguments come immediately to mind. First, Habermas might claim that this position remains outdated, perhaps even regressive. Much of the polemical thrust of his important "Tanner Lectures" was directed against authors—especially on the right—who attack the welfare state by highlighting its abandonment of classical legal forms. Similarly, in the early texts, *The Structural Transformation of the Public Sphere* and "On the Concept of Political Participation," Habermas showed an interest in pointing to the necessity and even advantages of much deformalized legal regulation.[32]

According to this position, amorphous law has helped make the welfare state possible. In undertaking the regulation of ever more complex spheres of social life, legislatures are forced to rely on broad "result" or "purpose-oriented" grants of power and the vague legal standards that accompany them. How else is the state to regulate social spheres involving complex and ever-changing scenarios? Nonformal law provides the flexibility that modern administrators and courts need if they are to grapple with the multifaceted problems intrinsic to contemporary capitalism, and an attack on them risks becoming an anachronistic and dangerous assault on the welfare state itself.[33] Traumatized by the fascist experience, Neumann—or so the argument might continue—was ultimately insensitive to all the real advantages of "soft" deformalized law under the more democratic conditions of the contemporary welfare state. Under democratic conditions, the sacrifice of formal law can result in greater social autonomy for broad masses of the population and buttress noncoercive processes of democratic will formation. In short, Weber was right to consider classical formal law characteristically bourgeois. In moving to regulate capitalism, social democrats and welfare state liberals were equally right to dismember it.

Despite some manifest strengths, this view seems to me too defensive and self-satisfied in character. Perhaps a concrete example best shows why. Let us take the following legal act, extreme but hardly atypical, passed by the U.S. Congress in 1970, which states: "the President is authorized to issue such orders and regulations as he deems appropriate to stabilize prices, rents, wages, and salaries . . . The President may delegate the performance of any function under this Title to such officers, departments and agencies . . . as he may deem appropriate."[34] In a simpler era, this statute might have been labeled an "enabling act," and conscientious liberals and Democrats would have worried about its parceling out of (ill-defined) authority to the executive and state bureaucracy. Should we now simply chalk it up to complexity, as Habermas occasionally seems to imply? Are we to believe that the "imperatives of the administrative system" today necessitate it and that it is somehow fundamentally modern in structure?

If Habermas is right, the process of legal rationalization would have culminated in rather paradoxical results. There can be no broad agreement about what the phrases "good morals," "good faith," or "unconscionable" action mean today. Yet welfare state law makes use of these curious moral categories as well as many similar ones. The language of these standards is strikingly akin to that of a premodern and antipluralistic substantive morality, and they arguably have no place in a legal order which can only be grounded in and oriented towards a disenchanted procedural ethics like that now advocated by Habermas. As the Nazi legal order's heavy reliance on such categories suggests, they may be a potential source of serious and even dangerous misunderstandings about the nature of modern law and politics, providing an opening for those social interests with disturbing antimodern conceptions of natural law and a morally homogeneous community. Indeed, even in postwar West Germany—and certainly elsewhere as well—legal standards of this type have been interpreted in accordance with worrisome traditional conceptions of morality.[35] Those legal scholars who would respond by pointing to the fact that the anachronistic moral language of these legal norms generally plays a minor rule in their employment are too eager to forget recent legal history.

Secondly, Habermas' too-quick concession to the necessity of far-reaching antiformal trends in the law tends to foreclose any real consideration of a variety of fascinating proposals for a more transparent and less discretionary system of law—none of which necessarily imply undermining the very much unfinished quest to broaden social and economic autonomy. A suitable analysis of legal development must steer its way between the Charybdis of a conservative Hegelianism blind to contemporary law's contingent features and too eager to demonstrate its hidden "rationality" and the Scylla of a naïve faith in classical law, which underplays the necessity of complex forms of state intervention. If Habermas is right in thinking that too many critics of deformalized law succumb to the latter, his own view too often takes on the contours of the former. Hardly an opponent of the welfare state, the political scientist Theodore Lowi has shown that some of the more impressive achievements of the American welfare state (like the introduction of social security) take a rather traditional legal form, whereas some of its biggest flops (including much of the "Great Society" regulation of the 1960s) failed in part because of their lack of traditional legal virtues. Classical formal law puts the rather impressive power of the state unequivocally on the side of a particular reform and the subordinate interests which it allegedly supports, and deformalized law sometimes hands out political authority to organized interests and, as in the case of Kennedy and Johnson-era reforms, cripples it. A reformed welfare state would do well to rely as much as possible on classical legal modes.[36] More persuasively, another rather diverse group of authors suggests the possibility of an alternative and more humane welfare state based on a set of universalistic social programs (most commonly, a guaranteed minimum income) which might avoid excessive legal discretion while simultaneously generating greater social and economic equality. Andre Gorz links a version of the guaranteed minimum income to a complicated defense of a "right to work" policy and convincingly suggests that it needn't require an intrusive or complicated bureaucratic form.[37] Left-liberals, such as Ralf Dahrendorf and a number of German Greens, offer distinct versions of the same idea.[38] Whatever their particular merits, the crucial insight here is that there is no a priori reason why state intervention needs to take a legally inchoate form. For example, it is not "complexity," but a particular configuration of power and privilege that probably prevents legislatures from institutionalizing a guaranteed minimal income; such a legislative act would have a great deal more legal integrity than most legislative acts can claim nowadays. A law demanding "that all citizens be given XXXX dollars each month" possesses greater legal coherence, and is less threatened by the specter of legal arbitrariness, than the sad example given above from the recent annals of American lawmaking.

What is striking about many of the blanket clauses that worry Neumann is that they generally appear in the most conflict-ridden of social spheres.[39] This should at least lead to a consideration of the possibility that the source of contemporary law's problematic structure lies in part in some of the most unnecessary and vicious social antagonisms that continue to characterize our political universe. Because of the tremendously antagonistic nature of social relations in spheres like the capitalist workplace, for example, there can be no clear agreement about how to regulate conflicts that emerge there; thus neither clear-cut formal parliamentary rules nor precise legal procedures with which to regulate labor-capital relations can be determined. Indeed, the seeming parallel identified by Neumann between everyday deformalized legal standards and terms such as "prerogative" or "national security" may reveal its full implications here. Just as emergency laws remain essential to an antagonistic and insufficiently "rationalized" international political setting, so too do blanket clauses appear to mirror, if fortunately more blandly, the more irrational and excessively conflict-ridden facets of contemporary social and economic life. As "martial law" or "national security" in the global arena too often become a front for a badly regulated exercise of power by the most privileged nation-states, so too have blanket clauses in social regulation too often worked to serve the interests of hegemonic social interests. In short, if existing democracies have to sacrifice some important features of classical formal law, this is as much a result of the profoundly unsatisfying organization of much of political and economic life as it is of social complexity. Might not a more egalitarian social world be able to do without some of the more disturbing features of existing welfare state law? Could an alternative global order generate political compromises more satisfying to the groups concerned, and might not these agreements take a form less akin to imprecise legal forms like "national security" which continue to pave the way for the most horribly barbaric forms of state action?

In *A Theory of Communicative Action*, Habermas tries to explain what he describes as the crisis of "juridification" as an expression of the antagonistic and problematic structure of the modern welfare state.[40] But the structure of the argument he presents there is distinct from mine in at least one crucial respect. Rather predictably, given his tolerance for the messy semantic structure of contemporary legal regulation, he highlights the dangers of "the generality of legal situation definitions ... tailored to bureaucratic implementation" as a threat to social autonomy. Classical parliamentary and bureaucratic rules subject the intricate and complicated problems of social life to an act of "violent abstraction."[41] Bureaucratically organized monetary compensations are not only inappropriate to the social problems they aspire to solve, but they also create new forms of dependency and undermine solidaristic relations in civil society. This happens in part because the structure of classical formal law is tied to "a system of action in which it is assumed that all individuals behave strategically," and which makes "explicit the form in virtue of which modern law can fulfill the functional imperatives of economic commerce regulated through markets"—as well as the "imperatives" of the state bureaucracy.[42] In this view, the problem with much of contemporary welfare state regulation is not its reliance on vague blanket clauses; it is, instead, its adherence to classical formal law, which is appropriate to the logic of strategic action in the economy or state administration but not to the regulation of many other spheres of social existence. This prognosis then leads Habermas to advocate an alternative model of legal "self-regulation": Some areas of social life should be regulated according to "procedures for settling conflicts that are appropriate to the structures of action oriented by mutual understanding—discursive processes of will-formation and consensus-oriented procedures of negotiation and decision making."[43] Decentralized participatory decision making guided by procedures appropriate to the problems of particular social spheres—Habermas mentions the family and school—are preferable to the "violent abstraction" of formal rules and bureaucratic regulation.[44]

The argument is revealing because it suggests that Habermas' hostility to formal law is greater than might at first seem to be the case. In some respects astonishingly reminiscent of Weber, Habermas too often sees general law more as a complement to capitalist and bureaucratic organization than, like Neumann, as an "ethical" instrument for humanizing state action. According to this view, not only is classical general law oftentimes anachronistic; it is the culprit as far as juridification is concerned. Yet there are competing and, in my view, richer empirical analyses of many of the same symptoms Habermas places under the rubric of juridification that instead locate their genesis in deformalized law. These alternative accounts also emphasize the manner in which the welfare state creates new dependencies in society. Yet in their view, this is more often the result of the tremendous and ill-defined authority blanket clauses put into the hands of administrators, judges, and corporatist-type set-ups than some vague "violent abstraction" allegedly intrinsic to formal law. Lowi, for example, shows how deformalized law spawns symbiotic relations between government bureaucracies and the social groups they regulate, and he defends the thesis that the legal structure of the War on Poverty reforms in part actually undermined African-American political power in the 1960s.[45] Ingeborg Maus argues that precisely those spheres of regulatory activity where blanket clauses and other types of deformalized law are dominant are the ones that Habermas sees as exemplary victims of juridification. Family or gender law, one of Habermas' crucial examples in *A Theory of Communicative Action,* is particularly revealing in this respect: "Among all spheres of the 'life-world', it is probably the family which is most strongly dominated by discretionary legal norms and relatively uninfluenced by [classical forms of] state law."[46] The fact that (male) judges act on the basis of open-ended and inappropriately moralistic standards may be the real problem in gender or family law, and not that "colonizing" (deflowering?!) formal law undermines its (virgin?!) "life-worldly" characteristics.

Still, if Habermas' proposed alternative could increase the cogency and regularity of regulatory lawmaking and generate something more than yet another ill-defined gift of legislative authority to administrators or privileged private elites, his proposal could be seen as compatible with my reformulation of Neumann's defense of classical formal law. In Chapter 6, we take a careful look at his more recent advocacy of what he now calls the "proceduralist paradigm" of law. Anxieties about the fragility of classical rule of law virtues should certainly not lead us to surrender our powers of institutional imagination. By the same token, Habermas still needs to show why his proposal for a relative decentralization of legal authority can grapple with the imposing problem of how inequalities are to be undermined in a particular social sphere so that conflict resolution there will constitute more than a front for the exercise of illegitimate power. What would procedures in the spheres of family life, for example, have to look like so that patriarchal power could be prevented from transforming an (allegedly) democratic procedures-oriented system of conflict resolution into a cruel joke on women? And in an educational system where military contractors and multinational corporations too often dominate discussion and policy-making, what types of procedures could counteract their rather impressive arsenal of weapons?

Part II

Jürgen Habermas, Globalization, and Deliberative Democracy

5 Between Radicalism and Resignation

Democratic Theory in Habermas' *Between Facts and Norms*

In 1962, a relatively unknown scholar published a contribution to democratic theory destined to generate something of a sensation in the still rather staid intellectual universe of postwar Germany. Appearing a mere thirteen years after the reestablishment of liberal democracy in Germany, the 33-year-old Jürgen Habermas' landmark *Structural Transformation of the Public Sphere* focused on precisely those features of contemporary democracy that the young author's more conservative scholarly peers tended to downplay.[1] Influenced significantly by the neo-Marxism of the Frankfurt School, Habermas argued that contemporary democracy exhibited a number of troublesome tendencies: A catastrophic fusion of state and society, unforeseen by classical liberal theory, had resulted in the disintegration of the very core of liberal democratic politics, a public sphere based on the ideal of free and uncoerced discussion. In Habermas' scathing account, mounting evidence suggested that liberal democracy was evolving towards a new and unprecedented form of authoritarianism, a mass-based plebiscitarianism in which privileged organized interests linked hands (by means of what Habermas polemically described as "neo-feudal" institutions fusing public and private power) in order to perpetuate social and political domination. Relying on the most advanced empirical American social science, Habermas argued that an ossified and inflexible political system, in which decisions increasingly were "legitimated" by means of subtle forms of mass persuasion, functioned alongside a profit-hungry mass media that trivialized public life in order to thwart democratic aspirations. The autonomous "bourgeois public sphere" of the late eighteenth and early nineteenth centuries had been jettisoned for the "manipulated public sphere" of organized capitalism.

Habermas' study struck a raw nerve in the young German polity. Particularly in the context of a political system in which traditional cleavages seemed increasingly muted—recall Willy Brandt's 1961 comment that "in a sound and developing democracy it is the norm rather than the exception that the parties put forward similar, even identical demands in a number of fields"[2]—Habermas' analysis of the decline of a critical public sphere seemed prescient. Within a few years, the influence of Habermas' work was already manifest in political tracts, sometimes far more radical in character than his own study, written by those who openly identified with Germany's burgeoning New Left.[3]

Thirty years after the publication of his first major work, Habermas' *Between Facts and Norms: Contributions to a Discourse Theory of Law and Democracy* revisits many of the core concerns of his original contribution to democratic theory.[4] Once again, Habermas hopes to offer a conception of *deliberative democracy* capable of providing a guidepost for a revised critical theory. Indeed, the analytical framework of his recent contribution to democratic theory is infinitely more subtle than its predecessor, chiefly because Habermas himself has conceded that *The Structural Transformation of the Public Sphere* was seriously flawed.[5] Thus, his recent works articulate a sophisticated neo-Kantian brand of contract theory in dramatic contrast to the Hegelian-Marxism at the core of his original foray into democratic theory. Even more striking, the normative and institutional specifics of the discursive conception of the "public sphere" introduced, but inadequately developed in Habermas' 1962 work, are elaborated in great detail here. *Between Facts and Norms* also breaks dramatically with what Habermas has recently described as a form of crude "holism" implicit in traditional democratic socialism, according to which a more or less homogeneous "macro-subject" ("the people") is outfitted with the task of establishing a perfectly transparent, democratically planned economy in order to achieve full autonomy; Habermas now believes that this ideal, which clearly motivated his 1962 inquiry, fails to provide sufficient independence for the "system imperatives" of modern markets and bureaucracies. For Habermas, radical democracy has to come to grips with the exigencies of social complexity. The failure to do so can prove disastrous, as demonstrated by Soviet-style state socialism.[6] Finally, missing from *Between Facts and Norms* is a problematic feature pivotal to the dramatic texture of his 1962 study: an exaggerated contrast between a stylized freewheeling "bourgeois public sphere," described in a surprisingly sympathetic light, and the bleak reality of contemporary capitalist democracy, described in tones reminiscent of the apocalyptic cultural criticism of the early Frankfurt School. To his credit, Habermas now avoids the oftentimes tortured historical claims that rightly garnered so much criticism for *The Structural Transformation of the Public Sphere*.[7] The democratic theory of *Between Facts and Norms* rests on an impressive attempt at rigorous political and social theorizing, not idiosyncratic myths about a liberal bourgeois golden age.

But my chief concern in this chapter is not with explaining the conceptual advances of Habermas' *Between Facts and Norms* vis-à-vis *The Structural Transformation of the Public Sphere*. Scholars sympathetic to Habermas' project have already done so.[8] Instead, I would like to pursue an alternative line of inquiry. Although widely discussed, Habermas' recent book has failed to ignite anything on the scale of the response generated by his 1962 study. One might simply chalk this up to its immense intellectual complexity; *Between*

Facts and Norms is accessible to only a minuscule group of scholarly experts. But it may also point to a weakness in Habermas' contemporary democratic theory, namely its failure to give adequate expression to legitimate unease and anxiety about the fate of representative democracy at the end of the twentieth and beginning of the twenty-first centuries. Despite rapidly growing evidence of widespread dissatisfaction with the operations of contemporary capitalist democracy, Habermas' work at times offers a surprisingly moderate and even conciliatory picture of "real-existing" democracy. In my view, Habermas' justified acknowledgement of the intellectual virtues of liberal and democratic thought à la Mill or Rawls, and his justified attempt to correct the theoretical failings of his early forays into democratic theory, seems to have generated a troubling side effect: an inadequately critical assessment of "real-existing" capitalist democracy.

Let me be more specific. In his eagerness to integrate a mindboggling array of alternative legal and political theories, *Between Facts and Norms* ultimately offers a deeply ambiguous account of modern democracy. Habermas' democratic theory now lends itself to two competing—and probably incompatible—interpretations, in part because he undertakes to develop his model of deliberative democracy by relying on a series of politically and intellectually inconsistent views. First, *Between Facts and Norms* at times seems to point to the outlines of an *ambitious* radical democratic polity, based on far-reaching social equality, and outfitted with far-reaching capacities for overseeing bureaucratic and market mechanisms. Yet Habermas never adequately develops this line of inquiry. Despite his repeated attempts to overcome a false juxtaposition of normativity to facticity, this model remains at the level of an abstract "ought." Second, Habermas simultaneously suggests a defensive model of deliberative democracy in which democratic institutions exercise at best an attenuated check on market and administrative processes, and where deliberative publics most of the time tend to remain, as Habermas himself describes it, at rest (*im Ruhezustand*) (379). In my view, this second model risks abandoning the critical impulses that have motivated Habermas' intellectual work throughout his impressive career.

I begin with a brief introduction to the general features of Habermas' model of deliberative democracy then turn to an analysis of its inconsistent "critical" and "uncritical" renditions. Finally, I point to the possible sources of this tension in the conceptual structure of *Between Facts and Norms*. In particular, I hope to suggest that Habermas never offers an adequate analysis of the interface between democratic and administrative authority.

HABERMASIAN DELIBERATIVE DEMOCRACY

For Habermas, the normative core of modern democracy is best captured by the principle that "[o]nly those laws can claim legitimate validity if they meet with the agreement of all legal consociates in a discursive law-making procedure that in turn has been legally constituted."[9] Despite the immense complexity of Habermas' attempt to explicate this (deceptively simple) statement in *Between Facts and Norms*, the broad outlines of his institutional vision of deliberative democracy are relatively straightforward. Habermas develops what he describes as a "two-track" model of representative democracy, in which an "organized public" (consisting of legislative bodies and other formal political institutions) functions alongside an "unorganized public," a broader civil society in which citizens rely on a panoply of devices (including political associations and the mass media) to take part in freewheeling political debate and exchange. Formal political institutions do play a key role by "focusing" the process of public opinion formation and then codifying the results of that process by giving them a binding legal form, but Habermas' model places special weight on the importance of civil society: It is the freewheeling character of discourse outside the formal political arena that now takes on the absolutely pivotal role of identifying, thematizing, and interpreting political concerns.[10] Indeed, Habermas tends to wax enthusiastic about what he describes as the refreshingly "chaotic" and even "anarchic" nature of deliberation in civil society.

Habermas repeatedly describes civil society as "anonymous" and even "subjectless" in order to break with a long tradition in political theory that misleadingly conceptualizes "the people," in an overly concretistic way, as a unitary, collective sovereign. By more fully acknowledging the profoundly pluralistic and decentered quality of public life in modern democracy, Habermas hopes thereby to respond to theorists of difference who have worried about the potentially antipluralistic implications of the tendency, probably most evident in *The Structural Transformation of the Public Sphere*, to privilege a single, homogeneous public sphere engaged in the quest for rational agreement or unanimity.[11] Now, Habermas openly concedes that it only makes sense to talk of a diversity of public *spheres*, and in *Between Facts and Norms* he seems eager to show that complex processes of bargaining and compromise—dramatically distinct from the Rousseauian model of politics that haunted some of his previous work[12]—have a legitimate and even noble role to play in modern democracy.

But the anonymous character of civil society by no means renders it impotent. Explicitly building on Hannah Arendt's famous delineation of power from violence, Habermas describes civil society as the prime generator of what he calls "communicative power," according to which deliberation and action in concert are essential for understanding the origins of political power, though by no means the exercise or use of power. For Arendt, "[p]ower corresponds to the human ability not just to act but act in concert. Power is never the property of an individual; it belongs to a group and remains in existence only so long as the group keeps together."[13] In Habermas' view, Arendt thereby identifies the roots of power in uncoerced communication; she grasps the centrality of "the power of communication aimed at mutual understanding" (148). Communicative power constitutes a "scarce good" that state administrators rely on but are unable to produce on their own (146–151). In this model, political power possesses a dualistic structure. Communicative power can only be effectively employed in complex modern societies by means of administrative bodies and forms of decision making that rest on strategic and instrumental-rational forms of action: "The legitimating ideals of administration are accuracy and efficiency. Administrators are to discover and undertake those actions that will be instrumental to the achievement of specific ends."[14] Thus, the nature of administrative power conflicts with the logic of communicative power, which is ultimately based—for Habermas as for Arendt—on relations of mutual recognition and respect.[15] Modern democracy thus seem paradox ridden to the extent that it requires forms of (administrative) power structurally incommensurable with the very (communicative) power which alone make democratic deliberation possible in the first place; for Habermas, this is one of the more obvious manifestations of the tension between facticity and validity which he thematizes in the extremely demanding theoretical reflections found in the work's initial chapters.

For Habermas, in some distinction to Arendt, the medium of law plays a central role in transforming communicative power into administrative power. Crucial to *Between Facts and Norms* is the simple idea that law lies at the very intersection between communicative and administrative power; one of the most important implications of this insight is that the fate of representative democracy and the rule of law are intimately linked. Insofar as law potentially functions as a successful connecting link or bridge between communicative and administrative power, the seeming paradoxes of modern democracy are surmountable. Communicative and administrative power should be able to cooperate fruitfully in the service of the plurality of deliberative "networks" that make up civil society. In this view, not only does Arendt fails to acknowledge adequately the autonomous dynamics of administrative power (and thus the paucity of legal analysis in her writings), but her republican streak leads her to envision "power" as a more or less spontaneous expression of a substantive common will.[16] In an extremely complicated discussion that I cannot do justice to here, Habermas tries to counter this view by arguing that communicative power combines otherwise distinct (in his terminology: "moral," "ethical," and "pragmatic") forms of deliberation: Politics concerns questions of moral fairness guided by a rigorous neo-Kantian criteria of universalizability, questions of cultural value and identity concerned with arriving at an "authentic self-understanding" and which legitimately allow for a loosening of the tough standards of moral discourse, as well as pragmatic attempts to reach practical compromises which give equal weight to all relevant interests (155). Thus, political deliberations involve the quest for reaching an uncoerced, reasonable common understanding on normative matters as well as somewhat less pristine processes of mutual bargaining and compromise. In any case, crucial to this process is that we have "a warranted presupposition that public opinion be formed on the basis of adequate information and relevant reasons, and that those whose interests are involved have an equal and effective opportunity to make their own interests (and the reasons for them) known.[17] Habermas thus deserves to be grouped among those defending what has come to be described as a "public reasons" approach in political theory.

RADICAL DELIBERATIVE DEMOCRACY

So much for the bare outlines of Habermas' democratic theory. What then is problematic about it?

At first, *Between Facts and Norms* seems to offer an ambitious interpretation of the idea of a two-track model of deliberative democracy. First, Habermas emphasizes that all manifestations of political power ultimately must derive from communicative power; even if indirectly, administrative power needs to legitimize itself by reference to discursive processes based in civil society (169). In particular, this is guaranteed by the principle of the legality of the administration. The medium of law merely transfers or translates communicative power into administrative power. The primacy of deliberatively derived law assures that communicative power effectively "determines the direction" (187) of the political system; in another formulation, Habermas claims that communicative power "maintains" or "asserts" (*behaupten*) itself against administrative and market mechanisms (299). Habermas by no means intends thereby to question the relative autonomy of complex markets and bureaucracies from the integrative force of communicative action. Nonetheless, some formulations in *Between Facts and Norms* suggest that their autonomy can legitimately be contained by means of a relatively far-reaching set of deliberatively derived democratic checks and controls on their operations. This is arguably a model not only, as Habermas himself tends to describe it, in which a "balance" has been achieved between communicative power, on the one side, and money and administrative power, on the other, but in which communicative power gains a pre-eminent position in relation to administrative and market processes (151), without thereby unduly impinging on the underlying dynamics of market and administrative subsystems.

Habermas builds on the work of socialist-feminist theorist Nancy Fraser, who has openly criticized his concessions to systems theory a la Luhmann and has often sought to rework Habermas' theory in a more explicitly anticapitalist gloss than Habermas himself.[18] Habermas' most obvious debt to Fraser is his use of her distinction between "weak" and "strong" publics. For Fraser, weak publics simply refer to those unburdened by the immediate task of formal decision making, whereas strong publics (most importantly: elected legislatures) are those "whose discourse encompasses both opinion formation and decision making."[19] In both Chapters 4 and 7 of *Between*

Facts and Norms, Habermas reproduces this formulation: For him as for Fraser, parliament at times is conceived of as an extension of the deliberative networks constitutive of civil society, as an "organized middle point or focus of a society-wide network of communication" (182). Parliament is merely a technical device necessary in large, complex societies to "focus" the process of political debate and exchange, but this technical feature need not extinguish parliament's own deliberative attributes.[20] The task of making sure that parliamentary bodies are, in Habermas' expression, "porous" to civil society, is thus eminently realistic in light of the fact that there is nothing structurally distinct between weak and strong publics. In both, communicative power is predominant.

Fraser's original essay never adequately addresses the possibility that strong publics might be forced to realize communicative power in a manner distinct from the "anarchic" associational life found in civil society. But one can imagine that she might accept Habermas' gloss on her views in certain passages of *Between Facts and Norms*: In parliament, time constraints necessitate that actors are less concerned with the "discovery and identification than the treatment (*Bearbeitung*)" of problems, "less with developing a sensibility for new problem positions than with justifying the choice of problems and deciding between competing solutions" (307). Parliament serves as a site for impressive debate and exchange, even if the imperatives of the formal decision-making process reduce the "wild" and "anarchic" features in civil society. Habermas also suggests that "deciding between competing solutions" is likely to heighten the importance of compromise within the "strong" parliamentary public. But he can be interpreted as arguing that this need not vitiate his (and Fraser's) ambitious view of parliament as a deliberative policy-making body. Here, a compromise is "fair" when in accordance with three conditions: (1) it provides advantages to each party; (2) it tolerates no "free riders"; (3) no one is exploited in such a way as to force them to give up more than they gain by compromise (166). As Stephen White has noted, this theory of compromise means that "it is the privileged agent who is confronted with the choice of . . . demonstrating to what degree his inequality can be discursively justified," of showing that it is in accordance with standards of procedural equality, participation, nondeception, and nonmanipulation.[21] In this model, the process of reaching and then defending any particular compromise seems unlikely to entail the suppression of deliberation. On the contrary, it seems destined to encourage debate insofar as citizens are required by it to consider whether compromise procedures actually compensate for "asymmetrical power structures" (177), as Habermas demands that they must.

For our purposes, this last condition is most telling. Crucial to Fraser's discussion of weak and strong publics is the insight that "where societal inequality persists, deliberative processes in public spheres will tend to operate to the advantage of dominant groups and to the disadvantage of subordinates."[22] Thus, the achievement of a truly freewheeling civil society, as well as a parliament responsive to its dictates, demands that we radically challenge asymmetries of social power; Habermas' discussion of "fair" compromise can be interpreted as an illustration of this more general—and implicitly quite ambitious—point. Here again, he reproduces Fraser's explicitly socialist argument: "*All* members of the political community have to be able to take part in discourse, though not necessarily in the same way" (182). In order for this requirement to gain substance, an egalitarian social environment needs to have been achieved: "Only on a social basis that has transcended class barriers and thrown off thousands of years of social stratification and exploitation" can we achieve a fully thriving civil society (308). At another juncture, Habermas describes the merits of a civil society "adequately decoupled" from class structures, and then he adds that "social power should only manifest itself [in civil society] to the extent that it *enables* and does not *hinder* the exercise of citizenship" (175).

Deliberative democracy, it seems, does in fact need to break with what Marx once described as the "prehistory" of class society. Although Habermas seems allergic to the conceptual paraphernalia of traditional left-wing political theory, he does imply at many junctures that the socialist tradition's aspiration to destroy illegitimate socioeconomic inequality is anything but exhausted. On the contrary, this undertaking arguably takes on renewed significance in his work given the tremendous emphasis placed on civil society in it. To the extent that civil society is especially vulnerable to the pathologies of class domination, it would seem incumbent on a democratic theory that places special emphasis on the importance of unhindered debate within civil society to salvage something of the socialist critique of the crippling inequalities of capitalist society, even if we now surely need to acknowledge the undeniable virtues of complex markets and bureaucracies in modern society.[23]

Habermas is right to follow Fraser in focussing on the social barriers to deliberative democracy: The idea of a freewheeling deliberative democracy remains ideological as long as avoidable social inequalities undermine the deliberative capacities of the vast majority of humanity. Unfortunately, *Between Facts and Norms* has nothing adequately systematic in character to say about "social asymmetries of power," let alone how we might go about counteracting them. Habermas points to the need for an account of how (a) capitalist domination undermines democratic deliberation and (b) some egalitarian alternative to existing capitalism alone can allow deliberative democracy to flourish. Alas, no such account is offered in his study. Indeed, matters may be complicated by the strikingly Weberian overtones of Habermas' definition of social power: "I use the expression 'social power' as a measure of an actor's chances to achieve his interests in social relations against the opposition of others" (192). Does this definition provide the best starting point for making sense of what Marxists have traditionally described as "structural" inequalities in economic power? I do not mean to trivialize the difficulty at hand here: In the wake of the demise of Marxist class theory, we still lack an adequate theory of social stratification.[24] Yet without some analysis of this sort, many of Habermas' more interesting proposals risk representing precisely what he seem so intent on avoiding in *Between Facts and Norms* in that normative aspirations have, at best, a tangential relationship to the operations of real-existing capitalist democracy (373).

Many political scientists would, of course, legitimately note that Habermas' model of parliament as a focal point for meaningful debate represents at best an *ideal* of how parliament should operate.[25] Many parliaments today continue to rubber stamp decisions that have been made elsewhere by the executive, upper divisions of the state administration, and representatives of powerful organized social groups, in a manner not altogether unlike that described by the young Habermas in *The Structural Transformation of the Public Sphere* in 1962. Similarly, we would be hard pressed to identify compromises in contemporary democracy that live up to the demanding standards of Habermas' model of just compromises. Amidst the vast economic inequalities of contemporary capitalism, compromise often inevitably means that some groups give up more than they gain: One only need recall the crippling "compromises" forced upon welfare state "clients" by neoliberal governments in recent years.

At worst, Habermas' comments about "social power" represent little more than a rhetorical leftover from the Hegelian-Marxism of *The Structural Transformation of the Public Sphere*. At best, they represent a starting point for a revised critical theory of contemporary capitalism—a critical theory that Habermas' *Between Facts and Norms* very much needs.

"REALISTIC" DELIBERATIVE DEMOCRACY

Habermas' theory of deliberative democracy also lends itself to an alternative reading, however. Especially in the final chapters of *Between Facts and Norms*, Habermas is intent on showing that his theory has "empirical referents and represents more than a series of normative postulates" (373). However understandable, this move generates a real problem for Habermas: it leads him to an interpretation of the two-track model that stands in a profound tension to his initial reconstruction of Nancy Fraser's socialist-feminist democratic theory. Moreover, this revised model makes too many concessions to the oftentimes woeful conditions of "real-existing" capitalist democracy—woeful realities, I should add, with which an ever-increasing number of our fellow citizens are rightfully becoming frustrated.[26]

The interpretation of Habermas' model along the potentially radical and socially critical lines indicated above suffers from an obvious flaw. Habermas' comments on the interface between communicative and administrative power are more ambivalent than I suggested above.[27] As I noted, at some junctures he argues that communicative power can rely on the medium of law to determine administrative power. Yet at many other junctures, Habermas offers a more modest view of the scope of communicative power: Communicative power "more or less"(!) programs, and merely "influences" and "countersteers" administrative power. In any event, communicative power "itself cannot 'rule' (*herrschen*), but only steers the use of administrative power in certain directions" (300, 444). In this second line of argumentation, the significance of deliberative democratic processes within his overall model seems substantially reduced. Here, communicative power functions to "lay siege" in a defensive manner to the exercise of administrative power. But it is utopian to hope that communicative power can gain the upper hand in relation to bureaucratic (and market) mechanisms. In the final section of this paper, I hope to show that this ambiguity stems from a fundamental conceptual tension within his argument. For now, let me just suggest that Habermas' institutional gloss on his two-track model of democracy in the concluding chapters of *Between Facts and Norms* takes a substantially less ambitious form than described above as well.

In Chapter 8, Habermas again elaborates on his two-track model. But now Nancy Fraser's radical democratic socialism fades into the background. In its place, Habermas relies extensively on the work of the late Bernhard Peters, a brilliant German sociologist who devoted much of his impressive intellectual ability to developing a critique of precisely those types of radical democratic arguments so important to writers such as Fraser. Habermas here relies on a study that Peters himself openly described as a contribution to a revised version of "realist" democratic theory, albeit of a "strongly modified normative" variety.[28] Like Habermas, Peters worried about the normative deficits of systems theory; in contradistinction to writers like Fraser, Peters thought that critical theory remains excessively mired in unrealistic, radical liberal, and radical democratic fantasies. In the spirit of Schumpeter, Peters posited that traditional normative interpretations of liberal democracy are essentially mythical in character: The idea of competent deliberative parliaments, deriving their authority from freewheeling political exchange among autonomous publics, and capable of determining administrative action by means of clearly formulated general rules, "has never even been approximately realized."[29] Despite its tremendous influence on democratic theory, "[i]t was not even defended as a normative political model—perhaps excepting certain short-lived constitutional doctrines influenced by Rousseau during the French Revolution (Sieyes, the Constitution of 1791)."[30] For Peters, the main source of the limits of every "idealized model of a democratic cycle of power" (like that described in Part I above) was "the extremely limited capacities for communication and problem resolution" intrinsic to the communicative channels described by it, in relation to the actual decision-making needs of modern representative democracy.[31] Thus, both traditional democratic theory—and radical contemporary proposals hoping to salvage its more ambitious normative aspirations—must be discarded. In its place, we need a model of democracy, a "very abstract, topological description of the political process," more in tune with the complex dynamics and exigencies of modern democracy.[32]

Peters was no conservative in the mode of Schumpeter. To his credit, Peters openly admitted that his description of the operations of real-existing democracy may include "contingent" elements.[33] But the polemical orientation of his book meant that he had little to say about such elements. Bent on purging the specter of radical democracy from critical theory, Peters at times seemed far more interested in pointing to the "rational" character of the democratic status quo than with elaborating its ills; the burden of proof lies with radical democrats critical of contemporary capitalist democracy. Although this view arguably provided a valuable immunization against irresponsible utopianism, it tended to lead him to downplay worrisome trends in contemporary capitalist democracy—just to name the most obvious: continued declines in participation rates, polls suggesting growing dissatisfaction with traditional legislative devices, and the resurgence of far-right wing movements pandering to xenophobia and racism.

Alas, Habermas opts to reproduce the core of Peters' realist-inspired model of democratic decision making by simply superimposing it onto Fraser's model (355). Inevitably, this produces a real set of tensions in Habermas' argument. The "two tracks" described by Habermas thus ultimately refer not only to Fraser's distinction between weak and strong publics but also to Peters' idiosyncratic delineation of the political "center" from the "periphery." In Peters' model, the "center" consists, most importantly, of parliament, the administration, and the judiciary. The "periphery" refers to a host of associations and organizations (a) concerned with "the definition, aggregation, and articulation of interests and demands in relation to the decision making processes of the center" or (b) functioning to bring about the "realization of public functions" within selected spheres of social activity.[34] Autonomous publics and communicative networks make up part of the periphery, but Peters generally seemed more interested in those actors emphasized by traditional political science, such as political parties, interest groups, and private associations. In order for decisions to take a binding form, they need to pass through the "channels" (*Schleusen*) of the center. But in contrast to traditional liberal democratic models, these channels are located at many different (administrative, legislative, and judicial) points within the "polycentric" decision-making center found within every modern representative democracy.

Even at this minimal descriptive level, Habermas' use of Peters leads the former to modify his initial account of the two-track model. Whereas his original gloss on Fraser made civil society the primary site for the "perception and thematization" of problems, here Habermas uses the same words to describe parliament's functions (307, 355). Moreover, now it is the administration that is seen as possessing the most impressive capacity for handling and resolving problems (*Problemverarbeitungskomplexität*); earlier in his study, that quality was attributed to parliament (307, 355). At first glance, this may seem a trivial shift. But in fact, it anticipates a dramatic revision that only becomes fully manifest in the proceeding stages of Habermas' argument: Parliament becomes the administration's junior partner in the legislative process, and deliberative civil society is removed an additional step from the actual decision-making process, thereby substantially attenuating its influence over the exercise of political authority. In light of Peters' unabashed attempt to break with traditional "myths" of parliamentary sovereignty, this move is unsurprising. Given Habermas' purportedly critical aspirations, it is far more surprising.

Peters openly argued that the political center inevitably gains independent status in relation to the periphery. Habermas accepts this view without showing sufficient concern for its potentially worrisome implications for democratic politics. In the course of what Habermas describes as "normal" politics, the deliberative periphery inevitably plays a minor role in determining the policymaking process. The autonomization (*Verselbständigung*) of the center vis-à-vis the periphery is inevitable considering the complexity of modern social life (356–359, 379–391). Most of the time, "courts reach decisions, bureaucracies prepare statutes and budgets, party organizations organize electoral campaigns, and clients influence 'their' administrators" (357), and civil society is unavoidably left at the wayside. Indeed, not only civil society, but even those elements of the "center" most closely tied to civil society, lose the central place attributed to them in traditional democratic theory: During moments of political normalcy, "the power and initiative to get problems on the agenda and then decide on them lies with the government and administration to a greater extent than the parliamentary complex" (380). According to Habermas, only during "exceptional" situations do communicative processes within civil society and parliament again seem to take on a renewed significance for decision making; during moments of heightened conflict, in periods of crisis, the legislature has "the last word" and then "*factually determine* the direction" of political decision making (357).

What concrete evidence does Habermas provide to demonstrate the empirical relevance of this model? Recall that Habermas wants to show that his vision of deliberative democracy has "long gained a footing" (317). This does not only mean that the self-understanding of modern liberal democracy is best captured by the idea of a two-track deliberative democracy; it also implies that empirical tendencies within contemporary democracy should correspond to his model. The proliferation of autonomous social movements in civil society over the course of the last decades (especially the peace, women's, and ecological movements) proves that (a) the periphery of civil society often can succeed in thematizing issues ignored by the decision-making center and (b) the political center remains "porous" to civil society, especially when a "growing awareness of a relevant societal problem generates a *crisis consciousness* on the periphery" (382).

Habermas' argument here represents an astonishing sleight of hand. Peters never claimed that his account is radical-democratic; Habermas

seems to think that it is. Nor does Habermas see any problem with synthesizing Fraser's democratic socialism and Peters' cautious brand of democratic realism. Not surprisingly, Habermas' model is Janus-faced. At times,
he speaks the language of radical democracy; at other junctures, his defense
of what amounts to an administratively dominated "normal" politics is
arguably less ambitious, in crucial respects, than the liberal democratic
models of classical authors like Mill or Tocqueville.[35] The paradoxes here
are striking: Habermas began his career as one of the most perceptive critics
of "realist" democratic theory.[36] Is he now willing to engage in a rehabilita-
tion of realist theory, as long as it is packaged in the impressive learning of
critical social theory?

Even if we ignore this analytical tension in *Between Facts and Norms*,
another problem becomes apparent as well. In short, this second version
of Habermas' two-track model exhibits a number of immanent flaws. No
systematic empirical argument is offered in support of the claim that it
actually corresponds to the workings of contemporary liberal democracy;
passing reference to a panoply of left-liberal social movements hardly constitutes adequate evidence for an empirical claim as ambitious as this one.
After all, one might legitimately interpret the proliferation of social movements in recent years (as well as the increasingly widespread dependence on
civil disobedience, which for Habermas represents the clearest instrument
by which social movements have mobilized public opinion) in a somewhat
less positive light as well. Whatever their undeniable merits, these movements may also provide evidence for worrisome tendencies within contemporary representative democracy: precisely because the "center" has gained
exorbitant power in relation to the "periphery," extraparliamentary social
movements, engaging in illegal action, have emerged to fill the gap left by a
formal political system increasingly dominated by ossified parties and organized vested interests. Similarly, civil disobedience often represents what
Habermas himself calls "the final instrument" (382) by which political
groups hope to ward off state action that they consider altogether unbear-
able; this would seem to be a rather defensive form of political action to
emphasize in order to demonstrate the continued vitality of civil society in
contemporary democracy. In a truly thriving deliberative democracy, one
would hope that citizens need not engage too often in peaceful lawbreaking
in order to gain attention.[37]

Habermas' argument here begs a host of unanswered questions. How
can we make sure that civil society will reactivate itself during moments of
crisis?[38] Habermas refers to the importance of liberal political culture as a
precondition for this (382). But as Ken Baynes has noted, Habermas has
very little to say about the specifics of such a culture.[39] Indeed, there may
be something downright unrealistic about the logic of Habermas' borrow-
ing from "realist" theory: Can a "public in dormancy" (*Öffentlickeit im
Ruhezustand*) effectively tolerate the exercise of de facto political power
by isolated political elites without risking its own disintegration (379)?

Tocqueville's warnings about "democratic despotism" come immediately to mind here: Why wouldn't political elites takes advantage of a situation characterized by a "public in dormancy" in order to exacerbate privatistic tendencies? Habermas claims that a political system temporarily dominated by the "center" by no means necessarily means that illegitimate social power has gained undue influence within the political complex (357). But his explanation here tends to be disappointing, particularly in light of the prescient concerns expressed elsewhere in his work about the dangers of social asymmetries of power for civil society: We can rest assured that social power will not be able to gain illegitimate influence as long as the periphery is able to identify outbreaks of illegitimate social power and then counteract them (358). What if social inequality simultaneously distorts the operations of civil society itself?[40]

Sometimes *Between Facts and Norms* does present a refreshingly honest assessment of worrisome trends within contemporary democracy. Habermas offers a clear-headed discussion of a capitalist mass media that trivializes public debate and cultivates cultural and political illiteracy; he notes that political parties too rarely serve as a meaningful device for guaranteeing the supremacy of communicative power; he concedes that cynical brands of systems theory have some real empirical correlates in contemporary democracy. In short, he still defends some of the critical elements of his empirical account of contemporary democracy in *The Structural Transformation of the Public Sphere*. But Habermas now seems so intent on proving that his own model "represents more than a set of normative postulates" that he ignores the possibility that his use of Peters' empirical description risks forcing him to make unnecessary concessions to the sad state of real-existing capitalist democracy.

COMMUNICATIVE AND ADMINISTRATIVE POWER: UNRESOLVED PARADOXES

For Habermas, law—and, more specifically, legislative bodies such as elected parliaments—mediates between communicative and administrative power. Lawmaking bodies depend on communicative power in order to issue norms, which then are rendered binding by the coercive apparatus of the modern state. The ambiguities that I have described in my exegesis above ultimately revolve around the nexus between communicative and administrative power. At some junctions, Habermas seems to point to parliament as the main site for lawmaking; at others, he accepts the "realist" view that parliamentary sovereignty is little more than a moldy liberal myth. Sometimes parliament is envisioned as an extension of a deliberative civil society; at other times, parliament's deliberative capacities are demoted in order to accentuate its pragmatic qualities and distinguish it from the "anarchical" processes of deliberation and exchange found within civil society. Habermas tends to emphasize the virtues of a deliberative civil society; at the same time, he is willing to admit that civil society inevitably has little real impact on state action during the course of "normal" democratic politics. Habermas hopes to show that communicative power can be "transcribed" into administrative power. But he does not seem altogether sure exactly how weak publics, strong publics, and administrative bodies should interact in order to bring about this translation.

The immediate source of this tension is not hard to find. Habermas conceives of his project as an attempt to overcome the one-sidedness of both normative theories allegedly blind to the exigencies of empirical reality (e.g., Rawls and Dworkin) and social-scientific theories lacking the most minimal normative sensitivity (e.g., the German systems theorist Luhmann). In the process, he devotes an enormous amount of energy to an immanent reconstruction of competing views in order to demonstrate how (a) they repeatedly succumb to one of these two flaws and (b) ultimately their underlying insights can best be integrated into his own thematization of the relationship between facticity and validity. As a consequence, most of Habermas' own ideas here are formulated by means of an exegesis and reconstruction of competing theories. There is no question that Habermas is a masterful practitioner of this craft. But in light of the fundamental dissimilarities among the theories Habermas discusses, there is a real danger that either (a) something essential is lost in the translation of these ideas into his own, or (b) the integrity of competing theories is preserved but at the cost of attempting a synthesis of that which probably cannot be synthesized. Indeed, is this not precisely what we find in Habermas' model of a two-track deliberative democracy, where radical democratic socialism and democratic "Realism" are oddly transformed into intellectual allies?

In this context, it is striking that Habermas' analysis of communicative power is derived from normative theorists (most important, Arendt), whereas his discussion of administrative power is drawn from a tradition of social scientific inquiry oblivious to normative questions (Luhmann). Habermas himself repeatedly emphasizes the incongruities between these two traditions; as he emphatically shows in *Between Facts and Norms*, both are blind to the merits of the other. In light of this, it should not surprise us that his occasionally forced attempt to integrate these traditions at times may reproduce something of the original incongruity between them. More specifically, Habermas' description of communicative and administrative power at many junctures tends to posit the existence of a fundamental dissimilarity between them. Communicative power rests on action in concert, and deliberation oriented towards mutual understanding; it depends on what Hegel famously described as "mutual recognition." In stark contrast, administrative action relies on strategic rationality, takes an unavoidably hierarchical form, and is concerned first and foremost with efficiency (145–151, 186–187). Given Habermas' insistence on a fundamental difference between these two forms of power, is not the task of translating communicative into administrative power inevitably destined to remain highly enigmatic? Does not this under-taking risk approximating the alchemist's attempt to "transform" simple metals into silver—that is, an inevitably doomed attempt to transform one set of elements into an altogether different set? No wonder Habermas at times stumbles in his description of the interface between communicative and administrative power: He may have defined the task in such a manner as to render it virtually impossible to solve.

Of course, the modern legal tradition long provided a plausible answer to the question of how communicatively derived legislative power could be successfully transformed into administrative action so as to guarantee that the latter does not infringe on the former: If we insist that legislation take the form of cogent, general norms, then we can make sure that administra-tive power can be effectively regulated in accordance with the preferences of democratically elected legislative bodies. In previous chapters, I have fol-lowed the work of one of Habermas' predecessors in the Frankfurt critical theory tradition, Franz L. Neumann, in arguing that much can still be said in favor of this classical model of the rule of law. As I argued in Chapter 4, Habermas' tendency to discount the strengths of this position generated some real problems for political and legal theory prior to the publication of *Between Facts and Norms*. To be sure, *Between Facts and Norms* offers a far more subtle and convincing discussion of some of the dilemmas I identi-fied there: Habermas now seems much more willing to admit that pervasive antiformal trends in the law pose disturbing normative and political ques-tions.[41] Nonetheless, he still claims, in a manner reminiscent of the rather one-sided spirit of his earlier work, that classical formal law remains impris-oned in the anachronistic "productivistic" assumptions of industrial capital-ism. Frankly, this still seems to me rather misleading.[42] Although I believe that Habermas remains too quick to dismiss the contemporary merits of formal law, he certainly is right to suggest that it at least seems anachronistic in light of the proliferation of vague and open-ended legal clauses and con-cepts in contemporary law. Antiformal legal trends have long been identi-fied at the domestic level; as I have argued earlier in this book, they are also proliferating at the global level.

For Habermas, such antiformal tendencies primarily suggest that we need to reconceive the traditional idea of the separation of powers in such a way so as to deemphasize the orthodox emphasis on generality within legal statutes; this view purportedly rests on an overly "concretistic" reading of the separation of powers (187–193, 526–537). So Habermas argues in the final pages of *Between Facts and Norms* for a restatement of the idea of a separation between distinct institutions (the legislature, judiciary, and administration branch) in terms of a distinction between alternative forms of communication and different ways of making use of reasons and arguments. Regardless of their concrete location within the state apparatus, forms of action deserve to be described as "legislative," "administrative," and "judicial" to the extent that they make use of forms of argumentation that Habermas sees as capturing the core of what traditional liberal theorists envisioned by means of each of the individual "instances" of the separation of powers. In turn, such forms of action then rightfully deserve to be institutionalized in such a way so as to correspond to the logic of the form of communication at hand:

> Laws regulate the transformation of communicative power into administrative power in that they come about according to a democratic procedure, ground a legal protection guaranteed by impartially judging courts, and withhold from the implementing administration the sorts of reasons that support legislative resolutions and court decisions. These normative reasons belong to a universe within which legislature and judiciary share the work of justifying and applying norms. An administration limited to pragmatic discourse must not disturb anything in this universe by its contributions; at the same time, it draws therefrom the normative premises that have to underlie its own empirically informed, purposive-rational decision making (192).[43]

Legislative power is best captured by the idea of communication involving the justification of norms which—as we have seen—makes use of diverse (moral, ethical, and pragmatic) forms of deliberation (192, 437–440). The gist of Habermas' rather complicated argument here is that we need to consider the possibility of extending communicative forms of this type whenever problems at hand require a legislative resolution—for example, when administrators are confronted with a choice of mutually incompatible collective goals in such a way as to explode the boundaries of traditional conceptions of administrative action. In order finally to do justice to a political system in which legislation occurs at many different interstices of the governmental apparatus, central parliaments need to consider the possibility of openly delegating and decentralizing legislative authorities and then organizing them in such a way as to subject them to deliberative democratic procedures (439–440).

Habermas' suggestion here is surely a provocative one. Indeed, if it could be successfully undertaken, it might very well serve as an antidote to some of my criticisms above: If deliberative democratic ideals could be institutionalized within the very core of the state bureaucracy, then Habermas' description of an administratively dominated "normal" politics might begin to seem somewhat less worrisome than I suggested above. Then the "normal" rule of the "state administration" need not necessarily entail a realist-inspired corrosion of deliberative democracy.[44]

But his argument here also points to a familiar weakness in *Between Facts and Norms*. Given the immense complexity of Habermas' text, it is easy to miss the tremendous significance of his discussion of a reformed separation of powers for the structure of his overall argument: It is supposed to represent nothing less than an institutional solution to the problem of transforming communicative power into administrative power. But, once again, Habermas has far too little to say about the specifics of his agenda here. Even if we are willing to concede the virtues of integrating deliberative democratic elements into the administration, does that necessarily solve the problem of how communicative power is to be effectively translated into administrative power? Habermas' proposal is not meant to deny that we still need to acknowledge the autonomous logic of the administrative system; instead, it only claims that what we today describe as the state administration or bureaucracy undertakes legislative tasks that should be organized in accordance with the principles of deliberative democracy. So perhaps this argument simply shifts the locus of the interface between communicative and administrative power from the nexus between parliament and the administrative apparatus to within the administration itself. If so, we still need an analysis of how deliberative processes then can effectively "steer" and "bind" decisions within the administration itself. In fairness, Habermas alludes to a growing number of experiments (for example: participation by clients in administrative bodies, ombudsmen, administrative hearings) with the "democratization" of administrative and judicial instances (440–441). But his examples have now long been established in many administrative practices of the advanced democracies of the west. Does anyone really believe that more Ombudsmen or administrative hearings can really protect us from what Habermas himself describes as the "crisis-tendencies" of modern representative democracy?[45]

What about more ambitious experiments in political and social democracy? Habermas does not a priori exclude them; he tells us that a careful brand of "institutional fantasy" is appropriate for the examination of such proposals (531). Unfortunately, it is just such "institutional fantasy" that too often is absent from Habermas' own argument—notwithstanding its tremendous importance for his own ambitious and in some ways pathbreaking quest in *Between Facts and Norms* to rethink the project of modern democracy.

6 Prospects and Perils of Proceduralist Law

The chapter on "Paradigms of Law" plays a significant role in Habermas' *Between Facts and Norms*. Throughout Habermas' intellectually demanding reworking of modern political and legal scholarship, the reader inevitably wonders whether Habermas ultimately intends to offer any concrete suggestions for how we might go about reforming contemporary legal practice in accordance with discourse theory. Can his brilliant yet indisputably abstract contributions to normative legal philosophy, political theory, and legal sociology help successfully guide legal reform? Is discourse theory capable of contributing to institutional change? Chapter 9 of *Between Facts and Norms* intends to answer such questions. As I hope to show, Habermas' attempt to do so, as always, proves creative and thought provoking. However, his defense of what he describes as "proceduralist law" raises at least as many new questions as it answers old ones.

THE CONCEPT OF A LEGAL PARADIGM

As we have seen, a central methodological preoccupation of *Between Facts and Norms* is the need to avoid an overstylized contrast between "ought" and "is" in thinking about democracy and the law. In this spirit, Habermas begins Chapter 9 by arguing that we need a workable conceptual instrument for describing the manner in which (normatively based) systems of law can be understand as integrally related to their specific social environments. The term "legal paradigm" is meant to serve this function. For Habermas, a legal paradigm is "not a scientific theory or a legal doctrine—it is an integrated set of cognitive and normative background assumptions about the relationship the law should establish between the state and society, and the form legal regulation must take."[1] Has Habermas thereby introduced yet another piece of unnecessary theoretical jargon into an already jargon-filled book? Not in his view. From Habermas' perspective, even a cursory look at the legal system calls out for such a conceptual framework: It is "clear that experts interpret individual propositions not only in the context of the legal corpus as a whole but also within the horizon of a currently dominant preunderstanding of contemporary society" (388). Legal practitioners typically operate with an implicit image of society according to which they make and interpret law. As Habermas also accurately recalls, many students of legal development have similarly argued that specific models of law rest on more or less implicit presuppositions about society. Both Karl Marx and Max Weber, for example, famously posited that classical "formal law" presupposed and indeed privileged a classical capitalist market economy, and subsequent mid-twentieth century legal scholars described recent breaks with legal formalism as necessarily linked to the emergence of the modern social welfare state. As we will see shortly, Habermas builds directly upon this tradition of thinking about legal and social change.

Yet, for Habermas, such background assumptions are by no means limited to the consciousness of the jurist or legal scholar. The foundational document of most modern legal systems, a written constitution, also contains relatively explicit references to specific visions of social life. Late eighteenth-century liberal constitutions promulgated the demise of feudal privilege and property forms, and post-World War II west European constitutions often contain explicit references to the welfare state. To be sure, such background images about the relationship of law to society are typically of greatest immediate significance to legal practitioners and experts. Thus, it should come as no surprise, Habermas observes, either that many contemporary jurists and legal experts have now become expressly aware that "an unavoidable background understanding of society" is indispensable to the legal system (393) or that a veritable academic cottage industry has emerged in response to the intellectual need to make sense of such background assumptions. Those scholars who rely on a vague idea of "legal culture" whose carriers are described as making up the entire population of any legal community potentially obscure the special place that legal paradigms play in the consciousness of legal experts. However, Habermas emphatically agrees that it would be mistaken to understand the notion of a legal paradigm as a practical and normative plaything of some set of expert legal "professional guardians":

> The dispute over the correct paradigmatic understanding of the legal system, a subsystem reflected in the whole of society as one of its parts, is essentially a political dispute. In a constitutional democracy, this dispute concerns all participants, and it must not be conducted only as an esoteric discourse among experts apart from the political arena (395).

Democratic citizens must ultimately be able to determine whether a particular legal paradigm guiding legal practice is normatively acceptable. Unless the popular sovereign's authority in this matter is given real significance in the political process, it is unclear how the legal system ultimately can plausibly claim to rest on the robust vision of democratic legitimacy Habermas seeks to defend. In Habermas' own view, a legal paradigm best suited to the exigencies of contemporary democracy would "satisfy the best description of complex societies; it should illuminate once again the original idea of the self-constitution of a community of free and equal citizens; and it should overcome the rampant particularism of a legal order that, having lost its center in adapting to the uncomprehended complexity of the social environment, is unraveling bit by bit" (393). Only a democratically constituted people, however, can rightfully determine which legal paradigm should guide the activities of lawmakers, judges, and administrators.

FROM LIBERAL FORMAL LAW TO MATERIALIZED WELFARE STATE LAW

Habermas then proceeds to use the notion of a legal paradigm as part of an attempt to offer a creative retelling of the history of legal development since the nineteenth century. Many others have described the shift in modern law from classical liberal formal law to "materialized" or welfare state law. Habermas' predecessor in Frankfurt political theory, Franz Neumann, for example, similarly chronicled the demise of classical formal law in the context of capitalist transformation. Habermas' account takes off from his own previous reflections about legal development as discussed earlier in Chapter 4 of this book. Characteristically, Habermas' latest version of this story includes a number of insightful observations and intellectual twists.

In the classical liberal legal paradigm, Habermas notes, the state was restricted to preserving the rudiments of public order and general presuppositions of a fundamentally self-regulating capitalist market economy. A minimum of state intervention was required in order to allow for individuals to exercise a maximum of negative liberty as well as pursue their respective conceptions of the good life. In this legal paradigm, individual liberty was assured by "personal rights and protection from torts, but above all freedom of contract (especially in the exchange of goods and services) and property rights (with the guarantees of use and disposal, including inheritance) allied with institutional guarantees for marriage and family" (397). State intervention in society was only legitimate if it could pass a demanding set of legal tests. For classical liberals, encroachments of state power on the private sphere always posed a threat to individual liberty; thus, it was necessary to rationalize the exercise of state power by means of a strict brand of legal formalism. Statutes were supposed to take the form of general and abstract rules with the aim of precisely determining typical "fact situations" and offenses in specific legal terms and linking them unequivocally to clear legal consequences. Although Habermas correctly points out that the notion of the generality of the law has occasionally been caricatured and distorted, especially among critics of the modern welfare state, for problematic political purposes (431, footnote 75),[2] his account also rightly underscores the crucial role played in the classical liberal model by clear and general statutes as a device for maximizing the likelihood of an impartial exercise of state power.[3] Only what Dworkin has described as a "rule-based" vision of law was thought capable of effectively minimizing state arbitrariness.[4]

Over the course of the last century, however, the classical liberal paradigm has lost its hegemonic position in legal practice and thinking. In lieu of clear general rules, we increasingly face what prescient observers of legal development since Weber describe as "materialized" or "substantialized" law, where law tends to take a vague and open-ended form: "The spectrum of legal forms has expanded to include special legislation, experimental temporary laws, and broad regulatory directives involving uncertain prognoses," as well as an "influx of blanket clauses, general clauses, and indefinite statutory language" (431). In some contrast to his previous and somewhat less critical discussion of such legal trends, Habermas now much more openly and accurately describes their perils. Statutory law no longer effectively binds or clearly "programs" the operations of the state administration or judiciary, and the result, according to a significant array of legal scholars whose work Habermas concisely summarizes, has been a notable increase in state discretion and even arbitrariness. To the extent that legislative statutes fail effectively to guide the administration or judiciary, the latter institutions are forced to engage in highly creative applications of the law that risk blurring any meaningful distinction between and among the practices of legislation, adjudication, and administration. Consequently, difficult questions are now raised for the traditional conception of the liberal-democratic separation of powers. In fact, a significant array of legal practices succumb to the dangers of "legal indeterminacy" that have so fascinated recent legal theorists: Statutory law often hands over relatively open-ended (or indeterminate) decision-making authority to institutions (courts, the state administration) which classical liberalism earlier had considered necessarily subordinate to the operations of the central parliamentary lawmaker. In contemporary liberal democracy, parliamentary legislation no longer effectively assures a normatively sensible division of labor between and among the three branches of government. Too often, Habermas asserts, we face "policies that are adopted in a manner that does not conform to the conditions for the [legitimate] democratic genesis of law" and are merely "cloaked" in judicial or administrative form (429).

In Habermas' retelling of this familiar story of modern legal development, such trends in the legal system need to be understood as part and parcel of a new social welfare state paradigm of law that emerged in the last century. "[A]s soon as the administration was enlisted by the social-welfare legislature for tasks of planning and political regulation, the statute in its classical form could no longer adequately program administrative practice" (431). Once the state takes an active role in ensuring economic subsistence and basic social services to all of its citizens, it becomes necessary for it to undertake ambitious and highly complex forms of regulatory and interventionist activity. As soon as the naïve liberal belief in the self-regulating market is abandoned, as Habermas thinks it rightly must be, classical liberal models of law lose their appeal. As Habermas points out, this shift has increasingly involved the state in complicated forms of forward-looking planning that mesh poorly with the quest to preserve traditional liberal legal ideals. Following the work of the Frankfurt jurist Erhard Denninger,[5] Habermas notes that many legislative undertakings now "have a dynamic character insofar as they reach far into the future, are dependent on prognoses, and require self-correction; the preventive norms of the legislature can only partially regulate these activities and link them to the democratic process" (432–333). Echoing neoliberal analysts (most prominent perhaps, Friedrich A. Hayek)[6] who adamantly insist that ambitious state intervention in social and economic life is simply inconsistent with classical liberal law, Habermas perceptively hints that the temporal preconditions of contemporary welfare state activity, especially in the context of risky forms of advanced technology and scientific research having profound implications for future generations, clash with the classical liberal paradigm of law. In the conceptual language I employed earlier in this volume: the process of time and space compression poses a significant challenge to the quest for traditional legal virtues like clarity, prospectiveness, and stability. Although Chapter 9 of *Between Facts and Norms* has little to say about the globalization of law per se, some of Habermas' comments astutely anticipate major challenges posed by globalization to law.

How then does Habermas' analysis of this familiar shift in legal development compare to that of Weber, Hayek, and others who have viewed it critically?[7] Habermas concedes, as noted, that the shift to a welfare state paradigm of law contains the possibility of heightened arbitrariness. He also forthrightly admits that the welfare state legal paradigm has occasionally resulted in new forms of paternalism. The specter of "welfare-state paternalism has raised the disturbing question whether the new paradigm is compatible with the principle of legal freedom at all," since the "welfare state obviously runs the risk of impairing individual autonomy, precisely the autonomy it is supposed to promote by providing the factual preconditions for the equal opportunity to exercise negative freedoms" (407). The most important source of this paternalism is probably the fact that the exercise of administrative power, *pace* traditional social democratic political theory, is by no means neutral. Yet the welfare state requires nothing less than an awesome employment of administrative power for the sake of guaranteeing retirement benefits, health care, a minimum income, housing, and employment. In Habermas' overall assessment, there are sufficient normative and political reasons to worry about recent legal trends in the advanced capitalist welfare states. Although it remains somewhat unclear in his discussion here how much remains of Habermas' earlier and somewhat misleading analysis of welfare state law as resting on a troubling form of juridification [*Verrechtlichung*] in which the "lifeworld" is "colonized" by market and administrative logics alien to it, *Between Facts and Norms* offers a relatively critical view of welfare state type of law, at least in comparison to many in the legal academy who have tried to defend it against its (primarily) neoliberal detractors.[8]

Not surprisingly, however, Habermas still offers a more balanced account of the welfare state legal paradigm than typically found in the work of neoliberal authors who see it as the harbinger of a horrific "road to serfdom." In striking contrast to Hayek and other neoliberal critics of welfare state law, Habermas underscores the numerous concrete institutional efforts undertaken in the last half century to tame the more problematic facets of welfare state law (for example, the emergence of new forms of legislative and judicial oversight over the state administration). Nor does he consider paternalism an essential facet of any attempt to develop a post-classical model of law. As we will see, he hopes that his own "proceduralist" paradigm of law can dispense with it. Most creatively, however, Habermas responds to writers like Hayek by pursuing the surprising explanation that "the weaknesses of the social-welfare model might be explained by the fact that it is still too closely attached to the premises of its liberal counterpart" (407).

In contradistinction to those who link the failings of welfare state law to the fact that it purportedly rests on a radical normative break with classical liberalism, Habermas instead underscores the fundamental normative continuities between classical formal law and materialized welfare state law. In his view, welfare state law represents a "more abstract" application of fundamental liberal legal ideals: With the emergence of the welfare state paradigm of law, "the idea of private autonomy, expressed in the greatest possible degree of equal liberty, did not change at all" (400). Classical liberalism offered a particular model of law in order to provide equal private autonomy to all. Yet the realities "of an organized capitalism dependent on the government's provision of public infrastructure and planning, and with a growing inequality in economic power, assets, and social situations" meant that "the universal right to equal individual liberties could no longer be guaranteed through the negative status of the legal subject" (402) and the classical model of formal law based on it. Given the empirical realities of modern capitalist society as they have emerged since the nineteenth century, it has become increasingly clear that core liberal legal normative aspirations could only be effectively achieved by means of the welfare state and the "materialization" of law that accompanied it. Liberal legal formalism would no longer suffice in order to maximize the private pursuit of individual interests. Only a just distribution of social and economic resources, undertaken by a state apparatus ready to intervene in far-reaching ways in the fundamental operations of the capitalist economy, might achieve an "equal distribution of individual liberties" in a factual as well as formal sense. Significantly, Habermas argues that classical liberalism presupposed both formal and factual equal liberties for each person "to do as she pleases within the framework of laws" (401). But this presupposition rested on a specific set of "sociological assumptions about the [relatively broad] distribution of wealth and an approximately equal distribution of social power, which was supposed to secure equal opportunities for exercising the powers conferred by private law" (402). Crucial to classical liberalism, Habermas posits, was the normatively attractive intuition that one could simultaneously guarantee both substantive social justice and extensive private liberty.[9]

With the appearance of organized capitalism, however, this aspiration soon proved vulnerable to empirical criticism. The alliance of classical formal law with capitalism failed because the latter did not, in fact, prove able to assure a broad dispersion of property or economic resources by means of its own immanent "natural" mechanisms. The basic liberty to "do as one pleases" can only be realized, in the context of organized capitalism, by new social rights in unison with many of the legal changes we have witnessed over the course of the last century. Notwithstanding the obvious institutional differences separating classical liberal formal law from welfare state law, both rest on a shared normative agenda, and "both are fixated on the question of whether it suffices to guarantee private autonomy through individual liberties [as in the classical liberal model], or whether on the contrary the conditions for the genesis of private autonomy must be secured by granting welfare entitlements" [as in the welfare state] (408). Unfortunately, both also "lose sight of the internal relation between private and political autonomy, and thus lose sight of the democratic meaning of a community's self-organization" (408).

We turn to examine Habermas' implicit claim in this statement that a normatively suitable legal paradigm will need to better acknowledge "the internal relation between private and political autonomy" in the following section of this chapter. For now, it is important to highlight what his provocative argument about the congenital normative links between classical formal law and materialized welfare state law has accomplished thus far. First, it allows Habermas to respond forcefully to critics of the latter who insist, in his view misleadingly, that it represents an abandonment of fundamental liberal ideals. In Habermas' view, there is no going back to a (nostalgically conceived) liberal model of strictly general rule-based liberal law. The abandonment of classical liberal economic practice and ideology has rightly rendered the early liberal model of law unavoidably anachronistic. At the same time, Habermas thinks that he has succeeded in preserving the normative kernel of classical liberalism by showing how the social welfare state has preserved its most worthwhile aspirations. The legitimate normative bearings for historical nostalgia (as prominently displayed, for example, in Hayek's legal theory) are thereby robbed from his intellectual and political opponents as well. In his own early defense of the welfare state and its legal apparatus in *The Structural Transformation of the Public Sphere*, Habermas undertook a strikingly similar argumentative move (1962, 263–287). There as well, Habermas underscored the normative links between the classical liberal rule of law as it emerged in the context of the "bourgeois public sphere" and more recent attempts to salvage a public sphere suitable to the contemporary era by means of welfare state type law. His earlier work also linked the fragility of liberal legal formalism to fundamental shifts in state-society relations and the emergence of organized capitalism. Yet his most recent version of the argument is more fully developed than the original, in part because it acknowledges the empirically problematic "implicit image of society" on which the classical liberal paradigm rests.

Second, this argument allows Habermas to defend the surprising conclusion that both liberal and welfare state paradigms of law rest on "the *productivist image* of a capitalist industrial society" (407). Contra neoliberal jurisprudence, Habermas not only sees welfare state law as a logical augmentation of classical liberalism, but he also places the blame for its failings at the doorstep of precisely that privatistic brand of political and legal philosophy embraced so enthusiastically by writers like Hayek. In his view, both the classical formalist and welfare state visions of law depict the relationship between state and state as a zero-sum game: Both oppose public and private autonomy and thereby obscure the relationship of fundamental mutual dependency between them (408). Despite appearances to the contrary, both legal paradigms privilege the quest for private autonomy and thereby miss the centrality of public autonomy and democratic citizenship. In somewhat blunter terminology than Habermas himself uses, the classical liberal paradigm of formal law tends to reduce human beings to the bourgeois market actor, while its social welfare state offspring risks transforming them into clients with social rights to a panoply of goods and services (education, health care, retirement benefits). In the latter, the question of justice tends to get reduced to the question of the proper distribution of goods (418). Habermas knows that the latter option, in broad historical terms, has proven vastly more satisfactory than the former. Yet both legal paradigms, he insists, tend to leave democracy at the wayside. For this reason, only a third alternative paradigm of law might successfully "illuminate once again the original idea of the self-constitution of a community of free and equal citizens" (393).

THE PROCEDURALIST PARADIGM OF LAW

As noted, Habermas hopes to overcome the simplistic is/ought methodological dichotomy characteristic of a great deal of legal scholarship by means of the formulation and subsequent application of the concept of a legal paradigm. He also seeks to move beyond this juxtaposition in another more immediately programmatic fashion as well: His own model of legal reform is already implicit, at least to some extent, in the course of contemporary political and legal development.

The purpose of Habermas' proposed legal reforms is to pursue the social welfare state project "at a higher level of reflection" (410). In concrete terms, this means that the continued struggle to tame capitalism socially and ecologically requires "the administration to employ mild forms of indirect steering; from the standpoint of legitimacy, it means linking the administration to communicative power and immunizing it better against illegitimate power" (410). As we have seen, existing forms of welfare state law too often prove heavy-handed, intrusive, and paternalistic. The move towards a more advanced, "reflexive" welfare state requires heightened democratic legitimacy for legal regulation. Paternalism can only be warded off when "the affected parties themselves . . . conduct public discourses in which they articulate the [legal] standards and justify the relevant aspects" of regulation (425) to a more meaningful extent than is presently realized in liberal democracy. In this vein, proceduralist law aspires "to secure the citizens' private and public autonomy *uno actu*: Each legal act should at the same time be understood as a contribution to the politically autonomous elaboration of basic rights, and thus as an element in an ongoing process of constitution making" (410). To a degree that Habermas believes is far too rarely the case in existing welfare state liberal democracies, the addresses of any particular example of legal regulation need to be able simultaneously to see themselves as the authors of lawmaking (417). In this model, the legitimacy of law depends on undistorted forms of communication "that *simultaneously* guarantee private and public autonomy *in the very conditions from which they emerge*" (409). Just as the classical liberal paradigm turned out to be an overly concretistic interpretation of the liberal normative intuitions on which it rested, so too is the more recent commitment to welfare state law a far too concrete reading of the internal relationship between private and public autonomy (437).

How then (a) does Habermas argue that his reform agenda is already implicit in contemporary political and legal trends, and (b) what precisely does the proceduralist paradigm of law require institutionally?

Habermas refers to many different ways by which present-day political and legal consciousness exhibits evidence of growing reflexivity. In a discussion of recent (mostly North American) feminist political and legal theory, he praises feminists for advancing a *"reflexive attitude* towards the successes of feminist reforms," and for astutely grasping that even seemingly successful welfare state programs concerning women have had at best highly ambivalent consequences for them (421). Too often, materialized welfare state law has proved counterproductive from the perspective of women, whereas any attempt to return to the classical formal legal paradigm is sure to generate serious dilemmas as well.[10] In part because of their allegiances to outmoded legal paradigms, Habermas insists, legislators sometimes arrive at misleading and oftentimes overgeneralized legal classifications and categories that harm rather than aid women. Here we have a paradigmatic case of welfare state paternalism, deriving from the fact that the relevant legal standards and categories too often normalize a particular vision of gender and family life so as to fail to match the needs of those affected by state regulation. What lessons can we draw from the failings of existing regulations concerning women? According to Habermas, public discussions must first clarify the aspects under which differences between the experiences and living situations of (specific groups of) women and men become relevant for an equal opportunity to take advantage of individual liberties. Institutionally defined gender stereotypes must not be assumed without question. Today these social constructions can be formed only in a conscious, deliberate fashion; they require *the affected parties* themselves to conduct public discourses in which they articulate the standards of comparison and justify the relevant aspects (425).

In short, the "reflexive" relationship of feminist activists to the welfare state points directly to the need for an alternative legal paradigm that does justice to the internal relation between public and private autonomy. What Habermas elsewhere elucidates in *Between Facts and Norms* as the core idea of the co-primordiality of public and private autonomy can only be realized by a legal paradigm that not only rests on the equal right to an autonomous private life, but simultaneously supports "the position of women in the political public sphere and thereby augments participation in forms of political communication that provide the sole arenas in which citizens can clarify the relevant aspects that define equal status" (426). Farsighted elements of the feminist movement have already anticipated, via their practical political work and hard-fought struggles for reform in the welfare state, the legal implications of his insistence of the relationship of mutual dependency between public and private autonomy.

Feminists not only anticipate the outlines of an alternative paradigm of law via their implicit acknowledgment of the necessity of novel forms of communication in lawmaking in which affected parties themselves would actively define what facets of their lives should be decisive for regulation. They also do so by underscoring the contingency of existing conceptions of the public/private divide. Of course, the dispute between the classical liberal and welfare state paradigms of law also concerns alternative conceptions of the proper way to separate the public and private spheres (415). According to Habermas, feminist challenges to traditional attempts to reify particular conceptions of the public/private divide represent concrete evidence of a growing contemporary awareness of how different conceptions of law contribute to particular visions of the public/private relationship. This, too, purportedly provides evidence that we are presently embracing an ever more "reflexive" view of different legal paradigms.

Last but by no means least, in his discussion of the concept of a legal paradigm itself, Habermas notes that contemporary legal experts are more conscious of their dependence on "implicit images of society" than their historical predecessors, for whom such background assumptions often possessed a nature-like (e.g., ideas of a "naturally" self-regulated market in classical liberalism) or at least a dogmatic form. Radicalizing this growing professional awareness of the relative contingency of background assumptions in the law, Habermas argues that a core element of the proceduralist paradigm of law is precisely a heightened sensitivity to the dangers of blindly privileging any specific legal paradigm. What this specifically entails is that the political legislator now must choose from among competing forms of legal regulation (including formal and materialized law) "according to the matter that requires regulation . . . Choosing among alternative legal forms reflexively does not permit one to privilege just one of these forms" (438):

> Dealing with the law reflexively requires that *parliamentary legislators* first make meta-level decisions: whether they should decide at all; who should decide in the first place; and, assuming they do want to decide, what the consequences will be for the further legitimate processing of their broad legal programs (439).

The proceduralist paradigm of law manifests its reflexive essence most immediately in the fact that it cannot be equated with any single vision of legal regulation. Instead, it requires that citizens and lawmakers deliberate on the specific regulatory task at hand and then make a meta-level decision about the appropriate way to tackle a particular policy aim. Unlike the classical formal-legal and welfare state paradigms of law, no specific model of legal decision making is favored by it.

From Habermas' perspective, more significant perhaps than any concrete proposal presently on the table for moving beyond the specific ills of either formal law or welfare state type law is that proceduralist law, regardless of the specific legal structure it takes, needs to do a qualitatively better job than previous legal paradigms at acknowledging the fundamental normative link between private and public autonomy. In the simplest terms: it needs to overcome the democratic Achilles' heel plaguing previous legal paradigms. Although at first glance counterintuitive, the proceduralist paradigm may in fact prove consistent with the employment of either formal or materialized law. But the lawmaker is only permitted to make use of such legal modes to the extent that they can be shown to avoid the demotion of public autonomy plaguing the classical liberal and welfare state paradigms. In other words, they should not be allowed to reduce the citizen to either the economistic liberal bourgeois or passive welfare-state administrative client. Whether or not any particular mode of regulation can live up to this difficult test, Habermas seems to believe, is typically a matter for institutional experimentation. The demanding empirical question of whether a particular type of regulation can best preserve an appropriate institutionalization of the co-primordiality of private and public autonomy will often depend on the specific situation or context at hand (437–438).

Habermas acknowledges recent calls for a reflexive model of law, along the lines proposed by the prominent German legal theorist and sociologist Gunther Teubner, as a possible alternative to classical liberal and welfare state law. In alternative regulatory models of this type, the centralized law-maker would delegate lawmaking authority to a specific set of bargaining partners and restrict itself to determining a set of abstract procedures and norms according to which they would operate. Legislators would "consti-tutionalize" particular arenas for legal decision making by promulgating a set of procedures which would determine the proper scope of self-regula-tion. Collective bargaining, for example, represents "a good example of the internal constitutionalization of a nongovernmental subsystem specialized for conflict resolution" (413). Habermas also appears to believe that there are specific situations potentially best served by means of such alternative forms of regulation. The proceduralist paradigm of law thus permits the lawmaker to make use of some variety of the "reflexive" model as well as the more familiar formal and material approaches (438).[11] However, Haber-mas refuses to attribute the status of a freestanding legal paradigm to reflex-ive law or any related model of reformed regulatory law, notwithstanding the many ways in which they might seem to represent a possible realization of his own hopes for a more reflexive form of state involvement in society. His main reason for this skepticism seems to be empirical: In those regu-latory arenas where we can already begin to discern the outlines of such alternative approaches to lawmaking, he thinks that we also find substantial evidence that they potentially suffer from those flaws plaguing the classical liberal and welfare state legal paradigms. Recent proposals for legally regu-lated "self-regulation" may also fail to realize adequately the co-primordial-ity of public and private autonomy. They may instead, as Ingeborg Maus has argued, undermine autonomy.[12] In the case of collective bargaining and labor law, the immediate institutional inspiration for Teubner's model of reflexive law, for example, delegations of lawmaking authority to bargain-ing partners sometimes fail to yield increased autonomy for the affected parties. On the contrary, like some forms of welfare state regulation affect-ing gender issues, they institutionalize problematic forms of normalization which paternalistically privilege a particular model of wage labor over a whole series of existing alternatives (413–414).

Habermas' most creative proposal for institutional innovation probably remains his attempted restatement of the traditional idea of the liberal-democratic separation of powers. Recall his worry that existing lawmaking too often is detached from a democratic legitimacy rightfully derived, in his theory, from a freewheeling process of communicative exchange, located in civil society but also potentially operative in core state institutions. In this view, too much of what presently passes for "administration" in fact constitutes legislation and thus must be rendered subject to forms of argu-mentation appropriate to lawmaking. Only by doing so can we hope to right the neglect of public autonomy characteristic of existing forms of legal regulation. In this account, the conventional idea of a separation of powers as referring to different institutions (the legislature, administration, and judiciary) requires reformulation in terms of a distinction between alternatives modes of communication as well as distinct ways of making use of arguments and reasons. Regardless of their specific location in the machinery of government, types of activity can be appropriately dubbed "legislative," "administrative," and judicial" to the extent that they make use of different forms of argumentation which Habermas interprets as capturing their core features. Legislative power is best conceptualized as resting on a model of communication concerned with the justification of norms. Moral, ethical, and pragmatic forms of discourse may be appropriate when the justification of norms is at stake; the crucial point is that the justification of norms draws its persuasive force from diverse and (ideally) inclusive forms of freewheeling communication. In contrast, administrative power should only properly rest on clearly circumscribed modes of strategic and instrumental rationality. When, in reality, the state administration is undertaking goals that require it to transcend narrow forms of strategic rationality—for example, when administrators find themselves forced to weigh different substantive policy goals—it is likely engaging in nonadministrative activities that require a corresponding dose of legitimacy from nonadministrative forms of communication. In such cases, modes of communication (along with the necessary institutional moorings) appropriate to legislation then need to be institutionalized within the sphere of "administrative" decision making. According to Habermas, de facto legislation already takes places at many interstices of the administrative machinery. It is now high time to acknowledge this fact of contemporary institutional life by permitting central legislatures to openly delegate lawmaking authority to the "administration," while insisting that the administrative apparatus then institutionalize mechanisms allowing it to claim a legitimate basis for such activities in identifiably "legislative" modes of communication. In a far more self-conscious fashion than hitherto has been the case, the legislature should be required to consider when legislative delegation is called for, and how it can be rendered normatively consistent with the strict requirements of a model of democratic legitimacy based in a communicative civil society. Doing so, in some situations, will require new forms of democratic decision making in which the central legislature is supplemented by any of a conceivable set of forums (ombudspersons, administrative hearings, new forms of participation) in which affected parties can gain a reasonable chance of seeing themselves as both the authors and addressees of law.

CRITICAL CONSIDERATIONS

Despite the evident strengths of Habermas' discussion, it inevitably generates legitimate critical observations even from those otherwise sympathetic to his work. As Andrew Arato has observed, the three legal paradigms are by no means fully parallel. Whereas the formal and welfare state paradigms favor specific types of legal regulation, proceduralist law does not.

In addition, precisely what "implicit image of society" is found in the proceduralist vision remains somewhat murky: Habermas' underdeveloped discussion of a reflexive welfare state, at the very least, lacks the same depth of his discussion of the social background assumptions of formal and welfare state law. In fairness, "such an asymmetry of course is part and parcel of the situation faced by any critical theory of society with 'emancipatory intentions,'" because proceduralist law remains a future-oriented and hitherto substantially unrealized project.[13] Not surprisingly, its precise contours and their background assumptions remain ambiguous at the present. According to Arato, however, Habermas still underestimates the potential virtues of "reflexive law" as a device for reforming the welfare state, and this lacuna means that "we do not know what exactly is the [legal] referent of the procedural or radical democratic paradigm." [14]As I have similarly argued elsewhere, when properly conceived and freed of the misleading antinormative connotations given it by Teubner, reflexive law properly has a significant role to play in reforming some arenas of regulatory law. Indeed, if effectively buttressed by a sufficient dosage of classical legal virtues, it might serve as a useful basis for experiments with novel forms of global economic regulation. Like few other available reform models, it seems normatively attractive and well-suited to the special empirical challenges posed by economic globalization. When properly designed, it might provide for much-needed experiments in novel post-classical legal regulation while still preserving classical legal virtues.[15] Habermas' reservations about reflexive law need to be taken seriously. Nonetheless, it is striking that those worries are empirical rather than of a principled normative nature. If we can figure out how we might minimize the empirical problems he astutely points to, reflexive law potentially offers a starting point for reform.

Because Habermas seems unduly skeptical of proposed alternatives to formal and welfare state models of legal regulation, one might fairly ask whether proceduralist law, in the form Habermas gives it, would entail any significant changes to the legal system at all. On one reading, Habermas simply leaves us with a call to undertake (cautious) democratic-spirited reforms of the existing legal system but hardly radical reform. However, his own clear-eyed diagnosis of the many pathologies plaguing existing law arguably demands nothing less than major changes to it. Here as well, we may have another example of Habermas' uneasy oscillation in *Between Facts and Norms* between "radicalism and resignation." The fundamental conceptual and political tensions plaguing his most recent contributions to political theory manifest themselves here as well: in the final analysis, Habermas' reader is left in the dark about the institutional and political bite of his otherwise impressive theoretical defense of proceduralist law.

Just as problematic perhaps, given Habermas' critical glosses on the formal and welfare state legal paradigms, it remains unclear why any sensible political legislator might opt to use such modes of regulation, unless they could be clearly distinguished from the original problematic background social and cognitive assumptions Habermas attributes to them. Not only does Habermas' cautious assessment of proposed reform alternatives to existing law (for example, reflexive law) undermine his promise to generate a sound theoretical basis for meaningful legal reform, but formal and welfare state law perhaps cannot be rendered easily congruent with the proceduralist paradigm to the extent Habermas posits. If this concern is justified, it would mean that the proceduralist paradigm risks being emptied of any concrete legal content whatsoever. After all, in his own vivid description of the fundamental characteristics of the formal and welfare state paradigms, their (purportedly enigmatic) background social assumptions are considered decisive. As we saw above, Habermas introduces the concept "legal paradigm" precisely in order to thematize such assumptions. If anachronistic notions of the "classical market" (in the case of formal law) and benign administrative power (in the case of welfare state law) are crucial to earlier legal paradigms, then why assume that formal and welfare state law can be neatly refigured in accordance with a proper proceduralist account of the law? At the very least, Habermas owes the reader a clearer explanation of how earlier forms of legal regulation can be legitimately disconnected from the problematic social and cognitive assumptions on which they once rested, and thereby rendered suitable instruments of a proceduralist paradigm essential to a reformed, more reflexive welfare state.

To be sure, Habermas' intuition that contemporary law would do well to make use of a panoply of alternative modes of legal regulation, along with his corresponding view that our choice among and between competing forms of legal regulation should be based on a firm understanding of the co-primordiality of private and public autonomy, are deserving of careful consideration. However, his own conceptual moves occasionally aggrandize the (already sizeable) difficulties we face as work to reform the legal system.

For example, it might seems odd to accuse Habermas of succumbing to a troubling "evolutionist" account of law, in light of his open acknowledgment of the need for the contemporary proceduralist lawmaker to make use of any of a variety of modes (formal, material, and reflexive) of regulation. However, his own discussion of the formal and welfare state paradigms, in which he retells the traditional story of the dismantlement of nineteenth-century "bourgeois" formal law by twentieth-century social-democratic welfare state law, suggests that Habermas' diagnosis, like so many others in contemporary legal scholarship, is by no means free of this tendency.[16]

Of course, Habermas' main endeavor is hardly a legal-historical one. Yet can we really be so sure that classical formal law, as Habermas here again tends to suggest, is fundamentally "bourgeois" in character? Should we accept his complementary assumption that formal law is somehow oblivious to the centrality of public autonomy? This is a complicated historical and theoretical matter, to be sure. Nonetheless, we would do well to recall that countless defenders of classical formal law have emphasized its eminently democratic attributes: Clear, public, prospective legal norms, along the lines endorsed by classical liberal jurisprudence, help guarantee the transparency and accountability of government, as well as a thriving civil society in which active citizens would be free from inappropriate forms of intrusive and arbitrary state action. Classical formal law serves indispensable democratic purposes no less than it helps assure "negative liberty" as well as legal security for rational economic actors. Consistent with this diagnosis, some social democratic thinkers have plausibly begun to disconnect the defense of formal law from its original background economic assumptions. When Franz Neumann stressed the "ethical function" of classical law, he was struggling to make this point as well. In contrast, Habermas' orthodox insistence on a necessary link between formal law and classical liberalism potentially obfuscates the important degree to which classical rule of law virtues continue to have a normatively indispensable role to play in contemporary law.

As Habermas himself is well aware, social welfare state law can be easily understood as an attempt to buttress and thereby ensure broad democratic participation. Recall that T. H. Marshall argued so powerfully in the middle of the last century that only the social welfare state could ultimately help secure basic civil and political liberties and thereby complete the liberal-democratic political revolution.[17] In this influential account, the welfare state is a necessary device for buttressing both liberal and democratic liberties. Of course, some welfare state programs have in reality proven to be paternalistic; Marshall himself probably recognized this danger. Yet to claim, with Habermas, that the welfare state legal paradigm is somehow blind to the centrality of public autonomy distorts not only the intentions of its most important defenders but probably legal and political history as well. The democratic preoccupations Habermas appears to consider special to his proceduralist paradigm have been constitutive of modern legal thinking at least since the nineteenth century. Arguably, both the formal and welfare state models of law have always been intimately linked to the modern quest to extend democracy.

If we start with this somewhat more nuanced portrayal of formal and materialized welfare state law, we can begin to understand, more clearly perhaps than Habermas himself, why both may potentially occupy legitimate stations within a reformed welfare state: When properly institutionalized, formal and welfare state law can potentially contribute to the more democratic welfare state we very much need today because both have always rested on a far-reaching commitment to the realization of public autonomy. Neither formal nor materialized law may of necessity be tied to the problematic social presuppositions described by Habermas. Only by downplaying some of those features Habermas considers essential to their "paradigmatic" nature is it possible in the first place, with Habermas, to salvage formal and materialized welfare state law for contemporary purposes. Along with potentially far-reaching experiments with novel forms of regulation that similarly take the co-primordiality of private and public autonomy seriously, "proceduralist" law will need to make use of them, depending on the particular regulatory matter at hand, in order to expand democracy and tame capitalism.

We may also need to consider possibilities for creatively synthesizing what, in Habermas' account, misleadingly appear as fundamentally incongruent models of law. Classical "formal" legal virtues should play a significant role in any model of reformed legal regulation, though they will likely need to do so in a fashion at odds with classical liberal visions of legislation and adjudication.[18] By setting formal law apart from competing legal paradigms, Habermas' argument seems to foreclose the possibility of creative fusions of this type altogether. Yet such fusions may be precisely what we need in order to salvage the rule of law.

Of course, this all presupposes that a reformed, radically democratic welfare state remains a historical possibility today. Yet as Habermas himself has acknowledged in his recent writings, this remains very much an open question in the context of neoliberal economic globalization, growing economic inequality, and the dangerous tendency—as evinced most clearly by the recent illegal U.S. invasion of Iraq—to discard the medium of law altogether in order to advance brutal power interests. More generally, whether Habermas' impressive recent contributions to democratic and legal theory can help us tackle the challenges of globalization remains an open question. Fortunately, both Habermas and his disciples have recently begun to tackle that question.

The most influential feature of Jürgen Habermas' wide-ranging contributions to political theory is his attempt to formulate a socially critical as well as empirically plausible conception of deliberative democracy. Both his earliest contribution to political theory, *The Structural Transformation of the Public Sphere* (1962), and his more recent *Between Facts and Norms: Contributions to a Discourse Theory of Law and Democracy* (1996), defend an ambitious deliberative model of political legitimacy, according to which normatively acceptable decisions are only those which meet with the agreement of affected parties in possession of far-reaching possibilities to subject them to critical debate. Not surprisingly, Habermas and those influenced by him have worked hard to outline the proper philosophical presuppositions of the basic intuition that only freewheeling argumentation can both justify the exercise of coercive state power and contribute to its reasonable character. In addition, they have taken important steps towards describing the appropriate institutional moorings of a vibrant deliberative democracy,[1] while struggling to demonstrate why deliberative democracy, when properly conceived, is the rightful intellectual heir of the early Frankfurt School.[2] Habermas' account of deliberative democracy is not only normatively distinct from competing liberal and communitarian models,[3] but it also purports to pose a more credible challenge to the social inequalities and injustices of contemporary capitalist society. In addition, Habermas and his followers repeatedly insist that their version of deliberative democracy remains realistic. It not only acknowledges the fact of modern social complexity, but we can even begin to see a rough outline of its proper operations in the otherwise depressing realities of present-day political practice.[4] Although maintaining a critical perspective of the status quo, it avoids a methodologically flawed juxtaposition of the "ought" to the "is," thereby offering relatively constructive guidance for those seeking to advance overdue radical reforms of the liberal democratic status quo.

The present-day critical theory obsession with deliberative democracy nonetheless seems surprising. With the notable but typically overlooked exception of Franz L. Neumann, the early Frankfurt School tended to neglect political and legal theory altogether. Implicit Marxist theoretical assumptions about the state and law led its most prominent representatives (Theodor Adorno, Max Horkheimer, and Herbert Marcuse) to discount normative political theory as well as creative intellectual approaches to the analysis of political and legal institutions. Only with Habermas' lifelong programmatic overhaul of critical theory—most important, his formulation of a theory of communicative action—was it possible for Frankfurt-oriented critical theorists to grasp the full significance of normative political theory to a critical theory of society.[5] Not surprisingly, Habermas and his followers have been at the forefront of recent efforts to develop critical models of deliberative democracy in which his ideas about uncoerced speech and communication typically loom in the background.

But should critical theorists continue to devote their intellectual energy to the project of deliberative democracy? Does deliberative democracy constitute the legitimate future—and not just the contemporary—focus of critical theory? In order to answer this question, we need first to consider another one. Is there some way by which we might sensibly test the capacity of Habermasian deliberative democracy to advance both critical theory and progressive politics?

Fortunately, Habermas and those influenced by him have themselves pointed to the existence of one possible test. Over the course of the last decade, Habermas and his sympathizers have turned much of their attention to the pressing question of how democracy needs to be reconfigured in light of the sizable challenges posed by globalization. Following the broad mainstream of present-day social science, they recognize that the multipronged process of globalization challenges both the normative legitimacy and effective regulatory capacity of the liberal democratic nation state. If democracy is to thrive, it needs to meet the numerous threats posed by globalization. Of course, critical theorists are hardly the only scholars busily examining the conflict-laden nexus between globalization and democracy. Distinct to the Habermasian approach, however, is the belief that its vision of deliberative democracy is best capable of providing persuasive resolutions of the normative and institutional quagmires of globalization. From this perspective, the most difficult challenge to contemporary democracy also provides an unambiguous corroboration of the impressive normative and empirical credentials of Habermasian political theory.

Although broadly sympathetic to this view, I would like to register a number of reservations. As I have tried to argue, Habermasian deliberative democracy remains profoundly ambiguous in its political and institutional ramifications. At some junctures, it points the way to a radical overhaul of the political and economic status quo; at others it makes its peace with present-day political conditions. This programmatic tension is reproduced in recent critical theory research on deliberative democracy and globalization. Unfortunately, this tension derives at least in part from conceptual slippage that we find in the Habermasian account. The potentially misleading imagery of an "anonymous" and even "subject-less" deliberative civil society sometimes contributes to a problematic conceptual bifurcation between deliberation and democracy. Deliberation without the meaningful (deliberative) involvement of concrete "subjects" is, in reality, no longer democratic. Lively deliberation is not, in fact, "subject-less," and the fact that lively argumentative give-and-take often makes it difficult for us to determine the genesis or initial "possession" of a specific insight hardly renders it altogether anonymous either. This conceptual slippage, I submit, opens the door to a troubling tendency to condone overly defensive models of deliberative democracy for the global stage.

BETWEEN RESIGNATION AND RADICALISM: GLOBALIZATION AND HABERMASIAN DEMOCRATIC THEORY

In Chapter 5 I argued that a striking programmatic oscillation can be identified in Habermas' most developed account of deliberative democracy. On the one hand, Habermas at times proposes an indisputably radical vision of deliberative democracy, where freewheeling deliberation would emerge in civil society but ultimately gain clear expression in the apparatus of government. Although Habermas follows Nancy Fraser in distinguishing weak from strong publics, with the latter culminating in binding legal decisions whereas the former fails to do so, there remains no structural difference between the two publics: In both, "communicative power" derived from spontaneous, unlimited debate and deliberation predominates. In this version of the argument, formal government institutions (most important, the central legislatures) are simply a technical extension of civil society, the "organized midpoint or focus of a society-wide circulation of informal communication" (182).[6] In turn, the principle of the legality of the administration guarantees that bureaucratic mechanisms are rendered unambiguously subordinate to processes of popular debate and deliberation which effectively "determine the *direction* in which political power circulates" via the medium of law (187). Of course, modern society still requires an administrative apparatus operating according to a distinct logic, but Habermas hopes that the "administrative state" might gain the requisite democratic legitimacy that it too often lacks. Even seemingly problematic forms of administrative discretion can be successfully subordinated to the legitimacy-generating power of deliberation in which "*all* members of the political community . . . take part in discourse" in a meaningful way. "Each must have fundamentally equal chances to take a position on all relevant contributions" (182). This equality of chances is by no means purely formal in character. For Habermas, it demands an egalitarian social and economic setting that "has emerged from the confines of class and thrown off the millennia-old shackles of social stratification and exploitation" (308). A normatively legitimate deliberative democracy, it seems, can only take the form of radical social (deliberative) democracy.

On the other hand, deliberative democracy periodically takes on somewhat more subdued hues in Habermas' discussion. He often seems so intent on emphasizing the necessity of complex markets that it remains unclear precisely what social and economic reforms—beyond some sensible improvements to the (increasingly fragile) welfare state—he has in mind. As argued in Chapter 7, the political and institutional implications of his proposed model of proceduralist law seem similarly ambivalent. He frequently describes popular deliberation as merely influencing, countersteering, or "laying siege" to the state administration, justifying this relatively modest aspiration with the claim that communicative power "cannot 'rule' of itself but only point the use of administrative power in specific directions" (300). He even endorses the possibility that a truly vibrant deliberative democracy necessarily plays a limited role in the actual operations of political decision making most of the time: Typically, "courts deliver judgments, decisions, bureaucracies prepare laws and process applications, parliaments pass laws and budgets, party headquarters conduct election campaigns, clients exert influence on 'their' administrators" with civil society necessarily left at the wayside (357). Even those facets of government most closely tied to civil society may have to accept a truncated role: under normal political conditions, "the initiative and power to put problems on the agenda and bring them to a decision lies more with the Government leaders and administration than with the parliamentary complex" (380). In this version of his model, only during unusual or exceptional conditions (as defined somewhat imprecisely by Habermas) can we expect a genuinely robust deliberative democracy, in which the argumentative give-and-take of civil society effectively dominates the political machinery, to surface.

In the second section of this chapter, I turn to consider one of the likely conceptual sources of this tension. For now, I merely hope to show how the ongoing critical theory debate about deliberative democracy and globalization reproduces it.

Contemporary critical theorists generally endorse the view that a deliberative model of democratic legitimacy is especially well suited to the demands of globalization. Indeed, this is one of the main reasons they adduce for the superiority of their approach. Habermas defends this position by noting that his model "loosens the conceptual ties between democratic legitimacy and the familiar forces of state organization."[7] Although democracy always needs some conventional (and typically state-based) forms of decision making and representation, the deliberative model "tips the balance" in precisely the right way by underscoring the centrality of a "functioning public sphere, the quality of discussion, accessibility, and the discursive structure of opinion- and will-formation," none of which is necessarily tied to a particular territory or nation's state-based political institutions.[8] For this reason, Habermas considers the paradigm of deliberative democracy especially fruitful for thinking through the possibility of developing and democratizing regional political and economic blocs (e.g., the European Union); it also helps us consider how such regional blocs might come to constitute core components of a broader cosmopolitan system of governance. Although, a centralized world-state is undesirable, a stronger and more democratic United Nations able to exercise peace-keeping and humanitarian functions, operating in conjunction with regional blocs outfitted with the decision-making muscle necessary for pursuing ambitious regulatory policies, are now called for. Whereas defenders of cosmopolitan democracy like David Held suggest that a refurnished United Nations might conceivably undertake ambitious forms of social, economic, and environmental regulation, Habermas would more cautiously limit global government to peacekeeping operations and the protection of fundamental human rights.[9] In lucky correspondence with the ongoing intensification of cross-border ties in countless arenas of social life, Seyla Benhabib notes in the same vein, deliberation "can emerge *whenever* and *wherever* human beings can affect one another's actions and well-being."[10] Deliberative democracy should prove adept at coping "with fluid boundaries" and producing outcomes across borders since human communication—especially in an age of high-speed communication and unprecedented possibilities for simultaneity—easily explodes the confines of conventional political and geographical boundaries.[11] In the same spirit, Jim Bohman defends a "public reason" model of decision making by noting that the profound pluralism characteristic of political affairs at the global level requires unrestricted communication along the lines encouraged by deliberative democracy. To be sure, Bohman thinks that Habermasians need to reconsider conventional ideas about the public sphere in order to liberate them from unnecessary Eurocentric baggage. Yet there is no reason to preclude the possibility of doing so successfully.[12] Whereas communitarian or republican accounts occlude the "fact of (rapidly growing) pluralism," deliberative democracy can grapple successfully with diversity.[13] In contrast to republican or participatory democratic decision-making models which privilege face-to-face political interaction (e.g., town meetings or mass demonstrations), deliberative democracy seems well-suited to exploit the virtues of relatively abstract forms of potentially cross-border communication. For this reason as well, it offers a fruitful starting point for theorizing about postnational democracy.

Despite this common starting point, Habermasian deliberative democrats take different roads in their approaches to globalization. Although the story is more complicated than I can acknowledge here, those roads ultimately mirror the tensions in Habermas' own discussion.

Echoing Habermas in his more radical moments, some of his sympathizers offer a vision of global (deliberative) democracy resting on the realization of ambitious new forms of transnational democratic decision making subject to global civil society, to be undertaken in conjunction with a plethora of radical social and economic reforms. In this version of transnational deliberative democracy, new formal institutions can be successfully established at the global level. Furthermore, the "commanding heights" of those institutions can be rendered directly subordinate to deliberatively derived communicative power. Thus, the late Iris Young argued that ultimately only "global institutions that in principle include or represent everyone" constitute the best institutionalization of the deliberative-democratic intuition that "dialogic interaction" can generate regulations that "take account of the needs, interests, and perspectives of everyone."[14] Given "the increased density of interaction and interdependence" of our globalizing universe, deliberative democracy—to be achieved in part by strengthening as well as democratizing the United Nations—is the only way to assure the legitimacy of "more global-level regulation of security, human rights, trade regulation, [and] development policy."[15] Young linked her defense of transnational deliberative democracy to the necessity of attacking the stark poverty that still plagues humanity, observing that transnational deliberative democracy is destined to founder if poverty continues to prevent the meaningful political involvement of hundreds of millions of our fellow prospective global citizens.[16]

Notwithstanding its many differences vis-à-vis Young's ideas, David Held's widely discussed model of a cosmopolitan democracy, which has been influenced by Habermas in numerous ways, can be placed under this rubric as well.[17] Held argues that "deliberative and decision-making centers beyond national territories are [to be] appropriately situated when those significantly affected by a public matter constitute a cross-border or transnational grouping, when 'lower' [local or national] levels of decision-making cannot manage and discharge satisfactorily transnational . . . policy questions, or when the principle of democratic legitimacy can only be properly redeemed in a transnational context."[18] He immediately links the call for novel modes of formal global government to the necessity of far-reaching social democratic social and economic reforms.[19] Last but by no means least, Habermas himself has recently taken on the role of an outspoken defender of relatively powerful forms of supranational European governance, and he has struggled to show why his discourse theory of democracy can help overcome the tired divisions between skeptics and defenders of the European Union. Only a refurbished European Union committed to the ideals of deliberative democracy, the argument goes, offers Europeans a way to preserve democracy and the welfare state. Habermas conveniently downplays some of the distinctive features of European regionalization, in part because he tends to interpret the European Union as part of a more general institutional trend towards more ambitious forms of transnational deliberative democracy.[20]

Yet critical theorists also offer models of transnational deliberative democracy which mirror Habermas' more cautious considerations about deliberative democracy. Although John Dryzek considers himself a left critic of many strands of Habermasian theory,[21] his work reproduces Habermas' own occasional suggestion that the "commanding heights" (e.g., existing centers of decision making, as well as novel sites as conceived by ambitious models of transnational democracy) of power are unlikely to be rendered effectively subordinated to communicative power. Dryzek offers a flattering account of transnational civil society as a site for spontaneous unconstrained communication, sharply contrasting it to the profound limitations on deliberation found in the formal political institutions of the capitalist state, where the dictates of globalizing capitalism truncate meaningful possibilities for deliberation.[22] This contrast leads Dryzek to favor global civil society as the central and perhaps exclusive site for transnational democratization. In contrast to other theorists of deliberative civil society who have emphasized the necessity of a "dualistic" strategy linking the democratization of civil society to democratic reforms of the formal apparatus of government,[23] Dryzek tends to emphasize the threat of cooptation posed by attempts to directly exercise, rather than merely influence, formal institutions.[24] In a similar vein, Jim Bohman asserts that "globalization processes are too large and complex, escaping not only the boundaries of the nation-state, but of all state-like institutions and their mode of exercising power."[25] In light of the necessary limitations of any state-centered strategy for democracy at the global level, Bohman tends to emphasize the virtues of a democratization strategy that extends the influence of emerging global deliberative public spheres to the existing potpourri of power holders presently operating at the global level.

Although much can be said in favor of this general approach, the question of the relationship between such influence and the actual exercise of power by the commanding heights of global authority still remains somewhat unclear. Bohman, in some contrast to Dryzek, appears to hold out the possibility of establishing more ambitious modes of firmly institutionalized transnational democracy; some of his observations suggest more far-reaching institutional aims. Yet his skepticism about conventional forms of state authority—including, it seems, conceivable postnational varieties—leaves unresolved the question of how conflicts between competing global publics ultimately might be mediated and given a binding legal form.

In these more cautious accounts of transnational deliberative democracy, understandable skepticism about the prospects of centralized global government, in conjunction with a hardheaded assessment of the pathologies of the contemporary capitalist state, risks generating a truncated vision of democracy. After all, influence is not, per se, equivalent to an effective exercise of power.[26] To be sure, extending the influence of civil society to existing sources of authority at the global level is an admirable political goal. Yet vassals also "influenced" feudal lords; children and wives influence patriarchal husbands and fathers. By neglecting the question of how the commanding heights of global power could be directed subjected to popular self-legislation, these models risk throwing out the baby with the bathwater. In contrast, the core idea of modern democracy requires the exercise of political power in accordance with rules and laws freely consented to by those affected by them. In this classical view, democracy requires autonomous self-legislation. In the context of deliberative democracy, this traditional democratic idea can be fruitfully reformulated as requiring that there can be "no rule of [deliberative] reasons apart from the self-rule of citizens by justified reasons."[27] Models of transnational democracy which reduce the unfulfilled quest for self-rule by deliberative citizens to the popular influence (or, in Habermas' appropriation of systems-theory jargon, countersteering) of seemingly impermeable global power blocs fail to pay proper fidelity to core democratic aspirations. To put the point more bluntly: deliberative influence does not a democracy make. Only the exercise of the commanding heights of decision making by deliberative citizens can achieve democracy. At the transnational level, this requires us to think even harder about how both existing and hitherto unrealized forms of transnational authority can be clearly subordinated to the preferences of deliberative self-legislating citizens.

POPULAR SOVEREIGNTY, DELIBERATION, AND TRANSNATIONAL DEMOCRACY

To what do critical theory analyses of deliberative democracy owe this now familiar oscillation between "radicalism and resignation"? Might not its ubiquity in Habermasian theory suggest the existence of a deeper conceptual weakness?

In Chapter 6, I traced the origins of this tension in part to Habermas' crucial conceptual distinction between communicative and administrative power. Another source appears to be a certain conceptual slippage plaguing Habermasian accounts of deliberative democracy. The problematic implications of that slippage are especially evident in recent discussions of transnational democracy.

Typically, Habermasians start with a bold account of the normative underpinnings of legitimate decision making. In this account, only those norms are legitimate when agreed to in a process of deliberation having the following attributes:

> 1) participation in such deliberation is governed by norms of equality and symmetry; all have the same chances to initiate speech acts, to question, to interrogate, and to open debate; 2) all have the same right to question the assigned topics of conversation; and 3) all have the same right to initiate reflexive arguments about the very rules of the discourse procedure and the way in which they are applied.[28]

If applied to the global arena, this normative ideal would probably have far-reaching and even revolutionary consequences. It seems to require the reconfiguration of global political and economic power so that *every one* of the planet's billions of inhabitants might possess equal and uncoerced chances to determine, via freewheeling deliberation resulting in a binding rule, the character of any decision influencing his or her activities. Not surprisingly, writers like Iris Young and David Held rigorously pursue this normative intuition by advocating fundamental alterations to the distribution of economic resources on the global level. But one might legitimately wonder whether even their sensible and impeccably humanitarian reform proposals—Held, for example, advocates redistributive policies and experiments with new forms of property and ownership—ultimately would suffice given the shocking inequalities plaguing present-day material conditions. Nor is it startling that some Habermasian deliberative democrats consequently embrace ambitious models of cosmopolitan democratic government, where supranational formal institutions would take on many tasks presently exercised by the nation-state. Given the transnational character of countless forms of human activity, such institutional aspirations would appear to make eminent sense.

At the same time, immediate problems present themselves to any serious defender of this approach. It seems fundamentally unrealizable given present economic and political conditions. Can anyone really imagine the United States peacefully surrendering its dominant military position within the international state system or, for that matter, any of the privileged rich countries acceding to a fundamental global redistribution of economic resources? Thus far, they have aggressively resisted even relatively modest (and inexpensive) efforts to reduce global starvation and disease. It remains unclear whether those who defend an ambitious application of Habermasian ideas to the global arena have sufficiently struggled with these practical questions. However normatively attractive, proposals of this type not only come up against the harsh realities of the existing global political economy, but they raise many difficult questions for political action. Even modest attempts to redistribute income from the rich to poor countries, for example, might easily trigger a reactionary backlash in the rich North. Cosmopolitan deliberative democracy might quickly find itself strangled in its cradle. In turn, a reactionary backlash might easily trigger violent revolutionary movements in the developing world, understandably angry at the rich North for its failure to pursue peaceful social reform but, for their part, far too willing to engage in morally irresponsible forms of political action. Of course, every radical agenda for reform faces such questions. But the Habermasian genre seems astonishingly disinterested in them.

On a more systematic level, applying Habermas' basic normative vision to the global arena also potentially undermines one crucial claim for its intellectual superiority vis-à-vis competing approaches. As noted above, Habermasians suggest that republican and participatory democratic models of decision making unrealistically exaggerate the necessity of relatively direct forms of small-scale face-to-face political exchange. But does not their model require an equally dramatic politicization of the (global) citizenry? Deliberative democracy in this account calls for a substantial quantitative increase as well as qualitative improvement to existing forms of political deliberation. Closer to republican and participatory democratic models than probably acknowledged, deliberative democracy demands a vast increase in participation and difficult old-fashioned "political work," because deliberation itself is obviously a form of participation. Revealingly, Benhabib speaks of "participation in deliberation," notwithstanding her attempts to contrast the deliberative model favorably to competing ones.[29] In fact, deliberation is an especially time-consuming and fragile form of participation, as it requires tremendous patience, a rare willingness to hear others out, and the careful evaluation of oftentimes ambiguous assertions and claims. The achievement of meaningful transnational deliberation is likely to be at least as arduous and demanding in terms of the scarce resource of time as many other transnational political endeavors.

Not surprisingly, many Habermasian deliberative democrats hesitate before embracing this radical interpretation of deliberative democracy. Other elements of Habermas' account offer a ready basis for a fall-back position. Yet those elements pave the way for an unsatisfactory account of transnational democracy.

Typically, the audacious normative model underlying the demand for deliberative democracy is quickly translated into the institutional demand for "a plurality of associations" or an "interlocking net of . . . multiple forms of associations, networks, and organizations" constituting "an anonymous 'public conversation.'"[30] Although formal institutions are necessary for the protection of deliberation and are expected to codify its results via binding general laws, the real site for creative political deliberation remains a decentered civil society characterized by a multiplicity of associations. Benhabib favorably contrasts this pluralistic model of "anonymous" deliberation to the traditional "fiction of a mass assembly carrying out its deliberations" in the form of one concrete unified body or institution. The concretistic and overly unitarian "fiction of a general deliberative assembly" fails to capture the properly pluralistic character of deliberation.[31] In undertaking this political translation of Habermas' deliberative model, Benhabib is simply following Habermas himself, whose *Between Facts and Norms* similarly announces the death of historically anachronistic ideas of a sovereign democratic macrosubject, in which society is conceived as a unified "body" or collective subject: Habermas repeatedly scolds traditional democratic thinkers for endorsing overly concretistic interpretations of the normative ideal of popular sovereignty. *Between Facts and Norms* is replete with references to the anonymous and even "subject-less character" of lively deliberative politics (136). Parallel descriptions of an anonymous deliberative civil society are now commonplace in the critical theory literature.

At first glance, this translation seems harmless enough. Popular sovereignty has indeed been interpreted in many unconvincing ways in modern political thought. Who could persuasively claim that a single deliberative legislature can either legitimately or effectively "stand in" for a pluralistic people and the "plurality of associations" they employ?[32] Habermas and his followers rightly praise the virtues of a vibrant civil society and lively process of deliberation in which ideas and arguments "move" and "flow" in an unpredictable and even anarchic fashion, and they understandably celebrate, in a postmodern spirit, the death of anachronistic ideas of a unitary sovereign macrosubject as the proper carrier of democracy. They are also right to follow Habermas in offering a proceduralist reading of the idea of popular sovereignty (287–328). Given this starting point, the appeal of such terms as anonymous and subject-less seems obvious. As we all know from the practical discourses in which we unavoidably engage, it often remains unclear who initiated a specific argument or to whom it "belongs." Many times we simply do not care: lively argumentative give-and-take can seem anonymous and even subject-less because fruitful deliberation often flows in complex and unexpected ways. We may be more interested in the practical resolution of whatever question or task is at hand than assigning credit for good arguments and blame for unproductive contributions. Our contributions to debate can generate unexpected consequences, taking on meanings or significance which we would never have imagined possible beforehand.

This translation of the basic normative model of deliberative democracy provides reason for concern, however. Its overstylized and potentially problematic contrast between unity and plurality, anachronistic macrosubjects and subject-less deliberation, and "concretistic" versus "desubstantialized" popular sovereignty helps obscure one of the most basic issues of democratic theory: How can the plurality of deliberative civil society undergo an effective funneling into a (unified) expression of democratically legitimate political power? If civil society is to result in coherent legislation to which deliberative citizens have agreed, if only in a relatively indirect institutional fashion (e.g., by representative bodies), subject-less discourse and debate must ultimately take a unified (that is, generally applicable) binding form. To the extent that political decision making requires that civil society ultimately speak with "one voice," political unity still must be achieved if "anonymous" and "subjectless" civil society is to speak coherently and decisively.[33] For traditional democratic theory, formal political institutions, of course, play a decisive role in generating this necessary moment of unity. Of course, both Habermas and his followers have proposed a number of thoughtful institutional innovations. Yet too little intellectual energy has been devoted to examining the proper role of those institutional mechanisms—most important perhaps, general lawmaking and the rule of law—which historically have played a decisive role in making sure that civil society can act effectively and coherently via binding legal norms. At times, an equally overstylized and misleading contrast between liberalism and radical democracy leads some of them to incorrectly see recent attempts within critical theory to do justice to classical models of the rule of law and constitutionalism as nothing more than a "political sellout."[34] However, this position risks reproducing the kneejerk anti-legalism that disastrously plagued the orthodox Marxist left and its most problematic political offspring.

To be sure, achieving even a minimum of such unity at the transnational level poses *enormous* hurdles in light of the unprecedented complexity and profound pluralism we find there. The United Nations, of course, constitutes an important attempt to do so. Yet one might legitimately wonder whether even a strengthened United Nations might successfully meet the stunning regulatory tasks at hand. How might we subject the "neo-feudal" power blocs (organizations like the WTO and IMF, international arbitration bodies, various forms of "soft" transnational legal regulation, etc.) presently operating on the global scene, in both a normatively satisfactory and institutionally realistic fashion, to democratic self-legislation? How might general legislation and the rule of law be effectively instantiated at the global level? Nonstate bodies will undoubtedly play a key role as we struggle to offer a real-life institutional answer to these questions. But an insufficiently critical homage to (nonstate) "governance" should not lead us to obscure the indispensable functions existing state and new state-like institutions will need to perform in achieving novel forms of self-legislation and the rule of law.

Whereas much of the critical theory work on these issues remains defensive and even anxiety-ridden, tending to emphasize the threats posed to democratic self-legislation and the rule of law by globalization, some recent work inspired by the Habermasian tradition suggests that we might tackle these issues in more constructive ways. In Chapter 6, I cautiously mentioned the merits of a reworked model of reflexive law as a possible launching pad for effective legal regulation. In a related vein, the German critical theorist Hauke Brunkhorst worries that transnational decision making is subject to weak but not yet strong publics. Civil society exercises moral influence, but only a "'loose coupling' between discussion and decision" can be found at the global level.[35] Arguing that we can separate the normative kernel of constitutionalism from its familiar carrier, the modern nation-state, Brunkhorst shares the understandable skepticism of grandiose proposals for new forms of extended state authority at the global level. Yet because normatively attractive legal and constitutional ideas can still be salvaged from the wreck of the declining nation-state, weak global publics might still successfully be transformed into strong (that is, legally enforceable) publics via "egalitarian procedures for the formation and representation of a global *volonte generale*, which would provide 'direct access . . . for all the interests concerned.'"[36] If modern democracy rests on the simple idea that the addressees of law must also be its authors, we undeniably suffer from a massive democratic deficit at the global level. As Brunkhorst reminds us, the global political economy rests on a complex network of both public and private legal instruments (e.g., WTO law, the legal infrastructure of international business arbitration, *Lex Mercatoria*, as well as the more familiar paraphernalia of public international law). Yet few of these instruments provide meaningful opportunities for democratic participation and deliberation. The good news, however, is that we also see substantial evidence of an emerging transnational civil society (e.g., human rights activists, so-called antiglobalization activists) or "weak public sphere," defined as an incipient form of democracy that has yet to realize institutional devices by means of which it can issue binding legal norms. Much of the task at hand then becomes outfitting transnational civil society with new instruments for binding lawmaking, and thus transforming it into a "strong public." As there is no necessary connection between the territorial state and the modern ideals of constitutional democracy, no a priori reason exists for excluding the possibility that democracy is realizable in novel and unprecedented ways beyond the confines of the existing nation-state. Despite its many flaws, the European Union already provides some preliminary evidence that we might achieve popular sovereignty at the supranational level. What we need is "real democratic representation" of the interests and voices of all those affected by global policies in transnational decision-making bodies.[37]

The important point for now is to recognize the potential perils of an interpretation of deliberative civil society that misleadingly generates an unwarranted neglect—and even skepticism—of the necessity of institutional mechanisms that will need to play a crucial role in realizing the legally binding and effectively accountable general results of freewheeling deliberation. Unfortunately, some strands of Habermasian deliberative democracy probably succumb to those perils. Not surprisingly, they ultimately engender a defensive account of transnational democracy in which global publics and civil society do little more than influence or countersteer the commanding heights of global authority. The self-legislation of the deliberative citizen is thereby reduced to one of its presuppositions, a freewheeling deliberative civil society. Without more effective institutional devices, however, existing global power holders will continue to disregard global civil society if they so desire.

Another potential error flows from the imagery of an "anonymous" and subject-less" civil society. Of course, a lively deliberative democracy is only anonymous and subject-less in a metaphorical sense. If a legitimate deliberative democracy rests on genuinely free and equal opportunities for everyone to deliberate about matters impacting them, the resulting deliberative process will in reality rest on the input of numerous subjects. Properly speaking, it is neither anonymous nor subject-less. Indeed, its core ideal makes it incumbent on us to ensure that everyone might have the opportunity to participate meaningfully in public debate and deliberation and shape decision making. As noted in the previous section, deliberative democracy is not per se the "rule of deliberative reasons," but instead should be properly understood as the "self-rule of citizens by (deliberative) reasons." The danger here is that the translation of deliberative democracy into anonymous and subject-less discourse risks downplaying indispensable democratic attributes of deliberative democracy; it may also lead those who reproduce this imagery to embrace correspondingly misleading institutional proposals. Deliberative democracy only deserves to be described as democratic if deliberation is undertaken by (concretely situated human) subjects for the sake of achieving self-rule or self-legislation. The peril at hand is that this translation unwittingly threatens to privilege ("anonymous," "subject-less") deliberation over democracy by downplaying the central place of self-legislating (and deliberating) subjects to democracy. As Ingeborg Maus similarly worries, by transforming the principle of popular sovereignty into freely fluctuating, subject-less deliberation, in Habermas' theory "communicatively generated power threatens to become nearly ubiquitous."[38] But this move potentially makes it difficult to assure the strict legal accountability of state actors to the sovereign people, which Maus rightly describes as a necessary precondition of democratic self-legislation. To whom exactly are state agents to be made accountable if the *demos* is always fluid and subject-less? How are its desires to be effectively funneled and ultimately given binding general legal form if communicative power is both ubiquitous and fundamentally fluid in character? How might it ever succeed in carefully regulating the exercise of administrative power?

Some of Habermas' recent writings on transnational democracy confirm the basic soundness of this concern. He has recently relied on a distinction between "democratic procedures whose legitimacy rests on the grounds that they are fair and open to all, and democratic procedures defended on the grounds that both deliberations and decisions have sufficiently rational character."[39] This distinction arguably parallels the general tendency to overstate the practical differences between participation and deliberation, as well as downplay the centrality of the actual (deliberative) participation of those concrete subjects affected by whatever norm or rule is under scrutiny in favor of the potentially misleading imagery of anonymous and subject-less deliberation. To put the point polemically (and rather crudely): if legitimate deliberation can be anonymous and somehow subject-less, perhaps we need not worry too much when actual deliberative input possesses a relatively limited participatory basis. In Habermas' own words,

> democratic procedure no longer draws its legitimizing force only, *indeed not even predominantly*, from political participation and the expression of political will, but rather from the general accessibility of a deliberative process whose structure grounds an expectation of rationally acceptable results.[40]

Many intergovernmental negotiating and transnational decision-making bodies lack the former. However, according to Habermas, they possess the latter. That is, they lack significant popular participatory input via conventional state forms, yet they nonetheless ground "an expectation of rationally acceptable results" and thus can perform, with some degree of success, what we might describe as useful epistemic functions, in the sense of generating "rationally acceptable results."[41] They raise the information level and contribute to rational problem solving because they include different parties and often adhere to arguing as a decision making procedure and not voting and bargaining. To various degrees such bodies inject the logic of impartial justification and reason giving into transnational bodies of governance.[42]

For this reason, Habermas concludes, the supposedly "weak" legitimation of some transnational bodies, when understood in light of his model of deliberative democracy, appears "in another [more positive] light."[43]

As Robert Fine and Will Smith point out, however, this argument downplays the indispensable role of democratic representative bodies and threatens to dissolve any link between deliberative civil society and formal political institutions. Discussing the implications of Habermas' ideas for the European Union, they worry that the development of a civil society "*in isolation from* such representative institutions might enhance the feeling of detachment" and alienation already widespread in relations between European citizens and institutions.[44] More generally, Habermas' distinction potentially opens the door to a relatively conciliatory reading of actual transnational decision-making bodies, many of which undoubtedly achieve useful "epistemic" functions but hardly rest on broad democratic deliberation. Many deliberative processes at the transnational setting arguably contribute to a measure of "rationally acceptable results." Unfortunately, few of them can claim to provide a sufficient institutionalization for deliberative global citizens who need to make sure that their preferences gain a binding legal form.

At the beginning of this chapter, I suggested that recent Habermasian attempts to tackle the normative and institutional quagmires of globalization offer a useful test for determining whether the paradigm of deliberative democracy should continue to occupy the energies of critical theorists. How then has deliberative democracy fared on this test? If I am not mistaken, the results look mixed. Although Habermas-inspired deliberative democracy has undoubtedly enriched the ongoing debate about the prospects of transnational governance, it remains both programmatically and conceptually tension-ridden. If it is to prove intellectually fruitful in the future, critical theorists will need to make sure to avoid the worrisome tendency to discount the indispensable democratic core of the idea of deliberative democracy. They will also need to move beyond disappointing defensive models of transnational democratization, while simultaneously showing why deliberative self-legislation can be meaningfully realized at the transnational level without succumbing to utopianism. Even though self-legislation has primarily been achieved within the confines of the nation-state in modernity, we now need to consider how it can be legally secured at the transnational level, most likely with only limited aid from novel forms of formal supranational state organization. Needless to say, these are difficult challenges. The basic intellectual richness of critical theory, however, suggests that it remains at least as well positioned as its main theoretical competitors to rise to those challenges.

8 Cosmopolitan Democracy
Democracy Without Law?

What are the likely consequences of globalization for democratic theory and practice? In a series of pathbreaking publications that have garnered a remarkable amount of scholarly attention in a brief span of time, the political theorist David Held and a group of interlocutors (most important, Daniele Archibugi and Anthony McGrew) have tackled this question by means of an audacious model of "cosmopolitan democracy," according to which the democratization of transnational politics now belongs at the top of the agenda.[1] Held and his intellectual compatriots argue that the ongoing globalization of key forms of human activity calls out for the development of no less transnational modes of liberal democratic decision making.[2] A host of recent social trends (the globalization of the economy, for example, as well as the growing significance of cross-border environmental problems) demonstrates not only that the existing nation-state is ill-prepared to deal with the regulatory imperatives of our times but also raises fundamental questions about the traditional attempt to weld liberal democracy onto the framework of the modern nation-state. Modern liberal-democratic theory typically presupposed the existence of substantial symmetry and congruence between citizen-voters and decision makers at the national level, and the key categories of consent, constituency, participation, and representation were accordingly conceived within the parameters of the nation-state. As national borders become ever more porous, however, a series of difficult and thus far unanswered questions force themselves onto the agenda of democratic theory: "What is the proper constituency, and proper jurisdiction, for developing and implementing policy issues with respect to...the use of nuclear energy, the harvesting of rain forests, the use of non-renewable resources, the instability of global financial markets, and the reduction of the risks of nuclear warfare" in light of their profound cross-border consequences?"[3] Their answer to this question is that we need to update the liberal-democratic vision by undertaking a series of dramatic institutional reforms. Stated in the simplest terms: those policy arenas whose transnational scope overwhelms existing nationally based liberal democratic institutions require a dramatic strengthening of nascent forms of transnational liberal-democratic authority (under the auspices of the UN but also regional organizations such as the EU or NAFTA) along with the establishment of new forms of transnational decision making (for example, cross-border popular referenda).

The resulting model of "cosmopolitan democracy" has generated significant interest among political theorists; a number of useful recent publications have already been devoted to critically analyzing Held's proposals from a host of different theoretical perspectives.[4] I cannot hope to offer here an adequate critical summary of that increasingly multisided debate, in which communitarian-inspired attempts to deflate cosmopolitan democracy's universalistic Kantian features play an especially prominent role.[5] Nonetheless, it is striking that little critical attention has been paid to cosmopolitan democracy's purported fidelity to classical conceptions of the rule of law. Held repeatedly suggests that "cosmopolitan democratic law" builds on the best of the western legal tradition, even going so far as to dub his updated version of liberal democracy a cosmopolitan "democratic *Rechtsstaat*."[6] As I hope to show in this chapter, this claim not only obscures the extent to which Held and his colleagues in fact break with defensible conceptions of the "rule of law," but the weaknesses of their legal argumentation also point to the existence of immanent flaws within their overall vision of transnational democracy. Both Archibugi and Held insist that one of cosmopolitan democracy's main appeals is that it circumvents the ills of unacceptable models of a hypercentralized "planetary Leviathan" or world-state likely to prove incapable of doing justice to cultural, religious, and ethical diversity.[7] They proudly assert that their model of "cosmopolitan democratic law" not only can succeed in effectively restraining the exercise of political power on the global level but that it would continue to provide significant room for decision making at the local and national levels. Presumably there is no legitimate reason to fear cosmopolitan democracy law as a potential cover for a new and potentially onerous form of imperialism, and opponents of centralized world government would do well to join forces with those committed to realizing transnational democracy in accordance with their ideas.[8]

Unfortunately, the legal ills of cosmopolitan democracy undermine precisely those features that initially make it so attractive. These flaws suggest that we would do well to pursue more modest—but nonetheless important—experiments in buttressing democracy at the global level. I first provide an exegesis of the conceptual foundations of the idea of a cosmopolitan democratic *Rechtsstaat* before turning to examine its conceptual weaknesses.

COSMOPOLITAN DEMOCRACY'S LAW

Cosmopolitan democracy is predicated on the plausible notion that a growing range of policy concerns explodes the confines of both the traditional nation-state and Westphalian system of international relations in which the nation-state has long been embedded. In light of a host of phenomena providing evidence of a "rapid growth of complex interconnections and interrelations between states and societies," along with the growing "intersection of national and international forces and processes," existing nation-states increasingly seem poorly equipped to tackle the most pressing political concerns of our times either unilaterally or by means of traditional forms of interstate cooperation.[9] National legislation too often is of limited effectiveness in the face of transnational problems; regulations passed by impressive second-tier powers (France, Germany, or Italy), or even a world power like the United States, are unlikely to immunize them against ozone depletion, or the problematic side effects of global trade. The heightened significance as well as the lasting character of many transnational policy tasks renders traditional forms of treaty making inadequate; the temporary and ad hoc character of most treaties meshes poorly with the regulatory undertakings at hand. From a normative perspective, the profound impact on domestic politics of global financial markets or the environmental crisis makes it difficult to accept the traditional view that international matters can be left in the hands of small groups of (typically nonelected) foreign policy elites. If we are to take liberal-democratic notions of legitimacy seriously, we need to conceive of new ways to democratize decision making concerning issues no longer narrowly "international" in the traditional sense of the term. In a similar vein, it is unclear how Realist "reason of state"—oriented views of interstate politics offer satisfactory conceptual resources for tackling the imperatives of transnational policy making, especially in light of the fact that Realism's dogmatic insistence on the primacy of the "national interest" decreasingly makes sense conceptually in a world in which the border between "national" and "transnational" interests becomes blurred.[10] Realist theories of international politics miss the boat in part because they reify precisely that institutional constellation, the modern nation-state, presently exhibiting signs of decay.

Inspired in part by Habermas, cosmopolitan democracy's exponents propose that

> [d]eliberative and decision-making centers beyond national territories are [to be] appropriately situated when those significantly affected by a public matter constitute a cross-border or transnational grouping, when 'lower' [local or national] levels of decision making cannot manage and discharge satisfactorily transnational...policy questions, or when the principle of democratic legitimacy can only be properly redeemed in a transnational context."[11]

Since many issues continue to affect constituencies primarily local or national in character, this recommendation should by no means entail the hypercentralization of decision making. Thus, Archibugi and Held repeatedly describe themselves as advocates of a multitiered political system in which new forms of transnational liberal-democratic authority, concerned exclusively with those issues possessing genuinely transnational effects, would complement existing forms of liberal democratic decision making. They also seem assured that this proposal amounts to more than yet another doomed "liberal idealist" pipe dream inconsistent with the fundamental laws of international politics. Though critical of its widely acknowledged democratic deficits, they not only see the European Union as an important stepping stone to more ambitious models of global governance, but they also interpret it as a present-day approximation of their own quest to develop transnational political authority "midway between the confederal and federalist models" of transnational governance.[12] Like the European Union, experiments in cosmopolitan democracy require closer ties among its units than those typically characteristic of loosely connected confederations of sovereign states (for example, NATO), because globalization increases the need for permanent forms of democratically legitimized transnational cooperation. Yet cosmopolitan democracy would avoid the relatively high degree of centralized power exhibited by existing federal systems (the United States, for example, or the Federal Republic of Germany) because "it is undesirable to go beyond a given threshold of centralization on a scale as vast as vast a global one." The EU example is also illuminating since it suggests the possibility of complex political institutions able to realize novel forms of sovereignty inconsistent with the traditional "hierarchical relationship between central institutions and individual states."[13] In this account, there is no principled reason to stress potential tensions between regional and global forms of political authority: Regional liberal-democratic political blocs not only represent useful experiments in transnational democracy, but regional decision making would also continue to play a decisive role in a more universal global network of liberal-democratic decision making when interests affected are genuinely regional in scope and thus require a regionalized solution.[14]

What then is the role of law in this model? Archibugi and Held advocate a system of cosmopolitan "democratic public law," which is in some contrast to existing international law, in part because they envision a more ambitious form of jurisprudence than implied by the traditional notion of a "law between states." Since the Nuremberg Trials, international rights protections have tended to demote the role of the nation-state while anticipating, albeit incompletely, the possibility of transnational citizenship built on an unmediated relationship between individuals and global institutions. A key task of cosmopolitan democratic law is to further this cause. New forms of regional and global liberal-democratic decision making would rest directly on an emerging transnational "community of fate," and an unmediated legal relationship between individuals and transnational decision-making bodies would come to operate in a manner thus far only hinted at within existing forms of international law. Transnational courts would ultimately gain jurisdiction over many key conflicts pitting individuals against existing nation-states. In order to help ground this transformation of international law into transnational law, Archibugi and Held appeal to Kant's famous notion that "universal hospitality" represents a universal right transcending the claims of particular nations and states and legitimately extending to all members of the human community.[15] But they radicalize Kant's claim by provocatively suggesting that "in a highly interconnected world" universal hospitality entails a more far-reaching set of rights than Kant originally had in mind. Given the process of globalization, universal hospitality today allegedly implies nothing less than the "mutual acknowledgement of, and respect for, the equal and legitimate rights of others to pursue their own projects and life-plans."[16] Reinterpreted in accordance with present-day social and economic imperatives, Kant's cosmopolitan right to hospitality points the way to an audacious model of transnational law committed to realizing an extensive set of basic rights.[17]

More fundamentally, cosmopolitan democracy builds directly on the liberal-democratic tradition insofar as it aspires to realize both the principles of self-determination and limited government. It promises protection from arbitrary power as well as meaningful possibilities for self-determination, individual self-development, and economic opportunity, and its commitment to upholding "cosmopolitan democratic public law" is essential to its liberal-democratic credentials.[18] Only by exercising political power in accordance with a legal "structure that is both constraining and enabling" can transnational liberal democracy, like its nationally based cousin, realize both self-determination and a commitment to the ideal of the rule of law.[19]

Held has gone furthest in offering a detailed account of the model of law at the base of this vision. In his view, cosmopolitan democratic law ultimately rests on liberal democracy's underlying "principle of autonomy," whose chief characteristics are already embedded in the liberal-democratic practices and traditions of the West. The principle of autonomy represents the "constitutive basis of democratic public law" and thus serves as an indispensable basis for political legitimacy in any liberal-democratic political community.[20] Influenced by John Rawls' conception of political liberalism, Held considers it possible to pursue his Kantian intuitions without committing himself to controversial philosophical justifications. Despite his deep intellectual debts to Habermas and the critical theory tradition in general, he distances himself here from Habermas' attempt to ground a similar model of democratic politics in a demanding "theory of communicative action."[21] In this view, the liberal-democratic vision of autonomy requires a commitment to diverse clusters of rights that alone make it possible for "people to participate on free and equal terms in the regulation of their own associations."[22] Making T. H. Marshall's famous account of the evolutionary dynamic of (legal, political, and social) rights look relatively cautious, Held argues that a legitimate interpretation of cosmopolitan democratic public law centers around a bold set of seven types of rights (health, social, cultural, civic, economic, pacific, and political). These include traditional liberal-democratic rights such as due process, equal treatment before the law, freedom of thought and expression, freedom of religion, adequate and equal possibilities for political deliberation, and universal political participation, as well as social-democratic, environmental, and even feminist rights to physical and emotional well-being, universal childcare, a guaranteed minimum income, a sustainable environment, control over one's own fertility, universal education, lawful foreign policy, political accountability, and a mixed economy consisting of diverse forms of consumption and production.[23]

Held is clearly aware of how unrealistic some of these rights are likely to appear in the existing political climate, and he concedes that it may be impractical to expect them all to be fully realized now. But this generates no real intellectual anxiety on his part: A substantial concretization of them is presently attainable, and thus they can legitimately function as a yardstick according to which political action should be evaluated. Although basic rights "must be defined broadly" in order to assure their abstract and general character "to guide and resolve disputes among...interests in particular conflict situations," they lay "down an *agenda* for democratic politics, but necessarily leave...open the exact interpretation of each of the items on the agenda."[24] The justiciable charter of rights proposed here constitutes the basis for a "rule of law" to the extent that it remains legitimate to expect "[r]ules, laws, policies and decisions" to be made within their confines.[25] Held clearly believes that they can successfully set "the form and limits of public power" in such a way as to make his vision deserving of the noble title of "democratic *Rechtsstaat*."[26] His proposed charter of rights thus offers "an agenda for change and direction for policy to which 'offending' institutions, laws and policies could, in principle, adapt if they are to claim justifiably the mantle of democracy."[27] To the extent that rights enable the exercise of political power by determining how it is to be properly channeled, while simultaneously limiting the exercise of power by focusing on its proper form and scope, this model allegedly offers an effective structure for a "democratic legal order—[a] democratic *Rechtsstaat*" in which political power is "circumscribed by, and accounted for in relation to, democratic public law."[28]

In the final analysis, this model of a transnational rule of law consists of the following core components. When faced with issues impacting on genuinely transnational groupings, supranational legislative devices should strive to act in accordance with a detailed—but by no means fully realizable—charter of rights, and these rights thus should "be enshrined within the constitutions of parliaments and assemblies."[29] In order to achieve this goal, transnational decision-making authorities would be empowered to pass "framework" legislation whose basic outlines would correspond to the aims of cosmopolitan democratic law, but whose application and implementation should be left in the hands of lower (national or local) levels of governance; on this point as well, Held has been inspired by the European Union and its relatively limited reliance on traditional forms of uniform general legislation, and he seems to accept the view that transnational leg-islation will need to take a relatively flexible form so as to deal effectively with the challenge of pluralism at the global level.[30] Transnational courts play a pivotal role in this conception as well. Although cosmopolitan demo-cratic law "empowers" legislators to pursue an ambitious policy agenda, the authority of courts will be extended "so that groups and individuals have an effective means of suing political authorities for the enactment and enforcement of key rights."[31] A system of judicial review would need to be established in order to make sure that legislators exhibit proper fidel-ity to the rights constitutive of cosmopolitan democratic law. In order to bring about this goal, Archibugi and Held propose that we build on Hans Kelsen's famous proposal to extend the compulsory jurisdiction of inter-national courts. Kelsen's courageous defense of a robust system of interna-tional justice has long been neglected, but Archibugi and Held believe that globalization provides Kelsen's hopes with a fresh impetus.[32]

GLOBAL LAW WITHOUT A RULE OF LAW

Archibugi and Held conveniently fail to mention a striking difference between their championship of compulsory jurisdiction and Kelsen's. To be sure, Kelsen hoped that international courts would undergo invigora-tion, and he proposed that individuals (for example, war criminals) could be held more or less directly punishable on the basis of international legal norms. Kelsen was no enemy of either an ambitious welfare state or social democracy.[33] Whereas cosmopolitan democracy institutionalizes mandatory jurisdiction for a vast range of political, social, economic, and environmen-tal rights, however, Kelsen's defense of compulsory jurisdiction for inter-national courts focused on the fundamental issue of war and peace, and a careful reading of his discussion of this issue suggests that he endorsed a more modest—yet indisputably innovative—model of compulsory jurisdiction for global courts.[34] Indeed, Archibugi's and Held's enormously ambitious proposals arguably leave them vulnerable to Kelsen's wise admonishment that the reformer of international law would do well not to compromise "great ideals" while simultaneously accommodating "his postulates to what is politically possible." Progress in international law is only achievable if we avoiding directing our suggestions "toward a goal which, if at all, can be reached only in a distant future; this is unreal and therefore politically less than nothing."[35] Archibugi and Held certainly offer "great ideals," but their recommendations for the international state system should at least raise the question of whether Kelsen's insistence on the virtues of a "slow and steady perfection of the international legal order" undertaken in a sober tone has been sufficiently heeded.[36] To the extent that cosmopolitan democracy means dismantling core components of the international state system, it points the way to revolutionary changes in contemporary political life.

My main aim here is to criticize neither cosmopolitan democracy's utopian overtones nor its misleading reliance on Kelsen. I mention these differences vis-à-vis Kelsen only in order to raise initial doubts about cosmopolitan democracy's legal credentials. As I hope to demonstrate, cosmopolitan democracy's legal weaknesses go well beyond a minor misappropriation of the leading light of twentieth-century liberal international law.

The notion of the "rule of law" has been widely contested in the history of legal thought.[37] Within the modern tradition, however, it generally has taken the form of requiring that state action rest on legal norms that are (a) general in character, (b) relatively clear, (c) public, (d) prospective, and (e) stable. In this standard view, only norms of this type assure a minimum of certainty and determinacy within legal decision making, help guarantee the accountability of power holders, promote the principle of fair notice, and contribute to achieving equality before the law. As pointed out many years ago, this model often coexists with a particular interpretation of the liberal-democratic commitment to basic rights. Liberalism rests on the notion of a "presumption in favor of the rights of the individual against the coercive power of the state."[38] The rule of law in part provides a minimal but indispensable standard for helping to determine the legitimate scope of state intervention in the sphere of individual rights. Although liberalism conceives of rights as essential for assuring liberty, rights nonetheless always require legal regulation or restraint, though they never can be obliterated by legal means; even ardent defenders of free speech, for example, must accept the necessity of regulating free speech, even if it only entails establishing minimal basic rules for registering demonstrations or publishing newspapers. By necessity, rights are interpreted, institutionalized, and contested by a panoply of state bodies and agents, and the task of making sure that the interpretation and regulation of individual rights can be rendered normatively acceptable traditionally has been linked to the notion of the rule of law. As Neumann noted, "individual rights may be interfered with by the state only if the state can prove its claim by reference to an indeterminate number of future cases; this excludes retroactive legislation and demands a separation of legislative from judicial functions."[39] Fidelity to the rule of law virtues noted above is essential if we are to make sure that the interpretation and regulation of basic rights (for example, free speech) takes a relatively predictable and consistent form. In contrast, if state bodies are permitted to regulate basic rights in accordance with inconsistent, ambiguous, open-ended, or retroactive norms, excessive discretionary authority is likely to accrue to state authorities, and the sphere of individual liberty will suffer significant damage. From this traditional perspective, the rule of law performs many admirable functions, but one of its more worthwhile purposes is to work alongside the liberal defense of basic rights in order to preserve meaningful possibilities for individual liberty.

Of course, even those of us sympathetic to this conventional interpretation of the rule of law must acknowledge its limitations; Neumann himself conceded that it was unrealistic to expect every aspect of the legal order to take the form of general, clear, public, prospective, and stable norms.[40] In addition, mainstream modern jurisprudence raises a host of difficult institutional questions, and the multiplicity of ways in which liberal democracy has sought to institutionalize the idea of the rule of law suggests that these questions are likely to remain controversial. Nonetheless, we would do well not to throw away the baby along with the bathwater, as too many critics of the traditional model of the rule of law tend to do. As I have tried to argue in previous chapters, a lack of traditional legal virtues in many areas of emerging global economic regulation contributes significantly to its most troubling attributes. Too often, it is the most powerful beneficiaries of a deeply unjust process of neoliberal globalization who prefer soft forms of law inconsistent with the rule of law as traditionally conceived. Despite the familiar dangers of overstating the merits of traditional jurisprudence, it provides a fruitful starting point for critically interrogating Archibugi's and Held's vision of cosmopolitan democratic law.

Notwithstanding constant appeals to the notion of the *Rechtsstaat*, Archibugi and Held seem unfamiliar with the traditional notion of the rule of law. At the very least, the only features of cosmopolitan democratic law overlapping with it are their demand for rights to due process and equal treatment before the law.[41] The account of the rule of law briefly summarized above is richer than theirs, however, to the extent that it better highlights key functions (for example, assuring fair notice and the accountability of power-holders) and more cogently underscores the importance of effectively harnessing the exercise of state authority by demanding that legal norms and standards take a clear, general, prospective, and stable form. From the perspective of traditional liberal jurisprudence, the potential danger with Archibugi's and Held's conceptual lacuna on this matter is that it may leave cosmopolitan democracy ill-equipped to ward off problematic forms of discretionary public and private authority. If Archibugi and Held are as worried by the specter of a "planetary Leviathan" as they repeatedly claim, one might expect them to pay closer attention to the traditional model's emphasis on the dangers of discretionary and even arbitrary state authority. Unfortunately, they occasionally associate traditional concerns of this type with economic "libertarianism" and the ideas of Friedrich Hayek.[42] A principled commitment to traditional rule of law virtues by no means necessitates loyalty to free-market capitalism, however.[43]

In a similar vein, it is also troubling that cosmopolitan democracy's exponents have little to say about how transnational "framework" legislation would be fleshed out at local and national levels. At one juncture, Held declares that local and national bodies would be outfitted with the authority to "implement" global laws, and that the European Union "embodies a range of relevant distinctions among legal instruments and types of implementation which are helpful to reflect on in this context."[44] Although there is no question either that the legal problem of "translating" transnational directives to the national or local arena is exceedingly complex, or that a great deal can be learned from the European Union about this matter, Held's appeal to the EU experience only begs the question at hand. Even those enthusiastic about the emerging EU legal system would likely consider it presumptuous to suggest that EU law in its present incarnation represents a fully satisfactory embodiment of traditional rule of law virtues.

Archibugi and Held undertake a conceptual move relatively familiar from recent jurisprudence: The notion of the rule of law is basically reinterpreted as a rights-centered model of jurisprudence in which courts are likely to gain substantial authority to determine a host of controversial matters.[45] At times echoing Ronald Dworkin's famous critique of a positivist "rule-book" conception of law and concomitant espousal of a rights-based jurisprudence in which courts are outfitted with generous interpretative authority, Archibugi and Held redefine the *Rechtsstaat* in terms of a set of basic rights purportedly able both to "empower" legal actors and effectively "circumscribe" them.[46] But here as well, courts ultimately are destined to take on weighty discretionary authority. As we saw above, the "rule of law" here basically means that legislators and courts are supposed to act in accordance with an ambitious set of basic rights. Given the fact that these rights "must be defined broadly," one wonders how they, in fact, might succeed in effectively binding or circumscribing state authority. On the surface, they would seem to provide tremendous leeway for both legislators and judicial actors, especially in light of the fact that Archibugi and Held seem uninterested in how a traditional model of the rule of law might contribute to the task of guaranteeing a modicum of consistency and calculability in the interpretation of basic rights. So how then would cosmopolitan democracy make sure that transnational authorities exercise authority in accordance with this charter of rights in a satisfactorily "circumscribed" way? In the final analysis, their answer seems to be that this determination should be placed in the hands of transnational courts: "[T]he influence of judicial 'review boards,' the courts, and designated complaints and appeal procedures has to be extended so that groups and individuals have an effective means of suing political authorities for the enactment or enforcement of key rights."[47] Although cosmopolitan democratic public law would probably grant impressive legislative power to a variety of transnational political actors, transnational judges would ultimately possess the impressive authority to determine how the rights constitutive of "democratic public law" are ultimately to be concretized and interpreted.

By commenting that we would do well to consider proposals to democratize the judiciary,[48] Held indirectly concedes that this vision risks placing substantial open-ended authority to interpret cosmopolitan democratic law in the hands of judicial personnel: Notwithstanding cosmopolitan democracy's alleged break with traditional concepts of sovereignty, it is such judicial experts who seem most likely to exercise far-reaching "sovereign" prerogative power. Discretionary rule by judicial personnel, however, is not the same thing as the rule of law.[49] Neither Held nor Archibugi seems to grasp the ways in which their view potentially conflicts with conventional ideas about the *Rechtsstaat* nor the fact that their account of cosmopolitan democratic law threatens to generate precisely the sort of unharnessed power which so worried classical theorists of the rule of law. In their model, that authority will now be exercised on a global scale, and thus ultimately backed up by the prospect of transnationally organized military force.[50] In a Dworkinian mode, one might praise this demotion of classical rule of law virtues by conceding that the architects of cosmopolitan democracy may be right to downplay the significance of clear, general rules for liberal-democratic jurisprudence. At the level of global decision making, classical conceptions of legislation and judicial interpretation undoubtedly face even greater challenges, in light of the complexity of the regulatory tasks at hand, than they do at the level of the nation-state. We need to undertake experiments with novel forms of global regulatory law, while working to make sure that they preserve a sufficient dose of traditional rule of law virtues. To his credit, Dworkin has at least devoted substantial energy to describing the proper scope of decision making for his famous Herculean judge, whereas Archibugi and Held say little about how their hypothetical transnational judges would be effectively "circumscribed" by cosmopolitan democratic law. The fact that they also claim that cosmopolitan democratic law presupposes no particular conception of the good and thus "does not require political and cultural consensus about a wide range of beliefs, values, and norms" seems reasonable given the challenges of pluralism on the global scale.[51] Yet it arguably compounds the weaknesses of their legal analysis by potentially opening the door to a vast diversity of alternative judicial interpretations of the basic framework of cosmopolitan law. If cosmopolitan democratic law is fundamentally neutral in the face of competing interpretations of the good, what is to prevent judges from fleshing out its complex and multifaceted charter of rights in a rich variety of potentially inconsistent ways? On this point as well, Dworkin's position is arguably superior: Whatever our final assessment of his restatement of natural law theory, Dworkin strives to provide a detailed gloss on how his conception of rights-based jurisprudence is to be properly embedded in a particular interpretation of liberal political morality.

It is also easy to see why this reinterpretation of the rule of law may initially seem so attractive. Many nation-states have already committed themselves to a set of ambitious international human rights agreements (for example, in the Universal Declaration of Human Rights). From a liberal-democratic perspective, this historical trend is a positive one; my criticisms here are not directed against the notion of universal human rights.[52] Nonetheless, a commitment to universal human rights is probably consistent with a rich variety of distinct institutional versions of liberal democracy, both on the global level and elsewhere. Whether the best way either to advance rule of law virtues or pursue transnational democracy is to demand the justiciability of a bold and indisputably controversial charter of rights by transnational courts remains open to debate. We should not conflate the protection of rights with the rule of law, nor should we ignore the ambivalent legal and political consequences of a model of transnational government probably destined to place massive discretionary decision making in judicial hands. Danilo Zolo has accused Held and his interlocutors of advancing a brand of judicial imperialism blind to the matter in which cosmopolitan democracy's model of basic rights masks western biases and exhibits indifference towards non-Western legal culture.[53] Although I see no reason for endorsing either Zolo's Realist international relations theory or his dismissive attacks on universalistic concepts of human rights, my argument suggests that he nonetheless may have stumbled onto a real failing here: In cosmopolitan democracy, judges would indeed be outfitted with impressive and arguably unprecedented authority concerning a rich variety of highly contestable political matters. The charter of rights making up the core of cosmopolitan democratic law includes issues (for example, ecological and feminist rights) still considered highly controversial even within the wealthy welfare state liberal democracies of Western Europe and North America. Since many of these rights are even more controversial on the global level, one might ask whether it makes much sense to try to advance transnational democracy by outfitting transnational judicial personnel with the authority to rely on an open-ended commitment to them as a starting point for an "agenda for change.[54] *Pace* Zolo, the weaknesses of this model hardly represent necessary byproducts of a universalistic brand of Kantianism. Instead, they derive from a questionable interpretation of the notion of the rule of law in which some of the core concerns of traditional liberal jurisprudence have simply been left at the wayside. Recall that Kant envisioned not only a cosmopolitan right of hospitality but that he also took the rule of law virtues of generality, publicity, and clarity seriously.[55]

This criticism also points to real problems for Archibugi's and Held's attempt to sufficiently distinguish cosmopolitan democracy from unacceptable models of a "planetary Leviathan" outfitted with enormous discretionary authority. Their vague statements concerning the precise scope of cosmopolitan law are only likely to fan such anxieties. As we noted earlier, Archibugi and Held tend to argue that issues "affecting" transnational groups would alone make up proper objects of transnational legislative and judicial activity. But this deceptively simple claim cloaks a host of complex normative and institutional questions. As Frederick Whelan has pointed out in an astute critical contribution to democratic theory, "[a]n obvious practical difficulty with the all-affected principle is that it would require a different constituency of voters or participants for every decision" in light of the fact that citizens are unlikely to be affected by every decision to the same degree or in the same way.[56] One of the more controversial aspects of many laws and policies is their likely impact on different categories of people;

political controversy often is concerned with determining which category of people should be affected by a policy. "Thus to say that those who will be affected by a given decision are the ones who should participate in making it is to...propose what is a logical as well as procedural impossibility."[57] A prior decision would be required in each case to determine who is to be affected and thus entitled to participate on whatever substantive issue is at hand. But how might this decision be made? It would have to be made democratically by those affected, "but now we encounter a regression from which no procedural escape is possible."[58]

Moreover, it is unclear that we can delineate transnational issues from those properly resolved on the local or national level as easily as cosmopolitan democracy's defenders claim, especially if it is correct to argue that

> [g]lobal governance knows no boundaries, geographic, social, cultural, economic, orpolitical. If...new trading partners are established, if labor and environmental groups in different countries form cross-border coalitions, if cities begin to conduct their own foreign commercial policies...then the consequences of such developments will ripple across and fan out at provincial, regional, national and international levels as well as across and within local communities.[59]

If we conceive of globalization as resting on a process of "time and space compression" in which instantaneousness and simultaneity increasingly make up constitutive features of human activity, it inevitably becomes difficult to specify a relatively limited arena for transnational policy. Given dramatic changes in the phenomenological horizons of present-day human activity, the scope of cosmopolitan democratic law thus is not only likely be characterized by ambiguity and flux, but it seems ultimately destined to cover a potentially enormous range of human activities.

In fairness, Held occasionally makes some brief suggestions about how he hopes to limit the scope of transnational legislation. A test of "extensiveness" would determine the range of people potentially affected by a collective problem; a test of "intensity" would assess the degree to which different groupings are affected by a collective problem; an "assessment of comparative efficiency" would focus on the practical pros and cons of grappling with a particular policy task at different levels of governance.[60] But here again, cosmopolitan democracy's proponents simply take their suggestions from the European Union and its tension-ridden experience with the difficult task of determining the proper relationship between transnational and national legislation. But they badly obscure the fact that the EU experience with "subsidiarity" raises at least as many difficult questions as it answers.[61] Unless much more is said about how we can properly delineate cosmopolitan democratic law from local and national law, there are legitimate reasons for worrying that cosmopolitan democracy is likely to fail in its noble quest to uphold the traditional liberal notion of a limited law-based government.

In light of its many jurisprudential flaws, should we abandon Archibugi's and Held's otherwise admirable quest to subject an array of transnational policy arenas to liberal-democratic ideals? Not necessarily. However, my argument does suggest that we will need to develop a concept of transnational democracy better equipped to take the legacy of traditional rule of law-virtues seriously. In light of the prospect of awesome forms of global political and economic authority that make the modern nation-state's power capacities pale in comparison, we abandon the traditional notion of the rule of law at our own risk. Traditional legal concerns about untrammeled power take on heightened significance as the prospect of global governance becomes real. A transnational democracy worth defending will have to find some way of preserving a substantial quotient of traditional rule of law virtues.

How might we accomplish that task? A host of more modest—yet potentially path breaking—proposals for democracy on the global level are now being discussed and deserve closer examination. Many of those proposals potentially cohere more clearly with traditional conceptions of the rule of law than the model criticized here. Those of us enamored of Kelsen's thoughtful warnings about the limits of "unreal and politically less than nothing" proposals for the international arena can easily identify many ongoing political struggles as good starting points for preparing the way for major changes in the international system.

The demand for an effective international criminal court should come immediately to mind, as should the possibility of altering the structure of the U.N. Security Council. Developing countries have understandably argued in defense of a modified Security Council that would be more representative of political, developmental, and demographic trends since 1945 as well as meaningfully democratic in the sense that some of its representatives would now be elected.[62] Phillip Schmitter proposes that nation-states accord each other seats in their legislatures to representatives of other nation-states with which they are intensely involved (for example, within free trade zones such as NAFTA).[63] One can easily imagine similar initiatives undertaken at the level of regional and local legislatures where, for example, the realities of economic integration mesh poorly with existing national boundaries. Voting rights need to better accord with the realities of "national" citizenries, which now consist to a growing extent of migrants and so-called "temporary" residents who tend to be unfairly disenfranchised by the dominant models of citizenship. Grassroots activists are legitimately demanding participation by NGOs and labor groups in the halls of the WTO and IMF and many other powerful interstate organizations that play significant roles in overseeing the global political economy. One can also begin to consider imaginative ways in which crucial forms of global business regulation—for example, international business arbitration—might be rendered publically accountable. Reforms of this type may seem relatively dull when compared to the dream of a full-scale global democracy committed to realizing an ambitious set of justiciable liberal, democratic, social-democratic, feminist, and ecological rights, but they better build on Kelsen's sound advice to pursue "a slow and steady perfection of the international legal order."[64] They may, in short, help us steer a path between the Charybdis of conservative political resignation and Scylla of unrealistic radicalism that has plagued too much recent Frankfurt School critical theory work on globalization.

9   Global Governance Without Global Government?

Since the mid-1990s, Jürgen Habermas has directed his critical acumen to the many challenges posed by globalization for democracy. Habermas' starting point is eminently political. Like many other principled democrats, he worries that the ongoing process of globalization threatens popular sovereignty at the local and national levels, where it alone has been more or less successfully established. As nation-states find themselves enmeshed in complex and increasingly dense networks of supranational decision making (e.g., the EU, WTO, or IMF), existing forms of political participation seem ever more remote from political and economic decisions "negotiated under asymmetrical relations of power" but having far-reaching ramifications. A committed social democrat, he also shares the worries of many on the left that globalization undermines the capacity of the welfare state to mitigate capitalism's harshest features. Conversant in the most advanced empirical research, he notes that national governments "still enjoy a range of options in policy areas that have an immediate impact on the covariant relationship between levels of employment and social welfare."[1] Nonetheless, globalization tends to lead to reductions in corporate tax rates and a general shrinkage of public finances. At the very least, it remains unclear whether small or medium states can realistically "withstand a creeping assimilation to the [neoliberal] social model being foisted upon them by the currently dominant economic regime."[2]

Motored by these anxieties, Habermas' intellectual energy has concentrated on explaining how democracy can "catch up" to our globalizing economy and the misfit between nationally based democracy and the realities of postnational decision making consequently be overcome. For better or worse, this programmatic starting point occasionally lends a defensive tone to his reflections. First and foremost, the political task at hand now appears to entail the preservation of the existing achievements of the democratic welfare state, albeit necessarily via novel experiments in self-government "beyond the nation-state." Globalization's challenge to the welfare state means that politically responsible intellectuals need to figure out how to conserve the personal, political, and social liberties to which those of us lucky enough to reside in the privileged countries of the North have become acclimated. Arguing against those who lament the lack of a wide-ranging constitutional debate along the lines of revolutionary France or America, Habermas asserts that the contemporary European political and intellectual situation is not akin to that of our Enlightenment republican predecessors:

> the challenge is less to invent something new than to conserve the great achievements of the European nation-state beyond its frontiers in a new form. What is new is only the entity which will arise through these endeavors. What must be conserved are the standards of living, the opportunities for education and leisure, and the social space for personal self-realization which are necessary to ensure the fair value of individual liberty, and thereby make democratic participation possible.

Despite its novel institutional form, the European Union's main normative justification is that existing levels of self-government and social policy can only be preserved at the supranational level: The European Union potentially allows us to see how political and economic institutions can adjust themselves to the realities of globalization. In spite of his own well-known enthusiasm for a European Constitution, for Habermas "the constitutional question is no longer the key to the problems we have to solve," in part because Europe's would-be constitutional architects are "merely treading well-worn paths." [3]

As always, Habermas' political instincts are sound and refreshingly hardheaded. In the face of a resurgent neoliberalism, the main intellectual undertaking for social democrats and welfare-state liberals indeed probably consists of determining how to preserve the fragile achievements of the welfare state amid accelerating globalization. Examined from the broader perspective of the Frankfurt School of critical theory, whose greatest representative Habermas undoubtedly has become, however, the defensive character of his recent reflections represents a substantial deflation of utopian energies. In his recent writings on globalization, Habermas has little to say about deepening or broadening self-government, rather than merely defending or salvaging it, let alone moving aggressively towards what *Between Facts and Norms* (1992) described as the necessity of a "reflexive" reform and extension of the welfare state. No mention is made of his earlier critical ideas about the existing welfare state or, for example, the pathological forms of "colonization of the lifeworld" that he attributed to it in *Theory of Communicative Action* (1981). As with many others on the democratic left, the ascent of neoliberalism has apparently left Habermas politically chastened.

More worrisome conceptually is the fundamental structure of an argument that commences from the assumption that democracy should "catch up" to economic and technological processes which remain in many decisive ways deeply pathological.[4] Why not instead begin with a critical-minded analysis of globalization that distinguishes between its historically necessary and transient attributes, as well as between its potentially positive and pathological features? If democracy is forced to catch up or adjust itself to the latter as well as the former, it will suffer: Democratic institutions made-to-order for global capitalism are unlikely to prove normatively attractive.[5] Of course, Habermas is no admirer of globalizing capitalism. Nonetheless, his formulation of the enigma at hand risks distorting the intellectual and political tasks we face. We need a political theory attuned to the ways in which globalization challenges democracy. Yet we also require a critical theory of the multipronged and contradictory processes that tend, sometimes misleadingly, to get lumped together under the catchall rubric of globalization.

Notwithstanding these dangers, Habermas' reflections remain impressive. His ideas on global democracy have undergone a number of significant modifications since he began articulating them over a decade ago. However, with the publication of his most recent collection of political essays, *The Divided West*, the basic contours of his model of global governance can now be discerned.[6] Habermas creatively defends a three-tiered system of global governance, where decision making at the level of the nation-state is complemented by novel modes of what he describes as *supranational* (e.g., worldwide or global) authority and *transnational* (chiefly regional or continental) democracy. At the cost of neglecting the much-discussed normative edifice—namely Habermas' conception of deliberative democracy and the theory of communicative action at its base—on which it builds, I highlight its main institutional features. Unfortunately, his particular rendition of the now theoretically fashionable view that we can realize global *governance* without substantial elements of global *government* proves overstated.[7] I start with Habermas' reflections on Kant's cosmopolitanism and its purported institutional weaknesses, before turning to critically examine Habermas' tripartite vision of global governance.

BEYOND KANT?

In Habermas' writings on globalization since the mid-1990s, Kant has served as a constant intellectual companion, both inspiring him and functioning as a friendly target against whom he has developed his own position.[8] *The Divided West* again revisits familiar debates about Kant's international political theory. Like many other recent cosmopolitan theorists, Habermas praises Kant's prescience in anticipating the now widely documented trend according to which "international law as a law of *states*" becomes an identifiably "cosmopolitan law as a law of *individuals*" in which "the latter are no longer legal subjects merely as citizens of their respective states, but also as members" of a universal or cosmopolitan constitutional order (124). As Habermas notes, however, Kant oscillated between envisioning the constitutionalization of cosmopolitan law in terms of a world republic and an institutionally more modest league or confederation of nation-states. Kant famously hesitated before consistently embracing the idea of a single world republic because he feared the dangers of a despotic world state: Even a world republic might devolve into a "universal monarchy."[9] Habermas is basically sympathetic to Kant's skepticism on this score, even though he sharply criticizes the traditional conception of indivisible state sovereignty on which Kant's original anxieties supposedly rested. "The democratic federal state writ large—the global state of nations or world republic—is the wrong model" for thinking about global governance (134). Unfortunately, the competing tendency to defend the virtues of a league or confederation founders as well. Even if we ignore the difficult exegetical questions raised by seemingly contradictory comments "over which generations of Kant interpreters have racked their brains," Kant's "idea of an ever-expanding federation of republics engaging in commerce which renounce wars of aggression" rests on untenable assumptions (125, 128). Inadequately cognizant of the pathologies of modern capitalism, Kant naïvely pinned his hopes on the pacifying influence of free trade and commerce, and his account was too closely tied, as many commentators have noted, to a dubious philosophy of history.

How then to overcome this bottleneck in Kant's theory and provide a secure constitutional basis for an emerging cosmopolitan system of rights? In Habermas' view, a vital lesson can be gleaned from Kant's internal ambiguities. Heavily indebted to the German political theorist Hauke Brunkhorst,[10] Habermas introduces a sharp conceptual distinction between "state" and "constitution":

> A "state" is a complex of hierarchically organized capacities available for the exercise of political power or the implementation of political programs; a "constitution," by contrast, defines a horizontal association of citizens by laying down the fundamental rights that free and equal founders mutually grant each other (131).

This simple but decisive conceptual clarification, he claims, allows us to overcome the immanent failings of Kant's cosmopolitanism. Relying on it, we can reject a series of false analogies that have misleadingly enticed many writers to envision "the constitutionalization of international law as simply a continuation of the development of the [nationally based] constitutional state at the global level," most likely in the form of a global, state-like federal system (134). In European history, the process of state-building and the rise of constitutionalism were, of course, intimately connected in complex and contradictory ways. However, there is no compelling conceptual reason for assuming that "state" and "constitution" will necessarily be married together in the same fashion at the international level. By missing this pivotal point, many defenders of enhanced global governance wrongly presuppose that its emergence must necessarily represent an extension of political and legal processes observable at the national to the transnational stage. They reify the history of modern state development and thus wrongly conceive of global governance as an extension of national government and thus as world government. The failure to distinguish clearly between "state" and "constitution" also leads them to obfuscate the fact that international law is already undergoing a process of "constitutionalization." Although by no means democratic in character, in the charters, agreements, and treaties that provide a legal basis for entities such as the United Nations, European Union, and World Trade Organization, we can already glean the makings of an emerging constitutional structure for "a decentered world society as a multilevel system that for good reasons lacks the character of a state *as a whole*" (134–136). Powerful global organizations lack a monopoly on legitimate violence, and they remain normatively and politically problematic for many reasons. Still, they issue binding rules and norms that tend to be widely respected by their constituent members. They represent, in an apt phase Habermas takes from Brunkhorst, emerging constitutional or "legal orders without a state" (138). From this perspective, the main chore at hand is to figure out how we might subject them to democratic legitimacy but not necessarily transform them into state-like institutions. In short, not only can we separate "constitution" from "state," we can also plausibly pursue the possibility of democratically legitimate legal and constitutional structures functioning without some crucial attributes of modern statehood.

The main programmatic attraction of a sharp conceptual division between "state" and "constitution" for Habermas is that it points to the possibility of a third path to constitutionalizing cosmopolitan law supposedly unrecognized by Kant and those who followed in his footsteps. In the broadest terms, this option would take the form of

> a politically constituted global society that reserves institutions and procedures of global governance for states at both the supra- and transnational levels. Within this framework, members of the community of states are indeed obliged to act in concert, but they are not relegated to mere parts of an overarching hierarchical super-state (135).

Furthermore, this vision constitutes no mere Kantian "ought" but has already been at least partially realized in the everyday realities of the existing system of global governance, where an impressive body of legal and quasi-constitutional materials undergird a complex network of institutions. Of course, pushing these institutions towards democratic reform will obviously require difficult and risky political battles. Nonetheless, Habermas here seems relatively hopeful that even relatively undemocratic international organizations—for example, the WTO—might ultimately find themselves subject to reform pressures. In support of this claim, he refers to the growth of global NGOs, transnational activism, and even an emerging global public sphere, as well as the fact that institutions like the WTO "increasingly take into account the protection of human rights" (140).

Habermas' most recent reflections can be interpreted as various attempts to work out the details of this vision. His model of "global governance without world government" would operate at three basic levels. At the global, or what he now describes as the supranational level, we would find a single world organization, essentially a reformed United Nations, outfitted with the capacity to secure basic human rights and preserve peace in a consistent and nonselective manner. In correspondence with his attempt to move beyond Kant, he argues that a modified UN need take the form of neither a world-state nor a loose league or confederation of states.

At the intermediate or transnational level, energy, environmental, financial, and economic policies, or what Habermas cleverly dubs "global domestic politics," novel modes of cross-border regulation would be hammered out by those global actors strong enough to bring about binding agreements as well as effectively check and balance their global rivals. Which global players might successfully undertake the weighty responsibility of promulgating transnational social and economic regulation, which necessarily should go well beyond the "negative" (and primarily neoliberal) integration pursued by most existing multilateral organizations? Because of their familiar democratic deficits, existing multilateral organizations are poor candidates for the requisite regulatory tasks, unless subjected more directly to democratic decision making. Although open to this possibility, Habermas tends to place his faith in democratized regional or continental regimes (e.g., a reformed EU, or NAFTA and ASEAN), though he sometimes suggests that great powers like the United States are already capable of getting the job done. In light of his understandable preoccupation with European political trends, this emphasis on highly integrated and democratized regional power blocs is by no means surprising: With the relatively positive case of the EU in mind, Habermas believes that not only are regional blocs most likely to garner the requisite democratic legitimacy, but that they also alone might possess sufficient power to implement policies across large territories and thus successfully tame globalizing capitalism.[11] Agreements among regionalized blocs, achieved in part perhaps via reformed multilateral organizations like the WTO or IMF, would require a complex system of negotiations and old-fashioned political wheeling-and-dealing. Nonetheless, if a fair international balance of power could be achieved (e.g., the EU could effectively challenge the U.S. or NAFTA), the major players might be expected "to fulfill expectations of fairness and cooperation" essential to the legitimacy of the negotiation process (142). International politics as we know it would continue to function at this level, as autonomous political units would still compete with one another and conflicts would inevitably ensue. A social-democratic EU, for example, could use its power to "counterbalance" the United States or NAFTA "at global economic summits and in the institutions of the WTO, the World Bank, and the International Monetary Fund," bringing "its influence to bear in shaping the design of a future global domestic politics" (42). Yet traditional international relations would nonetheless undergo substantial modifications in light of the fact that regionalized decision-making blocs would lack any possibility of resorting to war: they would still lack a constitutive attribute of modern statehood.

Finally, at the national level, states would maintain many core elements of sovereignty as traditionally understood, even though the right to wage war would be denied them. Yet transnational and supranational governance would ultimately remain dependent on the nation-state and its military muscle in order to enforce their decisions: "States remain the most important actors and the final arbiters on the global stage" (176). Habermas hopes that global governance can function effectively without necessarily taking the form of a world-state or perhaps even sovereign governments at the transnational or supranational levels. Simultaneously, he suggests that nation-states can still serve as sovereign governments even if crucial facets of governance have been relocated to the supranational and transnational levels.

GLOBAL GOVERNANCE WITHOUT WORLD GOVERNMENT?

How coherent is this model? At the risk of describing Habermas' ideas in an overly schematic fashion, I raise some critical questions by focusing on each of his three proposed levels of governance. Despite Habermas' claims to the contrary, it ultimately remains unclear that he has successfully overcome the institutional ambiguities that plagued Kant's original vision of cosmopolitan law.

Especially at the supranational level, Habermas appears to want to have his cake and eat it as well. He reminds his readers of the familiar limitations of the existing UN and especially the manner in which human rights and world peace are presently secured in an unfair and inconsistent manner to the advantage of the great powers. In the present-day UN, the hegemonic "law of the stronger" is legally entrenched in the Security Council and the veto with which it outfits each of its members (142). Like other contemporary theorists of a cosmopolitan and democratic bent, Habermas proposes far-reaching reforms: The Security Council needs to be democratized, and its constituencies updated in accordance with altered geopolitical realities; the General Assembly should be made more accountable to global public spheres and NGOs, and the political willfulness with which the Security Council tends to act (or, just as disastrously at times, fails to act) needs to be significantly reduced by constitutionally obliging it to act under certain specified circumstances. Lamenting the Security-General's lack of financial independence as well as the practices of "uncooperative governments that continue to enjoy exclusive control over military resources" (170), he argues that the UN executive branch "must be reinforced to a point where it can guarantee the effective implementation of resolutions of the Security

Council" (173). In this view, stronger transnational and supranational mandates for action require nothing less than effective "executive powers above the level of nation-states" (134). Only significant reforms to the UN, he asserts, can counteract the debilitating "selectivity" with which international law is presently enforced and ultimately open the door to a fair cosmopolitan legal order in which citizens of Burundi or Luxembourg, for example, might enjoy the same rights as those in the United States or Germany.

However appealing, Habermas' suggestions raise many familiar questions. How could "uncooperative governments"—including great powers like the United States or China—be rendered as accountable to international law as minor powers, unless the UN possessed sufficient independent military and political muscle to force its will upon them? When insisting on the need to reinforce the power of the Secretary-General, Habermas himself seems to concede this point. He sympathizes with proposals to provide the UN with more freedom to deploy troops than it presently enjoys. "Given that the UN is now involved in many urgent operations," for example, "it would be desirable if the larger member states were to maintain units in reserve for swift deployment in such cases" (163). But how might the UN consistently enforce world peace and secure human rights unless it increasingly took on some of the more familiar attributes of modern statehood? Even if it formally lacked a monopoly on the legitimate use of force, it would still need substantial political and military muscle if, as in the inevitable case of conflict, it tried to apply cosmopolitan norms (for example, against torture) in opposition to rogue states like the United States.[12] In other words, the nonselective application of cosmopolitan law understandably sought by Habermas inevitably engenders the specter, if not of a hypercentralized world-state, then at least of the possibility of a supranational order in which the UN operates, in the final instance, as a military arbiter. At least in this context, "constitution" and "state" remain more closely linked than Habermas wants to concede. Generality and consistency in law presuppose some capacity to enforce legal norms without undue dependence on those against whom they may need to be enforced.[13] If individual nation-states (or, for that matter, regionally based state units) remain "final arbiters" on a global stage plagued by deep military inequalities, as will likely remain the case for the foreseeable future, it seems improbable that such dependence could be easily reduced or made fair and calculable. Perhaps, as Habermas hopes, we might successfully achieve crucial elements of global governance without a single or unified global state. This, in fact, already seems to be happening, albeit in a highly undemocratic fashion. Yet it nonetheless seems problematic to downplay the likelihood that effective supranational governance will ultimately require the establishment of some core elements of global government.

A partial response to such criticisms can be gleaned from Habermas' brief appeal to constructivist International Relations theory: "We should not underestimate the capacity of international discourses to transform mentalities under the pressures to adapt to the new legal construction of the international community" (177). As the self-image of states adapts to experiences of growing interdependence, traditional state practices can be transformed as legal norms (e.g., the ban on war) are internalized. Shared legal norms and practices can dramatically transform the harsh "facts" of the existing international political universe. In an alternative global environment, great powers like the United States or China might still possess enough "hard" power to ignore the UN and cosmopolitan law. Yet just as contemporary Sweden and Japan undoubtedly have the requisite technical know-how to produce nuclear weapons but have opted not to do so, the great powers might refuse to employ their superior military muscle because of altered self-conceptions as well as the internalization of widely shared legal and constitutional norms.

Obviously, this is an attractive vision. Let us hope that Habermas—and the constructivists—are right. By the same token, in a political universe where political identities remain highly nationalized and particularistic, and even universally shared legal commitments (for example, the ban on genocide) still incite deep political controversy, there are sound reasons for doubting that the great powers will soon renounce the many power advantages they presently enjoy. National sovereignty is a historically variable legal "construct," but it remains a construct that justifies an impressive array of "real" or material advantages. For familiar reasons, powerful states are likely to jealously guard against any impositions on them.

Habermas probably only complicates matters further by arguing that UN reforms should take "account of the legitimate interests of a superpower that must be kept integrated into the world organization" (173). Of course, this is a sensible concession to political realities. Yet it hardly meshes particularly well with his demand for a UN capable of acting in a consistent and nonselective fashion. The basic conceptual problem derives perhaps from his initial reflections on Kant. As noted, Habermas insists on a sharp conceptual distinction between "constitution" and "state" in order to highlight the possibility of a constitutional order lacking the attributes of traditional statehood, and especially a system of multitiered global decision making that "lacks the character of a state *as a whole*" (136). Yet his arguably sound general defense of multilayered decision making occasionally gets conflated with a more general (and controversial) point: At times he endorses the view that supranational and transnational decision making can function effectively without possessing significant attributes of traditional statehood.

How might supranational governance be successfully democratized? Although Habermas wants reforms to the UN, he reassures his reader that the necessary minimum of democratic legitimacy is by no means "unfeasibly high" in light of the limited functional requirements of maintaining world peace and securing human rights (143). "At the supranational level, the enforcement of established law takes precedence over the constructive task of legislation and policy-making, both of which, on account of the greater scope for decision, demand a higher degree of legitimation, and hence more effectively institutionalized forms of citizen participation" (174). The fact that we are unlikely to achieve robust deliberative democracy at the supranational level should not worry us too much because

> [i]f the international community limits itself to securing peace and and protecting human rights, the requisite solidarity among world citizens need not reach the level of implicit consensus on thick political value-orientations that is necessary for the familiar kind of civic solidarity among civic-nationals. Consonance in reactions of moral outrage toward egregious human rights violations and manifest acts of aggression is sufficient (143).

Limited to protecting basic human rights and avoiding war, the UN rests on "clear negative duties of a universalistic morality of justice—the duty not to engage in wars of aggression and not to commit crimes against humanity." Correspondingly, supranational governance would not require full-fledged democratic legitimacy or the "thick" sense of solidarity and shared civic culture indispensable, in Habermas' view, to a robust democracy. Instead, a slender universalistic morality of justice that is both less controversial and more easily achieved would suffice (143). In a revealing contrast, he argues that at the intermediate or transnational level, where "global domestic policy" is to be hammered out, a thicker sense of solidarity and civic culture would in fact have to be achieved, because the ambitious legislative and regulatory tasks at hand go well beyond fidelity to the "negative duties of justice." Although we can realistically expand the powers of the UN as it concerns human rights and security without pushing for full-scale democratization, Habermas insists that at the intermediate or transnational level, democratization must take a more pronounced form. In this view, the fact that a "thick" civic political identity appears unachievable at the global level is in fact a main normative reason why social and economic regulation should be located at the level of continental or regional power blocs. An "ethical-political self-understanding of citizens of a particular democratic life" inevitably is "missing in the inclusive community of world citizens," yet the achievement of such a self-understanding remains realistic at the transnational and, of course, national levels (107). This gap need not worry us too much, however, since supranational governance chiefly involves the application and enforcement of basic rights already accepted as valid worldwide.

Habermas' argument here relies on a series of complicated distinctions between what he elsewhere describes as moral, ethical, and pragmatic forms of discourse. Rather than revisit familiar philosophical disputes generated by his complicated typology of discourses, let me just raise one skeptical political point. One hardly needs to be a Realist, let alone a protégé of Carl Schmitt, to observe that debates especially about the "existential" matter of war and peace typically represent the most controversial and fundamental of political questions. For precisely this reason, nation-states have been notoriously reluctant to hand over the right to determine when they will go to war to international organizations: Even after they formally sign off on the prohibition on aggressive war that makes up an essential component of the UN system, those countries capable of waging war effectively too often have worked to circumvent or even undermine the UN system. To imply that debates about war and peace or the enforcement of human rights are somehow less politically explosive than, for example, energy, financial, or social policies, and thus that the supranational realm can potentially get by with less democratic legitimacy than the transnational, fits poorly with historical and political experience. Lurking in the background here may be the quaint but basically incorrect old-fashioned left-wing political intuition according to which the heart of political conflict ultimately concerns issues of social and economic redistribution, but not war or peace.[14] Even if Habermas is right about the controversial point that an empowered UN would merely fulfill "clear negative duties," their application and enforcement would inevitably raise deeply controversial questions. The fact that the prohibitions on aggressive war or genocide are now universally accepted hardly ensures universal let alone uncontroversial agreement about what they concretely entail.[15] Unfortunately, the distinction between the "enforcement of law" at the supranational level in contrast to the making or promulgation of law at the transnational level is untenable.

Despite Habermas' claims, an empowered UN might plausibly demand a substantially democratized process of legitimation in which the voices of all those affected by security and human rights policies should be heard in a fair and impartial manner. Any institution claiming the authority to determine who should live and who should die—like the modern territorial state—requires far-reaching democratic legitimation. Now this demand may in fact be politically unachievable at the present time. Yet given the basic structure of Habermas' own theory, it remains normatively necessary. Habermas perhaps sees this tension. Yet his attempt to overcome it fails. In Chapter 7 I argued that both Habermas' earlier work on globalization and democratization and that of his disciples was plagued by deep internal political and institutional tensions. Unfortunately, *The Divided West* does not successfully resolve those tensions. Here again, we find radical arguments that cry out for nothing less than far-reaching democratization at the global level. Yet these more radical normative moments rest uneasily alongside institutional proposals that seem unduly cautious.

What then of Habermas' discussion of the transnational or continental level of decision making? Here as well, we can identify some revealing tensions. On the one hand, he sometimes appears to celebrate the fact that organizations like the EU lack a monopoly on force and thus conform well to his theoretical claim that "global domestic policy" can function successfully without global government. In his view, the EU lacks "the core element of internal and external sovereignty of the modern administrative and tax-based state" (137). Yet he simultaneously concedes that regionalized power bodies might evolve into "complex federal states on a continental scale" (141). Indeed, what he finds so praiseworthy about decision making at the regional or transnational level is precisely the fact that it possesses enough power to implement general policies across large territories. Yet recall his own definition of "statehood" as referring to "hierarchically organized capacities available for the *exercise of political power or implementation of political programs*" [my emphasis, WES] (131).

More fundamentally, in a slew of widely discussed writings on the EU, he proposes a federal model with striking similarities to a relatively traditional federal republic along United States or perhaps Swiss lines: Even if the democratic federal state is "the wrong model" for global governance at large, this is effectively what he proposes for the transnational level (134).[16] Many critics have in fact attacked his view for downplaying the idiosyncrasies of European development and especially the fact that a European state seems both normatively undesirable and politically unlikely.[17] Habermas has been no less adamant in defending the controversial view that Europeans can realistically expect to develop a sufficiently rich common political identity along the lines he considers essential to ambitious democratic self-government. Indeed, without such a shared civic identity, he argues, it is difficult to fathom any chance of legitimizing precisely those redistributive social and economic policies which continental blocs like the EU should pursue in order to salvage the welfare state.[18] The immediate issue is not whether Habermas or his critics are "right" on the matter of European political integration. But the fact that so many involved in the present debate interpret him, with good reason, as an advocate of a strong and relatively centralized model of the EU supports my intuition that he prefers to downplay the constitutive role that traditional elements of statehood would inevitably play in his vision of global governance.

Habermas has also become a prominent advocate among left-wing European intellectuals who share the view that the EU should pursue common foreign and security policies in order "to counterbalance the hegemonic unilateralism of the United States" (42). Unsympathetic commentators have attributed this position, and especially his eloquent and now-famous joint (with Jacques Derrida) condemnation of the foibles of recent U.S. foreign policy, to anti-Americanism (39–48). This is a surprising and in my view unfounded accusation in light of the profuse praise for U.S. political and legal culture found throughout Habermas' writings, as well as his long history of courageous public opposition to political revanchism at home.[19] In fact, the final section of *The Divided West* includes a fascinating attempt to defend the United States, though by no means the Bush Administration, against the fashionable view on the left that its foreign policy represents nothing more than an empirical confirmation of Carl Schmitt's cynical ideas about international law (179–193).[20] Such name-calling simply corroborate Habermas' anxieties, expressed eloquently in a thought-provoking 2003 interview with Giovanna Borradori, about the increasingly conformist contours of U.S. political culture after 9/11 (3–25).

More significant is the fact that Habermas' political stance presupposes, to a greater extent than he perhaps wants to admit, a rather traditional view of statehood. As Glyn Morgan has suggested with some plausibility, a coherent, shared European defense policy along the lines apparently desired by Habermas would demand of the EU not only that it shed some of its present-day institutional idiosyncrasies but also that it develop a capacity for effective independent military action. Doing so would inevitably require the EU to take on familiar virtues of modern statehood and probably a more centralized EU security apparatus.[21]

The Divided West is also filled with highly polemical comments about Realist international relations theory, which Habermas tends to read unsympathetically as a conservative defense of classical power politics in the tradition of Schmitt.[22] Yet he smuggles core elements of Realism into his own analysis. As noted, he envisions transnational regulation as emerging via an international negotiation system dominated by regionally based power blocs. In this account, guaranteeing that the results of interbloc political give-and-take represented more than the "naked" expression of global inequalities would require that the relevant global players possessed adequate power to check and balance one another. As those familiar with international political theory will immediately recognize, this argument might easily have come from the "arch-Realist" Hans J. Morgenthau, who emphasized the centrality of the balance of power to an effective system of international law without tying its operations intrinsically to the realities of the modern (for him, as for Habermas, historically transient) nation-state. As Realists have underscored, a "balance of power" on the international political scene has always been crucial to the consistent enforcement of international law. Habermas surreptitiously endorses a version of this old argument, because his model of transnational governance attributes a decisive role to political entities which, given the basic contours of his argument, would inevitably tend to take the form of relatively developed regional or continental states. Of course, there are many sources of power in the political universe, as even a Realist like Morgenthau always recognized. Military power only represents one, though undoubtedly crucial, resource for ensuring security.[23] Yet if an effective balance of power were to obtain between regional blocs, it would force some of them to acquire the impressive military prowess necessary to "counterbalance" the United States.

So much for "global domestic policy without government." As I have argued, Habermas' proposals require, at both the supranational and transnational levels, the enhancement of many traditional state capacities, even if he may be right to posit that no single centralized world state is necessary in order to achieve global governance. But no serious thinker today is advocating a single global Leviathan: If that's his main target, it's probably a straw man. As he promised, his model does not in fact look very much like a global federal republic. Whatever its other flaws, however, at least in a global federal republic the relationship between the different tiers of decision making would seem relatively transparent in legal and constitutional terms.[24] In Habermas' proposal, however, we instead arguably find a confusing and potentially problematic multiplicity of competing state-like entities at the national, transnational, and supranational levels.

Please note that I have said nothing about the normative desirability of achieving heightened levels of global government. As Habermas, following Kant, clearly understands, expanding formal governmental powers at either the transnational or supranational levels poses tough normative and institutional questions. On this point, by the way, they agree completely with sophisticated Realists. But let's not pretend, as I worry Habermas does, that we can have our cake and eat it too: If we opt to pursue "stronger transnational and supranational mandates for governance," as we very well may need to, let us not claim that we can do so without dramatically expanding relatively familiar forms of state power in arenas where they hitherto have been relatively limited (134). The inevitable result will be more global government, and not simply "multilayered governance." Only if we face this fact head-on can we realistically consider the full range of tough intellectual and political challenges we face.

Unfortunately, Habermas' brief comments on the third or national level of his multilayered system confirm the view that his account of global governance obscures its deep dependence on traditional modes of statehood, now likely to be located chiefly at the transnational and supranational levels. Although he insists that states would remain the final arbiters on the global stage, how any significant powers could realistically stay in the hands of the nation-state remains unclear. Significant forms of environmental, financial, and social and economic policy would have been transferred to the intermediate or transnational level of decision making. If peace and human rights are to be consistently secured, it is hard to see how this could be done without a sizable augmentation of the independent military prowess of the United Nations or, at the transnational level, of the state-like military capacities of regional blocs like the EU. States might indeed remain "the most important actors" in the global arena, but the states in question could hardly be nation-states. At least as far as the nation-state is concerned, it would apparently risk being "relegated to mere parts of an over-arching hierarchical super-state" (35). Its position would hardly seem superior to that typically occupied by individual regional units in federal republics. From the perspective of those who believe that the nation-state should continue to perform vital functions, a global democratic republic frankly might have more to offer than Habermas' model. California, after all, still possesses an impressive range of significant regulatory capacities, as the history of environmental reform in the United States might be taken to imply.

In a fascinating paper delivered in October 2005 at the University of Chicago political theory workshop, Habermas reiterates his view that global governance should be envisioned in terms of a three-tiered system of decision making, which would include a third or "lower level" of national decision making. Rather than offer a description of the specific functions remaining in the hands of the nation-state, however, the essay rapidly jumps to the stock argument that the global political economy overtaxes its normative and empirical capacities. His brief account of the "lower" or national level of decision making repeats the familiar view that nation-states must merge into novel forms of highly integrated, regionally based political blocs, along the lines of a democratized EU, alone purportedly capable of effectively navigating the harsh waters of the global political economy.[25] At a risk of polemical overstatement: the main function of the modern nation-state apparently consists in the task of ceasing to exist in any historically recognizable form. With the possible exception of a handful of great powers (and especially the United States), Habermas leaves the reader with the distinct impression that most nation-states are destined to go the way of the city-states and loose political confederations of the distant European past.

In defense of this position, one might point out that the nation-state is already being hollowed out by globalization and that its political latitude has become highly circumscribed even in the best of circumstances. But if this in fact is the case,[26] let us at least be forthright about the process at hand and openly admit that small and medium nation-states are now destined to play a role akin to Delaware or Rhode Island in the U.S. federal system, with large and relatively powerful nation-states perhaps realistically aspiring to the status of California or Texas. To describe this state of affairs as paving the way for a multilevel "politically constituted world society without world government," however, potentially misconstrues this remarkable historical shift more than it helps illuminate it.

For many good reasons, Habermas' ideas on deliberative democracy will continue to inspire scholars and hopefully also political activists struggling to determine the precise contours the emerging "post-national constellation" should take. Unfortunately, much work remains to be done in figuring out how his ideas might be instantiated in both a normatively desirable and institutionally plausible vision of reform.

Notes

INTRODUCTION

1. Globalization, of course, can be defined in many different ways. For the purposes of my discussion, I refer readers to the very helpful book by David Held, Anthony McGrew, David Goldblatt, and Jonathan Perraton, *Global Transformations: Politics, Economics, and Culture* (Stanford: Stanford University Press, 1999). Especially in Part I, I am mostly concerned with legal questions raised by economic globalization, whose relevant attributes I clarify when appropriate. For a more sociotheoretical definition than typically offered in the empirical literature, see my "Globalization" (http://plato.stanford.edu/entries/globalization).

2. I try to make some relevant constructive proposals, however, in my *Liberal Democracy and the Social Acceleration of Time* (Baltimore: Johns Hopkins University Press, 2004), pp. 210–227.

3. For (mostly European) responses to Habermas' work on globalization, see Peter Niesen and Benjamin (eds), *Anarchie der kommunikativen Freiheit. Jürgen Habermas und die Theorie der internationalen Politik* (Frankfurt: Suhrkamp, 2007).

4. A number of critical theorists are working on such a theory; much of their work is discussed in Chapter 8. But see also Max Pensky (ed), *Globalizing Critical Theory* (Lanham: Rowman & Littlefield, 2005) as well as Amy Batholemew (ed) *Empire's Law: The American Imperial Project and the 'War to Remake the World'* (London: Pluto, 2006), and the excellent essay by Jean L. Cohen, "Whose Sovereignty? Empire vs. International Law" *Ethics & International Law* 18 (2004), 1–24.

5. See Jürgen Bast, *Totalitärer Pluralismus* (Tübingen: Mohr, 1999); Mattias Iser and David Stecker (eds), *Kritische Theorie der Politik—Eine Bilanz* (Baden-Baden: Nomos, 2003); Duncan Kelly, *The State of the Political: Conceptions of Politics and the State in the Thought of Max Weber, Carl Schmitt, and Franz Neumann* (Oxford: Oxford University Press, 2003); William E. Scheuerman, *Between the Norm and the Exception: The Frankfurt School and the Rule of Law* (Cambridge, USA: MIT Press, 1994); Peter M. R. Stirk, *Critical Theory, Politics and Society: An Introduction* (London: Pinter, 2000); Rolf Wiggershaus, *The Frankfurt School: Its History, Theories and Political Significance* (Cambridge, USA: MIT Press, 1998). Martin Jay's work on the Frankfurt School remains indispensable, even though he tends to neglect Neumann (*The Dialectical Imagination* [Berkeley: University of California, 1973]).

6. For a useful discussion about how this model of the rule of law compares to others, see Brian Z. Tamanaha, *On the Rule of Law: History, Politics, Theory* (Cambridge: Cambridge University Press, 2004).

7. (Leamington Spa, UK: 1986 [1936]).
8. (New York: Oxford University Press, 1944).
9. (New York: Free Press, 1957). See also my recent collection, Scheuerman (ed), *The Rule of Law Under Siege: Selected Essays of Franz L. Neumann and Otto Kirchheimer* (Berkeley: University of California Press, 1996).
10. Neumann, "Change in the Function of Law" in *Rule of Law Under Siege*, pp. 117–118.
11. Note that I am referring here to global economic regulation or, in more conventional legal parlance, international economic law. I make no claims in this volume about international public law, which is plagued by antiformal trends as well but for reasons different from those analyzed here.
12. Such antiformalism is ubiquitous, for example, in the left in the U.S. legal academy, which—not surprisingly—tends to consider Neumann intellectually rather passé. This is a complicated matter, but let me just reiterate my view that such antiformalism tends to be overstated and problematic, as I argued in *Between the Norm and the Exception: The Frankfurt School and the Rule of Law*. It remains unclear to me why, as Martti Koskienniemi recently asserted (see *The Gentle Civilizer of Nations: The Rise and Fall of International Law 1870–1960* [Cambridge, UK: Cambridge University Press, 2001], p. 488, footnote 282), my defense of classical legal virtues in the context of globalizing law is "rather conservative." It is by no means politically conservative, because it is motivated by an abiding commitment to radical democracy and social justice. Nor is it institutionally conservative, as I believe the preservation of basic rule of law virtues is consistent with far-reaching legal experimentation. The only sense in which it is "conservative" is that, like the ideals of democracy or self-determination, it has deep roots in the western tradition and seems to me, like democracy, worth preserving. Of course, to preserve it we must adapt it to new political and social conditions. This may mean instantiating rule of law virtues, as suggested below in Chapter 6, in novel modes of legal regulation.
13. Hubertus Buchstein, "A Heroic Reconciliation of Freedom and Power: On the Tensions Between Democracy and Social Theory in the Late Work of Franz L. Neumann" *Constellations* 10 (2003), 228–240. Unfortunately, Buchstein's insightful criticisms lead him to throw the baby out with the bath water and miss what remains provocative about Neumann's work.
14. W. Rehg (trans) (Cambridge, USA: MIT Press, 1996).
15. See the powerful critical rejoinder to some of the arguments developed here by David Schneiderman, "Investment Rules and the Rule of Law" *Constellations* 8 (2001), 521–537.
16. (Boston: Beacon Press, 1981).

CHAPTER 1

1. See, for example, many of the essays collected in Joachim Perels (ed) *Recht, Demokratie und Kapitalismus. Aktualität und Probleme der Theorie Franz L. Neumanns* (Baden-Baden: Nomos, 1984); also, William E. Scheuerman, *Between the Norm and the Exception: The Frankfurt School and the Rule of Law*.
2. For an excellent critique of this view in reference to East Asia, inspired to some extent by Neumann, see Kanishka Jayasuriya (ed) *Law, Capitalism and Power in Asia: The Rule of Law and Legal Institutions* (London & New York: Routledge, 1999).
3. See David Held, Anthony McGrew, David Goldblatt, and Jonathan Perraton, *Global Transformations: Politics, Economics and Culture*.

4. William E. Scheuerman, *Carl Schmitt: The End of Law* (Lanham, MD: Rowman & Littlefield, 1999), pp. 141–174. But many German-language commentators long ago underscored the ominous political purposes of Schmitt's theory of international law; the English-language debate (and the works of Schmittians such as Paul Piccone and George Schwab) has badly lagged in this respect. Schmitt's anti-Semitism is now fully documented in Raphael Gross, *Carl Schmitt und die Juden. Eine deutsche Rechtslehre* (Frankfurt: Suhrkamp, 2000).

5. Carl Schmitt, *Völkerrechtliche Grossraumordnung mit Interventionsverbot für raumfremde Mächte* (Berlin: Deutscher Rechtsverlag, 1939). The economic and technological elements of the *Grossraum* theory are developed at many junctures: Schmitt, "Die Raumrevolution," *Das Reich* (29 September 1940), 3; Schmitt, "Reich und Raum. Elemente eines neuen Völkerrechts," *Zeitschrift der Akademie für Deutsches Recht* 7 (1940), 201–202; Schmitt, "Das Meer gegen das Land," *Das Reich* (9 March 1941), 17–18; Schmitt, "Raum and Grossraum im Völkerrecht," *Zeitschrift für Völkerrecht* 24 (1941), 145–149. More generally on the demise of traditional state structures: Schmitt, "Staat als konkreter, an eine geschichtlicht Epoche gebundenen Begriff" (1941), in Schmitt, *Verfassungsrechtliche Aufsätze aus den Jahren 1924–1954* (Berlin: Duncker & Humblot, 1973), pp. 375–385.

6. See his references to the *Planfeindlichkeit* of Anglo-American liberalism (Schmitt, "Die Raumrevolution," 3), as well as his comment about the "chaos" of British liberal universalism (in Schmitt, "Raum und Grossraum im Völkerrecht," 169). On the social and economic context and implications of Schmitt's theory, see the brilliant study by Ingeborg Maus, *Bürgerliche Rechtstheorie und Faschismus. Zur sozialen Funktion und aktuellen Wirkung der Theorie Carl Schmitts* (Munich: Wilhelm Fink, 1976).

7. Bauman describes the significance of the "new speed" in his *Globalization: The Human Consequences* (Cambridge, UK: Polity, 1998); Giddens talks of the "distanciation" of time and space (for example, in *The Consequences of Modernity* [Stanford: Stanford University Press, 1990]); Harvey analyzes "time and space compression" (*The Condition of Postmodernity* [Oxford: Blackwell, 1990]).

8. Franz L. Neumann, *Behemoth: The Structure and Practice of National Socialism, 1933–1944*, p. 160.

9. Neumann, *Behemoth*, pp. 199–200.

10. Neumann, *Behemoth*, p. 300.

11. Neumann, *Behemoth*, p. 331.

12. Neumann, *Behemoth*, p. 331.

13. Not the least because of a flurry of populist attacks on "western" human rights unleashed by political elites in the developing world (in particular, in East Asia eager to pursue an authoritarian developmental model without undue outside interference.

14. David Held, "The Transformation of Political Community: Rethinking Democracy in the Context of Globalization," in Ian Shapiro and Casiano Hacker-Cordon (eds) *Democracy's Edges* (Cambridge: Cambridge University Press, 2000), pp. 97–98.

15. Neumann, *Behemoth*, pp. 166–171.

16. The record of regional political blocs at the present time remains mixed, as evident by the contrast between the modest but worthy liberal-democratic achievements of the European Union vis-à-vis the vastly more problematic case of NAFTA.

17. Neumann, *Behemoth*, p. 130.

18. Franz L. Neumann, "Change in the Function of Law," in *The Rule of Law Under Siege: Selected Essays of Franz L. Neumann and Otto Kirchheimer*, p. 118.
19. For example: a legal standard determining the working day for one firm to be ten hours, whereas other firms are expected to respect the eight-hour day.
20. Neumann, "The Change in the Function of Law," p. 126.
21. Neumann, *Behemoth*, pp. 446–447.
22. Unfortunately, his discussion of contracts in competitive capitalism tends to focus on the history of political and legal ideas rather than legal history itself. Thus, Neumann tends to rely on an exegesis of Adam Smith's jurisprudence in order to discuss early contracts. See Franz L. Neumann, *The Rule of Law: Political Theory and the Legal System in Modern Society*, pp. 189–198.
23. Neumann, "The Change in the Function of Law," p. 132.
24. Neumann, "Labor Law in Modern Society" [1951], in *The Rule of Law Under Siege*, pp. 233–234.
25. John Braithwaite and Peter Drahos, *Global Business Regulation* (Cambridge, U.K.: Cambridge University Press, 2000), p. 30.
26. Braithwaite and Drahos, *Global Business Regulation*, p. 27.
27. See Claire Cutler's "Globalization, The Rule of Law, and the Modern Law Merchant: Medieval or Late Capitalist Associations?" *Constellations* 8 (2001), 480–502. More generally, Jarrod Wiener, *Globalization and the Harmonization of Law* (London: Pinter, 1999), 151–183.
28. For samples of this debate, see Albert Jan van den Berg, *International Dispute Resolution: Towards an International Arbitration Culture* (Hague: Kluwer, 1998); also R. Lillich and C. Brower, (eds), *International Arbitration in the 21ˢᵗ Century: Towards Judicialization and Uniformity?* (Irvington: Transnational Publishers, 1994).
29. On taxation, see Sol Picciotto, *International Business Taxation: A Study in the Internationalization of Business Regulation* (London: Weidenfeld and Nicolson, 1992).
30. Harry Arthurs, "Private Ordering and Workers' Rights in the Global Economy: Corporate Codes of Conduct as a Regime of Labour Market Regulation," unpublished manuscript, York University (1999); L. Compa and T. Hinchliffe-Darricarrere, "Enforcing Labor Rights Through Corporate Codes of Conduct," *Columbia Journal of Transnational Law* 33 (1995), 663–689.
31. Wolfgang Reinicke, *Global Public Policy: Governing Without Government?* (Washington, D.C.: Brookings Institute, 1998), p. 120.
32. Reinicke, *Global Public Policy*, pp. 99–100.
33. David Kennedy, "The International Style in Postwar Law and Policy: John Jackson and the Field of International Economic Law," *American University Journal of International Law and Policy* 10 (1995), 685. More generally on the legal structure of the WTO, John H. Jackson, *The World Trading System: Law and Policy of International Economic Relations* (Cambridge, MA: MIT Press, 1999).
34. L. Wallach and L. Sforza, *Whose Trade Organization? Corporate Globalization and the Erosion of Democracy* (Washington, D.C.: Public Citizen, 1999), p. 198.
35. Although critical of Marxist accounts of globalization, Braithwaite and Drahos tend to confirm this view in their massive *Global Business Regulation*. Reminiscent of Neumann, they see strict antitrust laws as essential to reforming both the global economy and global economic regulation (602–629). In this vein, see Claire Cutler, "Global Capitalism and Liberal Myths: Dispute Settlement in Private International Trade Relations," *Millennium: Journal of International Studies* 24 (1995), 377–397; Cutler, "Public Meets Private: The

International Unification and Harmonization of Private International Trade Law," *Global Society* 13 (1999), 25–48.

36. Judith N. Shklar, *Legalism: Law, Morals, and Political Trials* (Cambridge, MA: Harvard University Press, 1986), pp. 16–17.

37. Peter Schlechtriem, *Uniform Sales Law: The UN Convention on Contracts for the International Sale of Goods* (Vienna: Manzsche Verlags-und Universitaets-bibliothek, 1986), p. 1. More generally, see the symposium on commercial law in the *American Journal of Comparative Law* XL (1992).

38. Roy Goode, *Commercial Law in the Next Millennium* (London: Sweet & Maxwell, 1998), pp. 19–20.

39. Arthur Rosett, "Unification, Restatement, Codification and Reform in International Commercial Law," *American Journal of Comparative Law* XL (1992), 687.

40. Rosett, "Unification, Restatement, Codification and Reform in International Commercial Law," 695.

41. Lord Justice Mustill, "The New *Lex Mercatoria*: The First Twenty-Five Years," *Arbitration International* 4 (1988), 118–119.

42. Far more clearly than Neumann, the late Tim Mason demonstrated that this political option ultimately proved dangerous for some key business groups. Tim Mason, *Nazism, Fascism and the Working Classes* (Cambridge: Cambridge University Press, 1990), pp. 53–76.

43. David Harvey, *The Condition of Postmodernity*, pp. 121–200.

44. Harvey, *Justice, Nature & the Geography of Difference* (Oxford: Blackwell, 1996), pp. 240–241.

45. On the account of globalization implicit in the *Communist Manifesto*, see Harvey, *Spaces of Hope* (Berkeley: University of California, 2000), pp. 21–52.

46. Boaventura de Sousa Santos, "The Postmodern Transition: Law and Politics" in Austin Sarat and Thomas Kearns (eds) *The Fate of Law* (Ann Arbor: University of Michigan, 1993), p. 115.

47. International Institute for the Unification of Private Law (Unidroit), *Principles of International Commercial Contracts* (Rome: Unidroit, 1994), p. viii.

48. Kathyrn Sikkink, "Codes of Conduct for Transnational Corporations: The Case of the WHO/UNICEF Code," *International Organization* 40 (1986), 836.

49. John Kline, "Advantages of International Regulation: The Case for a Flexible Pluralistic Framework," in Carol Kline (ed), *International Regulation: New Rules for a Changing World Order* (San Francisco: Institute for Contemporary Studies, 1988), p. 36.

CHAPTER 2

1. Friedrich Hayek, *The Road to Serfdom* (Chicago: University of Chicago, 1944), pp. 220–239. Former General Counsel to U.S. Trade Representative Judith H. Bello and former Trade Representative Alan F. Holmer echo Hayek in their "After the Cold War?: Whither International Economic Law," *Harvard International Law Journal*, 32 (1991), 323–329. Within popular discourse, the idea of an "elective affinity" between globalization and the rule of law is typically expressed in a vague and somewhat unclear fashion. But in my reading of this discourse, many politicians and journalists mean substantially more than that globalization requires enforceable contracts and the maintenance of basic property rights. They often additionally suggest that globalization is likely to heighten legal predictability and regularity in many other arenas as well. Of course, from a historical perspective, this assumption

is plausible: The mainstream of modern political and legal theory (from Locke to Weber) accepted the tenet of an "elective affinity" between capitalist economics and a relatively robust conception of the rule of law.

2. This position can also be found in many of the essays collected in Peter B. Kenen (ed) *Managing the World Economy: Fifty Years After Bretton Woods* (Washington, D.C.: Institute for International Economics, 1994). From the left: Paul Hirst and Graham Thompson, *Globalization in Question* (Cambridge: Polity, 1996), pp. 191–194. Saskia Sassen offers a fine analysis of the legal structures of economic globalization, yet it is unclear to me that she fully appreciates how problematic they are from the perspective of a minimally defensible conception of the rule of law (*Losing Control?: Sovereignty in an Age of Globalization* [New York: Columbia University Press, 1996]).

3. But even this unification is hindered when MNCs and their political allies decide that they are more likely to benefit economically from a lack of such standards. Zacher, *Governing Global Networks* (Cambridge: Cambridge University Press, 1995), pp. 61, 98, 107, 133, 158–159

4. The term *Situationsjurisprudenz* stems from Neumann, who perspicaciously argued in the 1920s and 1930s that organized capitalism increasingly tends to rely on ad hoc, informal modes of jurisprudence inconsistent with the most defensible features of the rule of law.

5. Hayek, *Road to Serfdom*, p. 72. More generally: Joseph Raz, "The Rule of Law and Its Virtue," in Raz, *The Authority of Law* (Oxford: Clarendon, 1979), pp. 210–229.

6. James Rosenau, "Governance, Order, and Change in World Politics," in James Rosenau and Ernst-Otto Czempiel, *Governance Without Government: Order and Change in World Politics* (Cambridge: Cambridge University Press, 1992), p. 4.

7. Hirst and Thompson, *Globalization In Question*, esp. pp. 1–17, 195–201. For good discussions of the central place of the present-day "triadization" or regionalization of the international economy into three trading blocs: Linda Weiss, "Globalization and the Myth of the Powerless State," *New Left Review*, No. 225 (1997); Andrew Glyn and Bob Sutcliffe, "Global But Leaderless? The New Capitalist Order?" in *Socialist Register 1992*, Ralph Miliband & Leo Panitch (eds) (London: Merlin Press, 1992). Triadization is also an important theme in the now-classic study by Robert Gilpin, *The Political Economy of International Relations* (Princeton: Princeton University Press, 1987), pp. 364–405.

8. John Stopford and Susan Strange, *Rival States, Rival Firms: Competition for World Market Shares* (Cambridge: Cambridge University Press, 1991), p. 5.

9. The German political economist Joachim Hirsch has coined the apt term "national competitive state" to capture some of these trends. Joachim Hirsch, *Der nationale Wettbewerbsstaat. Staat, Demokratie und Politik im globalen Kapitalismus* (Berlin: Edition ID-Archiv, 1996).

10. According to most accounts, globalization has deepened trends towards economic concentration on the world level, in part because of the enormous start-up costs of many high tech industries. Stopford and Strange, *Rival States, Rival Firms: Competition for World Market Share*, pp. 6–72, 92–97. Robert Gilpin, *The Political Economy of International Relations*, pp. 215–216.

11. Ingeborg Maus, *Rechtstheorie und politische Theorie im Industriekapitalismus*. Munich: Wilhelm Fink Verlag, 1986.

12. For a good though somewhat outdated overview: Bernardo M. Cremades, "The Impact of International Arbitration on the Development of Business Law," *American Journal of Comparative Law*, 31 (1983).

13. I relied on a (popular) German translation: Jeswald W. Salacuse, *International erfolgreich verhandeln* (Frankfurt: Campus, 1992), pp. 111–138. Note that

anxiety here is not limited to legal irregularity resulting from dictatorship or political corruption. Salacuse rants against "bureaucracy," which seems to be a code-word for a host of ill-defined (both real and alleged) dangers to foreign investors.

14. Thomas E. Carbonneau, "The Remaking of Arbitration: Design and Destiny," in Carbonneau (ed) *Lex Mercatoria and Arbitration* (Dobbs Ferry, NY: Transnational Juris Publications, 1990), pp. 1–19.

15. Antonio Cassese, *International Law in a Divided World* (Oxford: Clarendon, 1986), pp. 50–51.

16. See Carbonneau (ed) *Lex Mercatoria and Arbitration.*

17. Harold J. Berman, "The Law of International Commercial Transactions (*Lex Mercatoria*)," *Harvard Journal of International Law*, 19 (1978). The *Lex Mercatoria* had a significant impact on the 1980 Vienna Sales Convention, which established minimal trade standards for international sales. Bernard Audit, "The Vienna Sales Convention and the *Lex Mercatoria*," in Carbonneau (ed) *Lex Mercatoria and Arbitration*, pp. 139–160.

18. Friedrich K. Juenger, "The *Lex Mercatoria* and the Conflict of Laws," in Carbonneau (ed) *Lex Mercatoria and Arbitration*, p. 224.

19. Benjamin Barber, *Jihad vs. McWorld: How Globalism and Tribalism are Reshaping the World* (New York: Ballantine Books, 1996), p. 271.

20. Left-wing proponents of a New International Economic Order have been vocal critics of the *Lex Mercatoria*. Stephen Zamora, "Is There Customary International Economic Law?" *German Yearbook of International Law* 32 (1989), 16–17. Cassese similarly notes that the chief opponents to customary international economic law in our century have been socialists, communists, and Third World countries. Cassese, *International Law in a Divided World*, p. 181.

21. Carbonneau, "The Remaking of Arbitration: Design and Destiny," p. 13.

22. See the English translation of the popular study by two journalists associated with the German newsweekly *Der Spiegel*. Hans-Peter Martin and Harold Schumann, *The Global Trap: Globalization and the Assault on Democracy & Prosperity* (New York: Zed, 1996), pp. 196–201.

23. My source here is the detailed study by Sol Picciotto, *International Business Taxation: A Study in the Internationalization of Business Regulation* (London: Weidenfeld and Nicolson, 1992), pp. 68–69.

24. Bernhard Grossfeld, "Multinationale Unternehmer als Anstoß zur Internationalisierung des Wirtschaftsrechts," *Wirtschaft und Recht* 32 (1980); Norbert Horn, "Die Entwicklung des Internationalen Wirtschaftsrechts durch Verhaltensnormen," *Rabels Zeitschrift für ausländisches und internationales Privatrecht* 44 (1980); Sol Picciotto, "The Control of Transnational Capital and the Democratisation of the International State," *Journal of Law & Society* 15 (1988).

25. Picciotto, *International Business Taxation*, esp. pp. xv-xvi, 38–69; on the taxation of intrafirm exchange, 171–221. Susan Strange, *The Retreat of the State: The Diffusion of Power in the World Economy* (Cambridge: Cambridge University Press, 1996), pp. 60–65, 77.

26. DeAnne Julius, "International Direct Investment: Strengthening the Policy Regime," in Kenen (ed) *Managing the World Economy*, pp. 280–284. Julius proposes that firms be given direct access to the dispute settlement procedures of the WTO. Thus far, only member-states have possessed this right.

27. Cassese, *International Law in a Divided World*, p. 103.

28. Tommaso Padoa-Schioppa and Fabrizio Saccomanni, "Managing a Market-Led Global Financial System," in Kenen (ed) *Managing the World Economy*, pp. 259–260; Hirst and Thompson, *Globalization In Question*, pp. 130–136.

29. The term is from Susan Strange's *Casino Capitalism* (New York: Blackwell's, 1980).

30. Strange, *The Retreat of the State: The Diffusion of Power in the World Economy*, pp. 122–146.

31. Timothy Sinclair, "Passing Judgment: Credit Rating Processes as Regulatory Mechanisms of Governance in the Emerging World Order," *Review of International Political Economy* 1 (1994), 139–141.

32. The most obvious democratic flaw of the IMF is that voting rights are largely proportional to the financial contributions of each country.

33. Joseph Gold, "Strengthening the Soft International Law of Exchange Arrangements," *American Journal of International Law* 77 (1983), 452.

34. Gold, "Strengthening the Soft International Law of Exchange Arrangements," 480.

35. Susan Strange, *Casino Capitalism*, p. 33; Robert Gilpin, *The Political Economy of International Relations*, p. 320.

36. Beyond the much-publicized summits featuring the political leaders of the United States, Britain, France, Germany, Japan (G-5) as well as Canada and Italy (G-7) and now Russia (G-8), the finance ministers of the involved countries also meet separately on a regular basis. The Director of the IMF also attends, but officially only in a personal capacity.

37. Harold James, *International Monetary Cooperation Since Bretton Woods* (Washington, D.C.: International Monetary Fund, 1996), pp. 422–425, 440–444.

38. One of the summit participants, Giscard d'Estaing, similarly described the group as "a private, informal meeting of those who really matter in the world." James, *International Monetary Cooperation Since Bretton Woods*, p. 267. Of course, at least the summits feature elected political leaders and thus are "private" only in the sense that their deliberations go on behind closed doors. This is a different sense of the term "private" than employed above in the discussion of international business arbitration and the *Lex Mercatoria*. Yet here as well, there is a strong trend towards what Norberto Bobbio has famously characterized as "invisible power." Norberto Bobbio, *The Future of Democracy* (Minneapolis: University of Minnesota, 1987).

39. James, *International Monetary Cooperation Since Bretton Woods*, p. 458.

40. Stephen Gill, "Globalization, Democratization, and Indifference," in James H. Mittelman, Ed., *Globalization: Critical Reflections* (Boulder: Lynne Rienner, 1996), p. 216.

41. On the legal evolution of GATT and WTO, see John H. Jackson, "Managing the Trading System: The World Trade Organization and the Post-Uruguay Round GATT Agenda," in Kenen (ed) *Managing the World Economy*, pp. 131–151.

42. At a U.S. Senate hearing in 1951, Senator Milliken commented that "Anyone who reads GATT is likely to have his sanity impaired." The jurist R. Gardner commented in 1966 that "only ten people in the world understand it, and they are not telling anyone" (cited in Cassese, *International Law in a Divided World*, p. 340).

43. Exceptions to the general rule of nondiscrimination in GATT are often facilitated by vague, open-ended legal clauses. Vagueness and nongenerality in law often go hand in hand, since vagueness allows decision makers to decide like cases in unlike ways. David Kennedy, "The International Style in Postwar Law and Policy: John Jackson and the Field of International Economic Law," *American University Journal of Law and Policy* 10 (1995), 685. I should add that extension exceptions are common to other international economic agreements of this type as well. The Vienna Sales Convention, for example, is plagued by them.

44. Ernest Preeg, *Traders in a Brave New World* (Chicago: University of Chicago Press, 1995), p. 224. The problem of what Preeg describes as "high tech nationalism/regionalism" is a common theme in general discussions of GATT. Gilpin, *The Political Economy of International Relations*, pp. 190–229.

45. David Kennedy, "Turning to Market Democracy: A Tale of Two Architectures," *Harvard International Law Journal* 32 (Spring 1991), 380–381. Unfortunately, Kennedy's perceptive diagnosis leads him to the worrisome conclusion that the traditional view of the rule of law as based on clear norms is anachronistic altogether.

46. Histories of GATT support this view. Jarrod Wiener, *Making Rules in the Uruguay Round of the GATT: A Study of International Leadership* (Aldershot: Dartmouth, 1995).

47. I do not mean to deny that there may be situations when particular firms are so dominant in a specific economic sector that they push for the principle of nondiscrimination. The reason here is familiar enough: "Free trade" is then likely to provide immediate benefits to the most developed and efficient firms. This is why certain American industries and their political allies have insisted on principled nondiscrimination in trade for specific industries (for example, film and telecommunications) in recent years. My point here is simply that the traditional assumption of an "elective affinity" between capitalism and general law badly overstates the significance of this scenario. First, even extraordinarily large, successful firms are likely to be outnumbered worldwide by aspiring and actual competitors, thus necessarily countering political pressures to extend the principle of nondiscrimination within international forms of governance. Political pressures to include exceptional clauses and vague standards, even within relatively codified forms of international economic coordination (GATT), are thus more often than not likely to prove decisive. Sol Picciotto makes a similar point when he observes that liberal legal forms are "continuously undermined by the operations of markets and competition," which inevitably lead economic actors to pursue advantages over their competitors. The exceptional clauses constitutive of GATT and other treaties of this type provide a paradigmatic illustration of this point (see *International Business Taxation: A Study in the Internationalization of Business Regulation*, p. 80). Although particular firms at specific junctures in the business cycle may seek general standards, globalizing capitalists as a whole seem to prefer informal mechanisms, particularly those (a) relatively free from potentially unfriendly political pressures and (b) run for and by international business.

48. I am forced to neglect the complex legal structure of the emerging regional economic and political blocs (NAFTA, ASEAN, and the EU) that are rapidly gaining in importance. But here as well, some preliminary evidence confirms the argument developed above. ASEAN, for example, is filled with vague norms and exceptional clauses intended to allow individual Asian member-states to cultivate "strategic industries" and so-called sensitive products. Legal uniformity gives way whenever individual countries strive to provide special protections to those firms being "armed" for international competition. Peter Kenevan and Andrew Winder, "Flexible Free Trade: The ASEAN Free Trade Area," *Harvard Journal of International Law* 34 (1993), 228, 235–236. NAFTA takes an unfortunate step towards outfitting firms with powers hitherto limited to nation-states. Chapter 11(B) allows private firms to submit complaints against member states to a three-member tribunal outfitted with the power to resolve conflicts and award damages. Corporations and nation-states have equal rights (!) to name members to the arbitration board: Each party names one member, and the third must be agreed to by both. DeAnne Julius, "International Direct Investment: Strengthening the Policy Regime,"

Kenen (ed) *Managing the World Economy*, pp. 282–283. In many ways, the European Union clearly represents a special case deserving of a careful, detailed analysis that I cannot undertake here. Nonetheless, it is striking that analysts of EU social policy have noted that business interests there have been trying to exploit the jurisdictional complexity of the EU, derived from its multitiered political and legal structure, in order to push Europe in a more neoliberal direction. Paul Pierson and Stephan Leibfried, "Multitiered Institutions and the Making of Social Policy," in Pierson and Leibfried (eds) *European Social Policy: Between Fragmentation and Integration* (Washington, D.C.: Brookings, 1995), p. 28.

49. For the numbers: Glenn Withers, "Migrations," in Kenen (ed) *Managing the World Economy*, p. 211.

50. See the revealing report put out by the German civil rights organization, the Committee for Basic Rights and Democracy: Till Müller-Heidelberg, Ulrich Finck, Wolf-Dieter Narr, Marei Pelzer (eds) *Grundrechte-Report* (Hamburg: Rowohlt, 1997).

51. On the globalization of organized crime, Susan Strange, *The Retreat of the State: The Diffusion of Power in the World Economy*, pp. 110–121. On the concomitant decline of the principle of legality within the criminal law: Francis A. Allen, *The Habits of Legality: Criminal Justice and the Rule of Law* (New York: Oxford University Press, 1996).

52. Nigel Purvis, "Critical Legal Studies in Public International Law," *Harvard International Law Journal*, 32 (1991).

53. Gunther Teubner, "'Global Bukowina': Legal Pluralism in the World Society," in Teubner (ed) *Global Law Without a State* (Aldershot, UK: Dartmouth, 1997), p. 13.

54. In light of the widespread tendency to caricature and dismiss formalist jurisprudence, we would do well to recall that even defenders of a relatively strong version of legal formalism typically admit that formalism may be of limited value in certain settings. Frederick Schauer, "Formalism," *Yale Law Journal* 97 (1988).

55. In his famous discussion of the common law, Max Weber suggested that legal determinacy within England was guaranteed to a great extent by common lawyers who constituted "a strong organized guild which, by corporate and economic interests, through a monopoly of the bench and a central position at the seat of the central courts" gained "a measure of power which neither King nor parliament" could ignore. Max Weber, *Economy and Society, Vol. I* (Berkeley: University of California, 1979), p. 794. Arguably reminiscent of the "guild" structure of traditional common lawyers, the homogeneity of international arbitrators probably functions to compensate for informality at the level of legal norms and standards. Of course, whether or not this state of affairs is defensible from a normative perspective is another matter altogether. My own view is that the ongoing renaissance of customary law within the global economy tends to point to the accuracy of some of the (traditional) formalist anxieties about the "Egyptian hieroglyphics" of customary law.

56. Yves Dezaley, "The *Big Bang* and the Law: The Internationalization and Restructuration of the Legal Field," p. 281, and Volker Gessner and Angelike Schade, "Conflicts of Culture in Cross-border Legal Relations: The Conception of a Research Topic in the Sociology of Law," p. 271, both in Mike Featherstone (ed) *Global Culture: Nationalism, Globalization, and Modernity* (London: Sage Publications, 1990); Sassen, *Losing Control? Sovereignty in an Age of Globalization*, pp. 16–21.

57. Interestingly, Law & Economics has abandoned the legal formalism of earlier variants of free market legal thought. Its embrace of antiformalism within the

law conveniently parallels actual legal trends within global economic law (see William E. Scheuerman, "Free Market Anti-Formalism: The Case of Richard Posner" *Ratio Juris* 12 [1999]).

58. Wolfgang Wiegand, "The Reception of American Law in Europe," *American Journal of Comparative Law* 39 (1991), esp. 234–235. Wiegand makes it clear that legal "Americanization" in Europe is highly ambivalent. In many areas, its impact (strengthened consumer protections and antidiscrimination laws) has been positive.

59. Malcolm Waters, *Globalization* (New York: Routledge, 1995), p. 55. I have learned a great deal from David Harvey's fascinating discussion of the compression of space and time: Harvey, *The Condition of Postmodernity* (Oxford: Basil Blackwell, 1989), pp. 201–326.

60. This is merely a simplified version of the traditional explanation of the sources of the "elective affinity" between capitalism and the rule of law.

61. Norbert Malanowski (ed) *Social and Environmental Standards in International Trade Agreements: Links, Implementations, and Prospects* (Münster: Westfälisches Dampfboot, 1997).

CHAPTER 3

1. Lance Compa and T. Hinchliffe-Darricarrere, "Enforcing Labor Rights Through Corporate Codes of Conduct" *Columbia Journal of Transnational Law* 33 (1995), 668–669.

2. See Terry Collingsworth, "American Labor Policy and the International Economy: Clarifying Policies and Interests" *Boston College Law Review* 31 (1989), 46–55; Katherine Van Wezel Stone, "Labour in the Global Economy" in William Bratton, Joseph McCahery, and Sol Picciotto (eds) *International Regulatory Competition and Coordination* (Oxford: Clarendon, 1996), pp. 448–453. Hard data supporting this claim is provided by the very useful report to the Secretariat of the Commission for Labor Cooperation (NAALC, 1996), which supports the claim that the threat of plant closing (and relocation to Mexico) is playing an increasingly important role in undermining labor's right to organize in the United States. (The report is available at www. naalc.org/english/publications/nalmcp.htm). More generally on the problem of globalization and domestic labor law, see Harry Arthurs, "Labour Law without the State" *University of Toronto Law Journal* 46 (1996), 1–45.

3. As Neumann grasped, a balanced appreciation of the traditional virtues of modern legality hardly entails subscribing to a crude hyperformalism, according to which legal decisions can be mechanically deduced from unambiguous norms. Of course, even cogent legal materials fail to predetermine a single correct answer, and it sometimes makes sense for a polity to delegate discretionary power to the administration or judiciary. Some measure of "indeterminacy" within the law is unavoidable. Nonetheless, indeterminacy can be managed and contained by a legal system committed to realizing the attributes of generality, clarity, prospectiveness, and publicity. For now, I refrain from repeating traditional normative arguments in defense of a model of law possessing these attributes; in the discussion that follows, many of these arguments should become evident.

4. Lon Fuller, *The Morality of Law* (New Haven: Yale University Press, 1964), pp. 155–156.

5. Karl Klare, "Judicial Deradicalization of the Wagner Act and the Origins of Modern Legal Consciousness, 1937–41" *University of Minnesota Law Review* 62 (1978), 344.

6. From one perspective, codes of this type represent nothing new for large transnational firms: Even the British East India Company and Hudson Bay Company were authorized to establish "special rules" regulating workplace conditions. Nonetheless, the significance of these codes seems to be gaining dramatically in recent years. On this and many other points concerning corporate codes of conduct, I am indebted to Harry Arthurs, "Private Ordering and Workers' Rights in the Global Economy: Corporate Codes of Conduct as a Regime of Labour Market Regulation," unpublished manuscript, York University, Toronto (1999).

7. See *International Labor Organization Working Party on the Social Dimensions of the Liberalization of International Trade Report* (1998; www.ilo.org/public/english/20gb/docs/gb273/sdl-l.htm#).

8. Reinecke, *Global Public Policy: Governing Without Government*, p. 90.

9. Harry Arthurs, "Private Ordering and Workers' Rights in the Global Economy: Corporate Codes of Conduct," pp. 10–11.

10. K. Tapiola, "The Importance of Standards and Corporate Responsibilities: The Role of Voluntary Corporate Codes of Conduct," OECD Conference on the Role of International Investments in Development: Corporate Responsibilities and the OECD Guidelines for Multinational Enterprises (Paris: OECD, 1995). (www.oecd.org/daf/conference/tapiola.pdf). Also, see *International Labor Organization Working Party on the Social Dimensions of the Liberalization of International Trade Report*.

11. See the numerous examples collected by the U.S. Department of Labor on its web site (www.dol.gov/dol/ilab/public/media/reports/apparel/5c.htm).

12. *International Labor Organization Working Party on the Social Dimensions of the Liberalization of International Trade Report*, para. 60.

13. See the materials provided by activists and labor unionists (www.sweatshop-watch.org). Saipan has become a major site of production for the garment industry because retailers can label products produced there "made in the USA," while at least thus far being able to get away with truly horrific labor practices (including indentured servitude). The territorial government has long been hostile to labor organizations and labor rights.

14. A revealing comparative case here is the Fair Labor Agreement, which similarly undertakes to tackle the problem of sweatshops in the apparel industry. Like the Saipan Agreement, the Fair Labor Agreement is a relatively detailed document; there is no question that the ambitious character of the Agreement stems from the fact that business, human rights lawyers, and labor activists scrambled to flesh it out so as to provide it with some substance. It clearly possesses more attributes of formal legality (clarity, transparency, and publicity) than many competing codes of conduct. At the same time, key labor and religious interests ultimately refused to sign off on the final agreement, arguing—in my view, correctly—that it ultimately fudges important wage and labor rights issues. The Saipan Agreement ultimately possesses more of the attributes of formal legality than the Fair Labor Agreement in precisely those matters of greatest importance to workers subject to sweatshop conditions.

15. For the most part, U.S. courts have been hostile to attempts to grant extraterritorial status to U.S. labor law (for example, in cases involving U.S. firms operating abroad). See J. Turley, "'When in Rome': Multinational Misconduct and the Presumption Against Territoriality" *Northwestern University Law Review* 84 (1999), 598–664.

16. See I. M. Destler, *American Trade Politics*, 2nd ed. (New York; Twentieth Century Fund, 1992).

17. Donald Pease and William Goold, "The New GSP: Fair Trade with the Third World" *World Policy Journal* 2 (1985), 351–366.

18. Terry Collingsworth, W. Goold, and J. Harvey, "Time for a Global New Deal" *Foreign Affairs* 73 (1994), 13.
19. Philip Alston, "Labor Rights Provisions in U.S. Trade Law: 'Aggressive Unilateralism'," *Human Rights Quarterly* 15 (1993), 7–8.
20. Alston, "Labor Rights Provisions," 17–18.
21. Alston, "Labor Rights Provisions," 11–12.
22. Alston, "Labor Rights Provisions," 19–23; H. Mandel, "In Pursuit of the Missing Link: International Worker Rights" *Columbia Journal of Transnational Law* 27 (1989), 465–481.
23. Terry Collingsworth, "International Worker Rights Enforcement: Proposals Following a Test Case" in Lance Compa and Stephen Diamond (eds) *Human Rights, Labor Rights, and International Trade* (Philadelphia: University of Pennsylvania Press, 1996), pp. 233–238; more generally, see Thomas Franck, *Political Questions/Judicial Answers: Does the Rule of Law Apply to Foreign Affairs?* (Princeton: Princeton University Press, 1992).
24. Collingsworth, "International Worker Rights Enforcement," pp. 230–231; J. Perez-Lopez, "Conditioning Trade on Foreign Labour Law: The U.S. Approach" *Comparative Labour Law Journal* 9 (1988), 263–264, 272–277.
25. Anonymous, "Review of Worker Rights Suspended" *Wall Street Journal* (February 17, 1994), A4.
26. Collingsworth, "International Worker Rights Enforcement," pp. 240–243.
27. Just south of the U.S.-Mexican border, an export-processing zone provides investors with a favorable business climate, including lax workplace regulations, low taxes, a cheap and plentiful labor supply, as well as a solid infrastructure and easy access to the United States. Although real wages in Mexico seem to have declined on average since 1993, employment at the Maquiladoras at the border is booming: Since 1986, employment there has grown at an annual rate of 12% (H. Williams, "Mobile Capital and Transborder Labor Rights Mobilization" *Politics & Society* 27 [1999], 139–140).
28. Public Citizen, "Global Trade Watch: School of Real Life Results" Washington, D.C. (1999). (www.citizen.org/pctrade/nafta/reports); J. Millman, "NAFTA's Do-Gooder Side Deal Disappointing: Efforts to Protect Labor, Environment Lack Teeth" *Wall Street Journal* (October 15, 2007), A19.
29. K. Brandon, "NAFTA at 5: Workers Say Enforcement is Lacking in Mexico" *Chicago Tribune* (November 29, 1998), Sects. 5, 1, 7.
30. H. Williams, "Mobile Capital and Transborder Labor Rights Mobilization" 154–56.
31. Van Wezel Stone, "Labour in a Global Economy," pp. 460–465. A copy of the NAALC can be downloaded at (www.naalc.org).
32. Of course, federalism complicates matters even further.
33. K. Hagen, "Fundamentals of Labor Issues and NAFTA" *University of California at Davis Law Review* 27 (1994), 925.
34. Van Wezel Stone notes: "[t]here is almost no instance, at least under USA labor law, in which government failure to enforce labor standards cannot be characterized so as to fall within one of these exceptions. These exceptions provide a legal excuse for almost all non-enforcement" ("Labour in a Global Economy," 462–463).
35. Stephen Diamond, "Labor Rights in the Global Economy: A Case Study of the North American Free Trade Agreement" in *Human Rights, Labor Rights, and International Trade*, p. 218.
36. Diamond, "Labor Rights in the Global Economy," pp. 217–218.
37. For an example of the former, see Diamond, "Labor Rights in the Global Economy: A Case Study of the North American Free Trade Agreement," pp. 214–221; of the latter, J. Castaneda and C. Heredia, "Another NAFTA: What

a Good Agreement Should Offer," in Ralph Nader, William Greider, and Margaret Atwood (eds) *The Case Against Free Trade: GATT, NAFTA, and the Globalization of Corporate Power* (San Francisco: Earth Island, 1993), pp. 86–87). Castaneda and Heredia rightly observe that an upward harmonization would force a reform of U.S. norms (occasionally inferior to Mexico's) and of Mexican enforcement (inferior to that of both the U.S. and Canada). Although typically dismissed as unrealistic, it is useful to keep in mind that the European Union has gone further than NAFTA in pursuing a system of harmonized labor standards. The European model is undoubtedly inadequate (see S. Simitis, "Dismantling or Strengthening Labour Law: The Case of the European Court of Justice," *European Law Journal* 2 [1996], 156–176; Wolfgang Streek, "The Internationalization of Industrial Relations in Europe: Prospects and Problems" *Politics & Society* 26 [1998], 429–459), yet it does tentatively suggest that support among low-wage countries for a modest upward harmonization of social and labor standards can be achieved if the richer members of a regional bloc are willing to make substantial side payments (for example, EU structural funds; see Peter Lange, "Maastricht and the Social Protocol: Why Did They Do IT?" *Politics and Society* 21 [1993], 21–24). Needless to say, it is difficult to imagine the United States acceding to an expensive system of "development funds" for its southern neighbor as a trade-off for maintaining a superior system of labor rights and standards.

38. Precisely for this reason, it seems to me that the European Union ultimately offers a more hopeful experiment in achieving what NAFTA perhaps cannot.

39. I am not arguing that those of us sympathetic to labor should abandon attempts to reform NAALC in light of the structural problems described here. (Similarly, activists sometimes can hope to use corporate codes of conduct to underscore the pathologies of corporate rule [as we see in the example of the Saipan struggles], and maybe even on occasion successfully employ flawed labor conditionality clauses in trade legislation.) But those of us committed to social change need to be honest about the likely limits of such strategies given the profound inequalities plaguing the global political economy. From the perspective defended here, the struggle to challenge those inequalities and the fight for enhanced formal legality constitute two sides of the same coin.

40. A system of this type will ultimately have to rest on "collective *decision-making* on policy and on operations, based upon clear rules," and these rules will have to specify unacceptable behavior and modes of collective action against those who violate them; finally, there must be "clear mechanisms for joint action to enforce the rules" (see Peter Gowan, *The Global Gamble: Washington's Bid for Global Dominance* [New York: Verso, 1999], p. 300).

41. The United States tried to raise the issue of labor standards within the WTO (and its predecessor organization [GATT]). During the 1999 WTO ministerial meeting in Seattle, the United States once again unsuccessfully reiterated its call for the WTO to link trading privileges to labor conditionality norms. For the background to the recent WTO meeting, see Virginia Leary, "The WTO and the Social Clause: Post-Singapore" *European Journal of International Law* 8 (1997), 118–122.

42. The Clinton Administration's advocacy of a WTO labor clause revealed significant rifts within its own ranks. Clinton clearly was trying to breach a compromise between organized labor (and the Department of Labor) and corporate interests (having ubiquitous institutional influence). It should come as no surprise that his balancing of these fundamentally divergent interests generated, as we have seen, dubious results. Most revealing was the lack of focused diplomacy to mobilize support for a labor clause; in contrast to the

impressive time and resources put into diplomatic efforts to advance U.S. positions on intellectual property rights, for example, or genetically manipulated foods, the administration did little on the diplomatic front to advance labor rights. This is hardly an oversight: it stems from (socially based) divisions within Clinton's own government.

43. Goete Hansson, *Social Clauses and International Trade* (New York: St. Martin's, 1983); P. Dorman, "Worker Rights and International Trade: A Case for Intervention" *Review of Radical Political Economics* 20 (1988), 241–46; Stephen S. Golub, "Are International Labor Standards Needed to Prevent Social Dumping?" *Finance and Development* 34 (1997), 20–23; A. Raynauld and J. Vidal, *Labor Standards and International Competitiveness: A Comparative Analysis of Developing and Industrialized Countries* (Cheltenham: Edward Elgar, 1998); OECD, *Trade and Labour Standards: A Review of the Issues* (Paris: OECD, 1995).
44. E. Lee, "Globalization and Labor Standards: A Review of the Issues" *International Labour Review* 136 (1997), 118–122.
45. See the WTO web page on "Ten common misunderstandings about the WTO," where fidelity to an ambitious version of democracy allegedly superior to what the WTO describes as "majoritarian democracy" and the rule of law are described as mainstays of WTO decision making (www.wto.org/wto/10mis)
46. J. H. Jackson, *The World Trading System: Law and Policy of International Economic Relations* (Cambridge, US: MIT Press, 1999), pp. 65–68.
47. Jackson, *World Trading System*, pp. 69–70.
48. Relevant here is Annex 2 of the WTO Agreement, available at (www.wto.org)
49. Lori Wallach and Michelle Sforza, *Whose Trade Organization? Corporate Globalization and the Erosion of Democracy* (Washington, D.C.: Public Citizen, 1999), p. 198.
50. An unsystematic survey of WTO rulings suggests that primarily the richest and most powerful capitalist countries are making the most effective use of the dispute resolution mechanisms (www.wto.org/wto/dispute/bulletin.htm)
51. G. Edgren, "Fair Labour Standards and Liberalisation" *International Labour Review* 118 (1979), 523–536; S. Charnovitz, "Fair Labour Standards and International Trade," *Journal of World Trade Law* 20 (1986), 61–78; Charnovitz, "The Influence of International Labour Standards on the World Trading Regime" *International Labour Review* 126 (1987), 565–584; R. Rothstein, "The Global Hiring Wall" *American Prospect* 17 (1994), 55–61.
52. Erika de Wet, "Labor Standards in the Global Economy: The Inclusion of a Social Clause in the General Agreement on Tariff and Trade/World Trade Organization" *Human Rights Quarterly* 17 (1995), 457.
53. Jackson, *World Trading System*, p. 182.
54. At this juncture, the ILO is able to do little more than direct moral suasion and critical public opinion at those countries which have formally agreed to abide by its conventions. See, for example, Victoria Leary, "Labor," in C. Joyner (ed) *The United Nations and International Law* (Cambridge: Cambridge University Press, 1997).
55. See Virgina Leary's discussion of some of these proposals (Leary, "Lessons from the Experience of the International Labour Organization" in Philip Alston (ed) *The United Nations and Human Rights* [Oxford: Clarendon, 1992], pp. 607–608). Difficult questions remain unanswered here. How might the ILO undertake effective punitive measures without succumbing to the potential ills of economic protectionism? What penalties would violators face? Although institutional and political fantasy is called for here, and the practical questions at hand are complex, I am unconvinced that the ILO experience implies an

unavoidable trade-off between practical efficacy and the pursuit of traditional rule of law virtues in transnational labor standards.

56. Alston, "Labor Rights Provisions," 32. There is some evidence of growing U.S. interest in relying on the ILO. Many activists remain skeptical, however.

57. The ILO rests on a tripartite decision-making structure in which representatives of member-states have twice the number of votes of business and labor combined; business and labor each have the same number.

CHAPTER 4

1. Franz Neumann, *The Governance of the Rule of Law* (1936); published recently as *The Rule of Law: Political Theory and the Legal System in Modern Society*, p. 213. For two very useful discussions of this volume, see Roger Cotterell, *Law's Community: Legal Thought in Social Theory* (Oxford: Oxford University Press, 1997), pp. 160–77; Fred Dallmayr, "Hermeneutics and the Rule of Law" in Gregory Leyh (ed) *Legal Hermeneutics: History, Theory, and Practice* (Berkeley: University of California Press, 1992), pp. 3–21.

2. In particular, "The Tanner Lectures," in S. McMurrin (ed) *The Tanner Lectures on Human Values, VIII* (Salt Lake City: University of Utah, 1988); *The Theory of Communicative Action, Vols. I & II* (Boston: Beacon, 1987), esp. Vol. I, pp. 243–272. More distantly: *Legitimation Crisis* (Boston: Beacon, 1975), part III; "Überlegungen zum Evolutionaren Stellenwert des Modernen Rechts," in *Rekonstruktion des Historischen Materialismus* (Frankfurt: Suhrkamp, 1976). As we will see in Chapter 5, in *Between Facts and Norms* Habermas modifies this position somewhat. In this chapter I focus on his legal ideas prior to its publication. As I hope to suggest, they are of more than antiquarian interest.

3. Neumann, *Governance of the Rule of Law*, p. 58.

4. They were reprinted in *The Democratic and Authoritarian State*.

5. Recall Weber's description of modern legal-rational authority as a "system of abstract rules" of "generalized formulation(s)"(Weber, *Economy and Society* [Berkeley: University of California, 1978], p. 217).

6. Neumann, "Change in the Function of Law in Modern Society," in *Rule of Law Under Siege*, p. 116.

7. Neumann, *The Governance of the Rule of Law*, p. 125.

8. Neumann, *The Governance of the Rule of Law*, p. 122. On this development path, also pp. 72–3, 117–125, 183–185, 219–222, 239–253, 263–265.

9. Neumann, *The Governance of the Rule of Law*, p. 124.

10. Neumann, *The Governance of the Rule of Law*, p. 257.

11. Neumann, *The Governance of the Rule of Law*, p. 150.

12. Neumann, *The Governance of the Rule of Law*, p. 50. On the nineteenth-century German response to legal disenchantment, see also pp. 138–150, 179–182, 199–205, 217–219, 257–266.

13. Neumann, "Change in the Function of Law," in *Rule of Law Under Siege*, p. 126.

14. Neumann, "Types of Natural Law," in *Democratic and Authoritarian State*, p. 79; *Governance of the Rule of Law*, p. 137. On this social democratic path: *The Governance of the Rule of Law*, pp. 126–137.

15. Neumann, *The Governance of the Rule of Law*, pp. 135, 138.

16. Neumann, *The Governance of the Rule of Law*, pp. 130, 137.

17. See, for example, Habermas, "Tanner Lectures," pp. 220–230.

18. Habermas, "Tanner Lectures," pp. 246–249, 275.

19. Neumann, *The Governance of the Rule of Law*, pp. 27–31.

20. Neumann, *Governance of the Rule of Law*, p. 8.
21. Neumann, "Types of Natural Law," in *The Democratic and Authoritarian State*, p. 76.
22. Weber, *Economy and Society*, p. 868.
23. For a persuasive argument along these lines: Seyla Benhabib, "In the Shadow of Aristotle and Hegel: Communicative Ethics and Current Controversies in Practical Philosophy" *The Philosophical Forum* 21 (1989–90).
24. Habermas, "Tanner Lectures," p. 269; *Communication and the Evolution of Society* (Boston: Beacon Press, 1979), pp. 183–188.
25. Weber early on identified "anti-formal" trends in law as resulting from the interventionist welfare state (*Economy and Society*, pp. 882–889). More recent authors have confirmed this observation: Roberto Unger, *Law in Modern Society* (New York: Free Press, 1976), pp. 193–194.
26. This claim is in some ways not all that distinct from the view of some of the more sophisticated classical defenders of general law. Rousseau argued that "the law may indeed decree that there shall be privileges, but cannot confer them on anybody in name;" Hegel tells us in *The Philosophy of Right* (para. 211) that the generality of law must be "determinate" in form (cited in Neumann, "Change in the Function of Law in Modern Society," *Rule of Law Under Siege*, pp. 106–107, 118). At least some of the defenders of classical law acknowledged the need for complex and specialized forms of state intervention: Neither Rousseau nor Hegel was a laissez-faire liberal. Nonetheless, they thought law should best be directed at a precise and clearly defined type or category of general objects. Even if seeming to regulate a "generality" of objects, vague legal standards (like "in good faith") embody a spurious generality insofar as they allow excessively discretionary modes of judicial and administrative action incompatible with the ideal of equality before the law.
27. See Friedrich Hayek, whose views are developed most fully in *Law, Legislation, and Liberty*, Vol. I-III (London: Routledge & Kegan Paul, 1973).
28. Neumann, "Change in the Function of Law," p. 131.
29. On this developmental path, see Neumann, *The Governance of the Rule of Law*, pp. 86–98; "The Change in the Function of Law," in *Rule of Law Under Siege*, pp. 132–138; *Behemoth: The Structure and Practice of National Socialism*, pp. 440–476.
30. Habermas, "Tanner Lectures," p. 275; "Volkssouveränität als Verfahren: Ein Normativer Begriff der Öffentlichkeit," in *Merkur* 43 (1989), 466–468.
31. Habermas, "What does Socialism Mean Today? The Rectifying Revolution and the Need for New Thinking on the Left" *New Left Review* 183 (1990), 18.
32. Habermas, *The Structural Transformation of the Public Sphere*, pp. 178–180, 225. Also, Habermas "Zum Begriff der politischen Beteiligung," in Habermas, *Kultur and Kritik: Verstreute Aufsätze* (Frankfurt: Suhrkamp, 1977).
33. For an influential statement of a similar view: Philippe Nonet and Philip Selznick, *Law and Society in Transition: Toward Responsive Law* (New York: Harper & Row, 1978).
34. Cited in Theodore Lowi, *The End of Liberalism* (New York: Norton, 1979), p. 275.
35. Gunther Teubner, *Standards and Direktiven in Generalklauseln* (Frankfurt: Athenaeum, 1971), pp. 13–23. Teubner nonetheless thinks that blanket clauses have a positive role to play in the legal order. See his "Generalklauseln also Sozionormative Modelle," in *Generalklauseln als Gegenstand der Sozialwissenschaften* (Baden-Baden: Nomos, 1978). Unger also sees in such standards the anticipation of a (very worrisome and ill-defined) "communitarian" utopia in *Law in Modern Society*, pp. 210–211.

36. Lowi, *The End of Liberalism;* also his "The Welfare State, The New Regulation, and the Rule of Law," in A. Hutchinson and P. Monahan (eds) *The Rule of Law: Ideal or Ideology?* (Toronto: Carswell, 1987).
37. Andre Gorz, *Critique of Economic Rationality* (New York: Verso, 1989), pp. 191–215.
38. Thomas Schmid (ed) *Befreiung von falscher Arbeit: Thesen zum garantierten Mindesteinkommen* (Berlin: Wagenbach, 1986).
39. Neumann, *The Governance of the Rule of Law,* pp. 275–286; Maus, *Rechtstheorie und politische Theorie im Industriekapitalismus,* pp. 280–291.
40. Habermas, *Theory of Communicative Action, Vol. II,* pp. 356–373.
41. Habermas, *Theory of Communicative Action ,Vol. II,* pp. 362–363.
42. Habermas, *Theory of Communicative Action, Vol. I,* p. 260.
43. Habermas, *Theory of Communicative Action, Vol. II,* p. 371.
44. Unfortunately, Claus Offe repeats this argument uncritically and without offering any additional empirical basis (*Contradictions of the Welfare State* [Cambridge: MIT Press, 1987], pp. 280–281).
45. Lowi, *End of Liberalism,* pp. 234–238.
46. Maus, *Rechtstheorie und politische Theorie im Industriekapitalismus,* p. 303 (my translation—WES).

CHAPTER 5

1. Jürgen Habermas, *The Structural Transformation of the Public Sphere,* trans. Thomas Burger (Cambridge: MIT Press, 1989).
2. Cited in Otto Kirchheimer, *Politics, Law, & Social Change: Selected Essays of Otto Kirchheimer,* Frederic S. Burin and Kurt L. Shell (eds) (New York: Columbia University, 1969), p. 331.
3. See, for example, Johannes Agnoli and Peter Brückner, *Die Transformation der Demokratie* (Frankfurt: EVA, 1968).
4. Jürgen Habermas, *Between Facts and Norms: Contributions to a Discourse Theory of Law and Democracy,* William Rehg (trans) (Cambridge, USA: MIT Press, 1996). Unless otherwise noted, all internal references in this and subsequent chapters refer to this text. At times, I have altered the translations.
5. Jürgen Habermas, "Further Reflections on the Public Sphere," in Craig Calhoun (ed) *Habermas and the Public Sphere* (Cambridge, USA: MIT Press, 1992), pp. 421–461.
6. See also: Jürgen Habermas, "What Does Socialism Mean Today? The Rectifying Revolution and the Need for New Thinking on the Left," *New Left Review,* no. 183 (September-October 1990).
7. Wolfgang Jäger, *öffentlickeit und Parlamentarismus* (Stuttgart: Kohlhammer, 1973) is interesting on this score. For some historically minded critical discussions, see Craig Calhoun (ed) *Habermas and the Public Sphere.*
8. For a helpful brief overview of Habermas' study: Peter Dews, "Agreeing What's Right," *London Review of Books* (13 May 1993). More ambitiously: Kenneth Baynes, "Democracy and the *Rechtsstaat*: Habermas' *Faktizität und Geltung,*" in Stephen K. White (ed) *The Cambridge Companion to Habermas* (Cambridge: Cambridge University Press, 1995); James Bohman, "Complexity, Pluralism, and the Constitutional State: On Habermas' *Faktizität und Geltung,*" *Law and Society Review* 28 (1994); Michel Rosenfeld, "Law as Discourse: Bridging the Gap Between Democracy and Rights," *Harvard Law Review* 108 (1995). These thoughtful discussions address many elements of Habermas' complicated argument, which I necessarily leave unexamined here. See also the special issue of *Philosophy and Social Criticism Vol. 20* (1994)

devoted to Habermas' legal theory. See also the collection of collected essays by Rene von Schomberg and Kenneth Baynes (eds), *Discourse and Democracy: Essays on Habermas' Between Facts and Norms* (Albany, NY: SUNY Press, 2002).

9. The translation from Habermas (110) is from Ken Baynes, who offers a fine introductory discussion of its broader complexities, including the question of its relationship to Habermas' conception of communicative rationality. For Habermas, communicative rationality refers to the basic idea that:

Communication is not reducible to getting someone to believe something. For Habermas, it consists (paradigmatically) in reaching an understanding with someone about something, where 'reaching an understanding' draws upon (unavoidable) suppositions constitutive for a weak and fragile (but nonetheless socially effective) form of mutual recognition: To reach an understanding with someone about something implies that one is also prepared to provide warrants for the claims raised ... should they be contested and that one recognizes the other as someone who is free to take a Yes/No position with respect to those claims. Baynes, "Democracy and the *Rechtsstaat*," pp. 203, 208.

Here, I have chosen to bracket many of the fundamental questions concerning the normative roots of democratic politics in Habermas' concept of communicative rationality, not because I consider them unimportant, but because I think that an adequate vision of modern democracy ultimately should offer a convincing institutional model as well as an impressive account of its normative core. In addition, it seems to me that Habermas scholarship too often downgrades "mere" institutional questions: Too often, something of the academic philosophers' traditional snobbishness towards their empirical-minded cousins in political science can be detected here.

10. Habermas has been influenced here by the superb study by Jean Cohen and Andrew Arato, *Civil Society and Political Theory.*

11. Nancy Fraser, "Rethinking the Public Sphere: A Contribution to a Critique of Actually Existing Democracy," in Calhoun, *Habermas and the Public Sphere*, pp. 109–142. In a more general vein: Iris Young, *Justice and the Politics of Difference* (Princeton: Princeton University, 1990). For a discussion of *Between Facts and Norms* that claims that Habermas' recent work remains inadequate on this count: Bohman, "Complexity, Pluralism, and the Constitutional State: On Habermas' *Faktizität und Geltung*," 920–928.

12. Seyla Benhabib, *Critique, Norm, and Utopia: A Study of the Foundations of Critical Theory* (New York: Columbia University, 1986), pp. 309–316. I will discuss Habermas' model of a "fair compromise" in greater detail below.

13. Hannah Arendt, *On Violence* (New York: Harcourt Brace & Jovanovich, 1970), p. 44. Habermas here downplays elements of Arendt's conception of the public sphere that conflict with his emphasis on uncoerced dialogue (Seyla Benhabib, "Models of Public Space: Hannah Arendt, the Liberal Tradition, and Jürgen Habermas," in Calhoun (ed) *Habermas and the Public Sphere*). More generally on Arendt and Habermas, the study by Maurizio Passerin d'Entreves, *The Political Philosophy of Hannah Arendt* (New York: Routledge, 1994).

14. Jerry Mashaw, *Due Process in the Administrative State* (New Haven: Yale University, 1985), cited in Habermas (187).

15. Thus, Habermas argues that radical democracy today must take a "self-limiting" form: Neither administrative bodies nor markets can be immanently organized in accordance with the principles of communicative power.

16. See also: Habermas, "Hannah Arendt's Begriff der Macht," in his *Philosophisch-politische Profile* (Frankfurt: Suhrkamp, 1981).

17. Baynes, "Democracy and the *Rechtsstaat*: Habermas's *Faktizität und Geltung*," p. 216.
18. Nancy Fraser, *Unruly Practices: Power, Discourse and Gender in Contemporary Social Theory* (Minneapolis: University of Minnesota, 1989), pp. 113–190. On the ills of systems theory for Habermas, also: Thomas McCarthy, "Complexity and Democracy: The Seducements of Systems Theory," in his *Ideals and Illusions: On Reconstruction and Deconstruction in Contemporary Critical Theory* (Cambridge: MIT Press, 1991).
19. Fraser, "Rethinking the Public Sphere: A Contribution to the Critique of Actually Existing Democracy," p. 134
20. This comes out most clearly in Habermas' detailed discussion of parliament in Chapter 4. There, he explicitly locates different (moral, ethical, and pragmatic) forms of political argumentation within formal parliamentary bodies and then suggests that each form of deliberation has particular implications for the institutionalization of deliberative legislative bodies. Pragmatic activities (concerned primarily with reaching compromises) justify a system of fair, equal, and secret elections, "[f]or the participation in a fairly organized system of compromise demands the equal representation of all affected." Ethical debate concerning the "authentic self-understanding" and "collective identity" of a particular people requires that "*[a]ll* members of the community . . . take part in discourse." Thus, deliberations of this type, "which are only representative in character because of technical reasons," cannot be organized according to a traditional model of an elected representative as a "stand in" for those represented. Parliamentary debate can only constitute "the organized middle point or focus of a society-wide network of communication." A similar vision of the legislature as a deliberative extension of civil society derives from the nature of moral discourses: "Here representation can only mean that the choice of representatives should function to guarantee the broadest conceivable spectrum" of interpretative perspectives, particularly those of marginal groups. The strict universalizability requirements of moral discourse for Habermas demand that the voices of even those groups which may not even make up a particular community (for example, refugees or resident aliens) need to be heard within the halls of parliament (181–182).
21. Stephen K. White, *The Recent Work of Jürgen Habermas: Reason, Justice, & Modernity* (Cambridge: Cambridge University Press, 1988), pp. 76–77.
22. Fraser, "Rethinking the Public Sphere: A Contribution to the Critique of Actually Existing Democracy," pp. 122–123.
23. For an important recent attempt of this type: Alec Nove, *The Economics of Feasible Socialism* (London: Routledge, 1991). It would be interesting to know Habermas' view of this genre; he ignores it.
24. Jean Cohen, *Class and Civil Society: The Limits of Marxian Critical Theory* (Amherst: University of Massachusetts, 1982).
25. The literature here is vast. For a recent summary: E.N. Suleiman, ed., *Parliaments and Parliamentarians in Democratic Politics* (New York: Holmes and Meier, 1986). For an argument suggesting that even the relatively impressive American Congress exhibits evidence of parliamentary decay: Theodore Lowi, *The End of Liberalism* (New York: Norton, 1979).
26. What I have in mind here is a massive empirical literature that suggests two different points: First, democratic processes continue to be undermined by social and economic inequalities which too often mean that the voices of the socially vulnerable are inadequately represented in the halls of government. A good deal of the political science literature on this topic suggests that this familiar problem has been exacerbated over the course of the last twenty years, as economic inequality has increased and neoliberal governments have dismantled

welfare state-type decision-making devices that often provided real—though inadequate—representation to socially subordinate groups. Second, growing evidence suggests that contemporary liberal democracy may be experiencing a crisis of legitimacy of sorts: Even in the most stable liberal democracies, voting rates are on the decline, and many polls suggest growing unease and dissatisfaction with the workings of parliamentary government. In short, a growing number of citizens are seeking to "disengage" themselves from the workings of representative democracy to an extent arguably unprecedented since World War II. How serious this crisis will turn out to be in the developed capitalist democracies of Western Europe and North America remains to be seen; in newly democratized countries, this crisis is likely to have far more dire consequences.

27. For a discussion based on similar concerns: Jim Bohman, "Complexity, Pluralism, and the Constitutional State: On Habermas' *Faktizität und Geltung.*"

28. Bernhard Peters, *Die Integration moderner Gesellschaften* (Frankfurt: Suhrkamp, 1993), p. 352. For a thoughtful discussion and criticism of this work: Jim Bohman, "Review of Bernhard Peters, *Die Integration moderner Gesellschaften,*" *Constellations* 1 (1995).

29. Peters, *Die Integration moderner Gesellschaften,* p. 329.

30. Peters, *Die Integration moderner Gesellschaften,* p. 329.

31. Peters, *Die Integration moderner Gesellschaften,* p. 344.

32. Peters, *Die Integration moderner Gesellschaften,* p. 351.

33. Peters, *Die Integration moderner Gesellschaften,* p. 345.

34. Peters, *Die Integration moderner Gesellschaften,* p. 341.

35. For an interpretation of Mill and Tocqueville along such lines: Carole Pateman, *Participation and Democratic Theory* (Cambridge: Cambridge University, 1970). On the surface, Habermas' use of Peters leaves him with a two-track model resembling Bruce Ackerman's, for whom "normal" democratic politics is substantially less ambitious in scope than "exceptional" political moments when the liberal democratic polity engages in alterations of its fundamental constitutional structure. But Ackerman is arguably more of a radical democrat than Habermas here; he may not be willing to accept the "realist" insight that elected democratic legislatures, even during the course of normal liberal-democratic politics, should be satisfied with taking on a secondary role vis-à-vis their administrative brethren. Bruce Ackerman, *We the People: Foundations, Vol. I* (Cambridge: Harvard University Press, 1991).

36. Jürgen Habermas, "Zum Begriff der politischen Beteiligung," in his *Kultur und Kritik* (Frankfurt: Suhrkamp, 1973).

37. Ingeborg Maus, *Zur Aufklärung der Demokratietheorie* (Frankfurt: Suhrkamp, 1992). This is not meant to criticize Habermas' normative defense of civil disobedience; it *is* meant to suggest that the empirical implications of its proliferation may be quite different from those he suggested.

38. What exactly, for that matter, is a "crisis" in this context?

39. Baynes, "Democracy and *Rechtsstaat*: Habermas' *Faktizität und Geltung,*" p. 218.

40. There is a similar ambivalence in Habermas' assorted comments about corporatist decision making here. At times, he repeats a traditional left-wing version of the argument (central to *The Structural Transformation of the Public Sphere*) that corporatist decision making represents a potential threat to popular sovereignty; at other junctures, he seems willing to concede the unavoidability of corporatism. What protections are there against its ills? He says that "[t]here are no easy recipes. In the final instance, only a suspicious, mobile, alert, and informed public . . . serves as a check against the emergence of illegitimate power . . ." (532). But what if autonomous processes within civil

society itself have been undermined by forms of corporatism that privilege the powerful and wealthy?

41. Ingeborg Maus, whose work has been heavily influenced by Neumann and who clearly shaped Habermas' discussion of contemporary regulatory and welfare state law in *Between Facts and Norms*, undoubtedly played a positive role in bringing about this modest but praiseworthy shift.

42. See Chapter 7. Habermas' position here also shares some surprising similarities with free market jurisprudence, which claims that the traditional liberal rule of law can only be preserved if competitive capitalism is maintained.

43. The translation here is from Baynes, "Democracy and the *Rechtsstaat*: Habermas' *Faktizität und Geltung*," p. 214. The passage also points out that Habermas sees courts as part of the lawmaking process (see Chapters 5 and 6). I have bracketed this complex issue here for two reasons: (1) Habermas tends to see courts as playing at most a secondary role in this process; (2) it would raise complicated jurisprudential issues that I simply cannot do justice to here.

44. Interestingly, he admits that this suggestion may imply that "my picture of a democratic 'state of siege' directed against the apparatus of the state" has been rendered inappropriate (440). It seems to me that this argument potentially moderates Habermas' (in my view, unduly harsh) criticisms of authors such as Joshua Cohen, who are more willing to accept a far more ambitious democratization of social and political institutions than Habermas tends to (304–308). Joshua Cohen, "Deliberation and Democratic Legitimacy," A. Hamlin and B. Pettit (eds) *The Good Polity* (Oxford: 1989).

45. See also the rather modest reform proposals outlined on p. 533: increased possibilities for the exercise of direct democracy as well as the "constitutionalization" of the mass media by means of a set of legal procedures counteracting asymmetries of social power.

CHAPTER 6

1. Jean L. Cohen, *Regulating Intimacy: A New Legal Paradigm* (Princeton: Princeton University Press, 2004), p. 143.

2. He is wrong, however, to claim that Neumann imported Carl Schmitt's tendentious interpretation of the idea of the generality of law into critical German legal scholarship. In fact, Neumann offered a devastating critique of the Schmittian notion of general law. See Scheuerman, *Between the Norm and the Exception*, pp. 97–156.

3. See also the important work of Ingeborg Maus, *Rechtstheorie und politische Theorie im Indistriekapitalismus*, who has exercised an important influence on Habermas' ideas on the history of regulatory law and the separation of powers.

4. Ronald Dworkin, *Taking Rights Seriously* (Cambridge, USA: Harvard University Press, 1978).

5. Erhard Denninger, *Der gebändigte Leviathan* (Baden-Baden: Nomos, 1990).

6. See especially Hayek's *Constitution of Liberty* (Chicago: University of Chicago Press, 1960).

7. His recent "Tanner Lectures," reprinted in the German editions of *Between Facts and Norms* (549–599) explores this relationship in more detail than can be found in Chapter 9.

8. See Habermas, *Theory of Communicative Action, Vol. II* .

9. Much of this sociological account echoes Neumann's earlier account of the transition from classical to monopoly capitalism, though Neumann is never mentioned by Habermas here.

10. See Cohen's book *Regulation of Intimacy* for an ambitious attempt to build on this insight as part of a Habermasian-feminist legal theory.
11. Thus, he notes that the properly proceduralist legislator might decide to make use of formal, material, or "procedural" modes of regulation (440). The formulation is confusing; "procedural" law is not equivalent to the broader proceduralist paradigm defended in Chapter 9. "Procedural" law refers to proposals—such as Gunther Teubner's—that call for the central legislator to determine a set of basic organizational norms and procedures for specific spheres of regulation. The proceduralist paradigm may opt for "procedural" forms of regulation (438), but it need not do so, and it is by no means conceptually equivalent to them. Nor does the proceduralist model necessarily favor them.
12. Maus, "Perspektiven 'reflexiven Rechts' im Kontext gengenwärtige Deregulierungstendenzen" *Kritische Justiz* 19 (1986), 390–405.
13. Andrew Arato, "Procedural Law and Civil Society: Interpreting the Radical Democratic Paradigm," in *Habermas on Law and Democracy*, p. 28. The most ambitious attempt to creatively defend reflexive law is found in Cohen's *Regulating Intimacy*.
14. Arato, "Procedural Law and Civil Society," p. 27; more generally, see Cohen, *Regulating Intimacy*.
15. Scheuerman, *Liberal Democracy and the Social Acceleration of Time*, pp. 210–226.
16. My comments here are indebted to a thoughtful essay by Erhard Blankenburg, "The Poverty of Evolutionism: A Critique of Teubner's Case for 'Reflexive Law'," *Law and Society Review* 18 (1984), 273–289, who leveled a similar criticism against Teubner's original proposals for "reflexive law."
17. T. H. Marshall, *Citizenship and Social Class* (London: Pluto, 1992).
18. For concrete suggestions along these lines, see Scheuerman, *Liberal Democracy and the Social Acceleration of Time*, pp. 210–227.

CHAPTER 7

1. See Simone Chambers, "Deliberative Democratic Theory" *Annual Review of Political Science 2003* (Washington, D.C.: APSA, 2003); John Dryzek, *Deliberative Democracy and Beyond: Policy, Politics, and Political Science* (New York: Cambridge University Press, 1990).
2. James Bohman, *Public Deliberation: Pluralism, Complexity and Democracy* (Cambridge, USA: MIT Press, 1996).
3. Rainer Forst, "The Rule of Reasons: Three Models of Deliberative Democracy" *Ratio Juris* 14 (2001), 469–487.
4. Seyla Benhabib, "Toward a Deliberative Model of Democratic Legitimacy," in Benhabib (ed) *Democracy and Difference: Contesting the Boundaries of the Political* (Princeton: Princeton University Press, 1996); Bohman, *Public Deliberation*; Emily Hauptmann, "Can Less Be More? Leftist Deliberative Democrats' Critique of Participatory Democracy" *Polity* 33 (2001), 397–421.
5. See Thomas McCarthy, *The Critical Theory of Jürgen Habermas* (Cambridge, USA: MIT Press, 1982); Stephen White, *The Recent Work of Jürgen Habermas: Reason, Justice and Modernity*.
6. Unless otherwise noted, all internal page references come from Habermas' *Between Facts and Norms*.
7. Jürgen Habermas, *The Postnational Constellation* (Cambridge, USA: MIT Press, 2001), p. 111.
8. Habermas, *The Postnational Constellation*, pp. 110–111.

9. Social, economic, and environmental issues—what Habermas describes as "global domestic politics" [Weltinnenpolitik]—would be dealt with by transnational, but not necessarily global, political actors. Habermas suggests that regional blocs such as the European Union should play a decisive role at this transnational level. See Chapter 9.

10. Seyla Benhabib, *The Claims of Culture: Equality and Diversity in the Global Era* (Princeton: Princeton University Press, 2002), p. 147.

11. Dryzek, *Deliberative Democracy and Beyond*, p. 129; also Rainer Schmalz-Bruns, "Deliberativer Supranationalismus; demokratisches Regieren jenseits des Nationalstaats" *Zeitschrift für Internationale Beziehungen* 6 (1999), 184–244.

12. James Bohman, "Globalization of the Public Sphere: Cosmoplitanism, Publicity, and Cultural Pluralism" *Modern Schoolman* LXXV (1998), 101–118; "Citizenship and the Norms of Publicity: Wide Public Reason in Cosmopolitan Societies" *Political Theory* 27 (1999), 176–201.

13. James Bohman, "The Public Spheres of the World Citizen," in *Perpetual Peace: Essays on Kant's Cosmopolitan Ideas*, p. 185; Dryzek, *Deliberative Democracy and Beyond*, p. 129.

14. Iris M. Young, "Modest Reflections on Hegemony and Global Democracy" *Theoria* 103 (2004), 3, 11. Of course, Young has been highly critical of some important features of Habermas' own account of deliberation. This is also true of other authors discussed in this essay. However, I do believe that they all share enough of Habermas' general approach to be fairly described as "Habermasian."

15. Young, "Modest Reflections," 4. Also, Young, *Inclusion and Democracy* (Oxford: Oxford University Press, 2000), pp. 271–275.

16. Young, "Modest Reflections," 8.

17. The influence is reciprocal, since Habermas refers favorably to Held's ideas on occasion. There are, however, normative and programmatic differences between the two approaches. See Chapter 8 for a discussion of the implicit jurisprudence of Held's influential model.

18. Held, "Democracy and Globalization," pp. 22–23.

19. Held, *Democracy and the Global Order*, pp. 239–266.

20. See Habermas, *The Postnational Constellation; The Divided West* (Cambridge, UK: Polity Press, 2006); "A Constitution for Europe?" *New Left Review* 11 (2001), 5–26. For the critique, Adam Lupel, "Regionalism and Globalization: Post-Nation or Extended Nation?" *Polity* 36 (2004), 153–174.

21. He worries that Habermasian critical theory has made too many concessions to liberal constitutionalism (see Dryzek, *Deliberative Democracy and Beyond*, pp. 8–20, 115–16). Dryzek is right to emphasize the many ways in which capitalism potentially restrains global institutional decision making. He is also right to worry that some critical theorists tend to downplay those restraints. However, he seems unduly skeptical of the "radical "reformist" possibility that far-reaching institutional reforms at the global level (for example, a dramatically strengthened U.N.) might threaten the social and economic status quo and thereby contribute to its radical transformation.

22. Dryzek, *Deliberative Democracy and Beyond*, p. 13.

23. Jean L. Cohen, for example, argues that transnational citizenship "involves the exercise of power and not only of influence," and she suggests a relationship of codependence between a vibrant civil society and effective formal channels of political power at the transnational level ("Changing Paradigms of Citizenship and the Exclusiveness of the Demos" *International Sociology* 14 [1999], 263).

24. Dryzek, *Deliberative Democracy and Beyond*, pp. 107–114.

25. Bohman, "International Regimes and Democratic Governance: Political Equality and Influence in Global Institutions" *International Affairs* 75 (1999), p. 88 [my emphasis added].
26. Ingeborg Maus, Vom Nationalstaat zum Globalstaat oder: der Niedergang der Demokratie" in Bachmann and Bohman (eds) *Weltstaat oder Staatenwelt?* (Frankfurt: Suhrkamp, 2002), pp. 226–259.
27. Forst, "Rule of Reasons," p. 374. To be sure, the question of the relationship between the concepts of deliberation and democracy raises profound philosophical questions. Unfortunately, I cannot fully address those questions here. But I think it pivotal that we underscore their mutual dependence: Democratic self-legislation without (rational) deliberation is normatively unattractive and probably impossible; deliberation without democracy (that is, without the approval of those impacted by resulting binding decisions) may produce more or less interesting and insightful epistemic results, but it cannot legitimately claim to justify binding decisions on those affected by them.
28. Benhabib, "Toward a Deliberative Model of Democratic Legitimacy," p. 70.
29. Benhabib, "Toward a Deliberative Model of Democratic Legitimacy," p. 70. For a critical discussion, see Hauptmann. "Can Less Be More?"
30. Benhabib, "Toward a Deliberative Model of Democratic Legitimacy," pp. 73–74.
31. Benhabib, "Toward a Deliberative Model of Democratic Legitimacy," p. 73.
32. To be sure, this argument has something of a straw man quality to it. Defenders of a simple parliamentary model of rule—the obvious target of Benhabib's comments—are few and far between today. In an important critique of Habermas' own formulations of this argument, Ingeborg Maus argues plausibly that this criticism rests on a caricature of the classical theory of popular sovereignty articulated most clearly by the Enlightenment theorists Rousseau and Kant (Maus, *Zur Aufklaerung der Demokratietheorie*; "Liberties and Popular Sovereignty: On Habermas' Reconstruction of the System of Rights" *Cardozo Law Review* 17 [1996], 874–875).
33. Of course, speaking with "one voice" may mean agreeing to disagree (as in the case of liberal abortion laws), or even agreeing to the necessity of relatively complex and even differentiated forms of legal regulation.
34. The present volume should be taken as an intended exception to this tendency. Dryzek's hostility to the resurgence of legal theorizing in critical theory, for example, rests on an overstated contrast between liberalism and radical democracy. Any desirable variant of the latter will also require individual rights, the rule of law, constitutional mechanisms channeling the exercise of political powers, and independent courts.
35. Hauke Brunkhorst, "Globalizing Democracy Without a State: Weak Public, Strong Public, Global Constitutionalism" *Millennium* 31 (2002), 679.
36. Brunkhorst, "Globalizing Democracy," 686.
37. Hauke Brunkhorst, *Solidarity: From Civic Friendship to a Global Legal Community* (Cambridge, USA: MIT Press, 2005), p. 125.
38. Maus, "Liberties and Popular Sovereignty," 875.
39. Robert Fine and Will Smith, "Jürgen Habermas' Theory of Cosmopolitanism" *Constellations* 10 (2003), 476–477.
40. Habermas, *Postnational Constellation*, p. 110 [my emphasis–WES].
41. Habermas, *Postnational Constellation*, p. 110; Fine and Smith, "Habermas' Theory of Cosmopolitanism," 476.
42. E. O. Eriksen and J. Weigard, *Understanding Habermas: Communicating Action and Deliberating Democracy* (New York: Continuum, 2004), p. 251.
43. Habermas, *Postnational Constellation*, p. 111.
44. Fine and Smith, "Habermas' Cosmopolitanism," 477.

CHAPTER 8

1. The literature is vast and constantly growing. See Daniele Archibugi, "Models of International Organization for Perpetual Peace Projects," *Review of International Studies* 78 (1984), 607–621; Archibugi,"Cosmopolitical Democracy" *New Left Review* 4 (2000), 137–151; Archibugi and David Held (eds) *Cosmopolitan Democracy: An Agenda for a New World Order* (Cambridge, UK: Polity Press, 1995); Archibugi, Held, and Martin Koehler (eds) *Re-imagining Political Community: Studies in Cosmopolitan Democracy* (Stanford: Stanford University Press, 1998); David Held, "Democracy, the Nation-State, and the Global System," in Held (ed) *Political Theory Today* (Stanford: Stanford University Press, 1991); Held, "Democracy: From City-States to a Cosmopolitan Democratic Order?" *Political Studies* 40 (1992), 10–39; Held, *Democracy and the Global Order: From the Modern State to Cosmopolitan Governance* (Stanford: Stanford University Press, 1995); Held, "The Changing Contours of Political Community: Rethinking Democracy in the Context of Globalization," in Ian Shapiro and Casiano Hacker-Cordon (eds) *Democracy's Edges* (Cambridge: Cambridge University Press, 2000); Held and Anthony McGrew, "Globalization and the Liberal Democratic State," *Government and Opposition* 28 (1993), 261–285; McGrew, *The Transformation of Democracy? Globalization and Territorial Democracy* (Cambridge: Polity Press, 1997); McGrew, "Realism vs. Cosmopolitanism," *Review of International Studies* 24 (1998), 387–398.
2. The project is interdisciplinary in scope, and a number of other scholars (including David Beetham, Mary Kaldor, Martin Koehler, Andrew Linklater, and Richard Falk) have played important roles in contributing to the theory of cosmopolitan democracy, whose fundamental core has been sketched out most clearly by Archibugi and Held in a number of essays, books, and jointly edited volumes. I should also note that the theory of cosmopolitan democracy has influenced some of Habermas' recent reflections on globalization.
3. Held, "Democracy and Globalization," in *Reimagining Political Community*, p. 22.
4. See especially Richard Bellamy and Dario Castiglione, "Between Cosmopolis and Community: Three Models of Rights and Democracy within the European Union," in *Reimagining Political Community*, pp. 152–178; Tony Coates, "Neither Cosmopolitanism nor Realism," in Barry Holden (ed), *Global Democracy: Key Debates* (London: Routledge, 2000), 87–102; Robert Dahl, "Can International Organizations Be Democratic? A Skeptic's View," in *Democracy's Edges*, pp. 19–36; Christoph Görg and Joachim Hirsch, "Is International Democracy Possible?" *Review of International Political Economy* 5 (1998), 585–616; Will Kymlicka, "Citizenship in an Era of Globalization: Commentary on Held," in *Democracy's Edges*, pp. 112–126; Ingeborg Maus, "From Nation-State to Global State or the Decline of Democracy" *Constellations* 13 (2006), 465–484. Danilio Zolo, *Cosmopolis: Prospects for World Community* (Cambridge: Polity Press, 1997).
5. Bellamy and Castiglione, "Between Cosmopolis and Community"; Will Kymlicka, "Citizenship in an Era of Globalization: A Commentary on Held," in Shapiro and Hacker-Cordon (eds), *Democracy's Edges*, pp. 112–126 Dailio Zolo, *Cosmopolis: Prospects for World Community* (Cambridge: Polity Press, 1997). See also the essays collected in Archibugi (ed) *Debating Cosmopolitics* (New York: Verso, 2003). Archibugi responds to many critics there.
6. Held, *Democracy and the Global Order*, pp. 221–238; "Changing Contours of Political Community," pp. 106–107.
7. See Archibugi, "From the United Nations to Cosmopolitan Democracy," in *Cosmopolitan Democracy*, pp. 132–135; "Principles of Cosmopolitan

Democracy," in *Reimagining Political Community*, p. 215. Most participants in the ongoing debate on transnational democracy share similar reservations about world government.

8. In a similar vein, Ingeborg Maus endorses neo-Kantian models of international relations, but she worries that contemporary Kantian models of global governance suffer from substantial conceptual and political confusion (see "Volkssouveranitaet und das Prinzip der Nichtintervention in der Friedensphilosophie Immanuel Kant," in Hauke Brunkhorst (ed) *Einmischung Erwünscht? Menschenrechte und Bewaffnete Intervention* [Frankfurt: Suhrkamp, 1998]). Like Maus, I am worried that core features of the idea of the "rule of law" are obscured by Held.

9. Held, "Democracy and Globalization," p. 12. In this account, globalization is a multidimensional (economic, environmental, cultural, legal, and political) phenomenon (see David Held, McGrew, David Goldblatt, and Jonathan Perraton, *Global Transformations* [Stanford: Stanford University Press, 1999]).

10. Held, "Democracy and Globalization," p. 22; Archibugi, "Principles of Cosmopolitan Democracy" in *Reimagining Political Community*, pp. 205–206.

11. Held, "Democracy and Globalization," pp. 22–23. Much of Held's early work was devoted to Frankfurt-based critical theory, and its influence can be detected here in many ways.

12. Archibugi, "Principles of Cosmopolitan Democracy," p. 215.

13. Archibugi, "Principles of Cosmopolitan Democracy," p. 216.

14. Many other observers are less sanguine about the relationship between regional and global law.

15. Kant was already able to observe that "[t]he peoples of the earth have thus entered in varying degrees into a universal community, and it has developed to the point where a violation of rights in *one* part of the world is felt *everywhere*. The idea of a cosmopolitan right is therefore not fantastic and overstrained; it is a necessary complement to the unwritten code of political and international right, transforming it into a universal code of humanity" (see Kant, "Perpetual Peace" [1796], in Hans Reiss (ed) *Kant's Political Writings* [Cambridge: Cambridge University Press, 1970], pp. 105–106).

16. Held, *Democracy and the Global Order*, p. 228.

17. On Kant's relevance for contemporary models of global governance, see the important essays collected in Matthias Lutz-Bachmann and Jim Bohman (eds) *Perpetual Peace: Essays on Kant's Cosmopolitan Ideal* (Cambridge, USA: MIT Press, 1997).

18. Held, *Democracy and the Global Order*, p. 150.

19. Held, *Democracy and the Global Order*, p. 147.

20. Held, *Democracy and the Global Order*, pp. 153, 163.

21. Held, *Democracy and the Global Order*, p. 166.

22. Held, *Democracy and the Global Order*, p. 191.

23. Held, *Democracy and the Global Order*, pp. 190–201.

24. Held, *Democracy and the Global Order*, pp. 200–201.

25. Held, *Democracy and the Global Order*, p. 205.

26. Held, *Democracy and the Global Order*, p. 216.

27. Held, *Democracy and the Global Order*, p. 205.

28. Held, *Democracy and the Global Order*, p. 106.

29. Held, *Democracy and Global Order*, p. 272.

30. Held, *Democracy and Global Order*, pp. 255, 274–275. See also Michael Zürn, *Regieren jenseits des Nationalstaates* (Frankfurt: Suhrkamp,1998), p. 345.

31. Held, *Democracy and Global Order*, pp. 200, 272.

32. Held, *Democracy and Global Order*, p. 272; Archibugi, "From the United Nations to Cosmopolitan Democracy," pp. 146–148; Hans Kelsen, *Peace Through Law* (Chapel Hill: University of North Carolina Press), 1944.
33. Hans Kelsen, "Foundations of Democracy," *Ethics* LXVI (1955), 1–103.
34. See Kelsen's famous discussion in *Peace Through Law*, pp. 71–123.
35. Kelsen, *Peace Through Law*, p. viii.
36. Kelsen, *Peace Through Law*, p. ix.
37. Norberto Bobbio, *The Future of Democracy* (Minneapolis: University of Minnesota Press, 1987), pp. 138–156; Franz L. Neumann, *The Rule of Law: Political Theory and Legal System in Modern Society*.
38. Neumann, "The Concept of Political Freedom," in *Rule of Law Under Siege*, p. 198.
39. Neumann, "The Concept of Political Freedom," p. 200.
40. Neumann, "The Concept of Political Freedom," pp. 203–204.
41. Held, *Democracy and the Global Order*, p. 193.
42. Held, *Democracy and the Global Order*, pp. 241–244.
43. Raz, *The Authority of Law*, pp. 210–229; William E. Scheuerman, "The Rule of Law and the Welfare State: Towards a New Synthesis," *Politics and Society* 22 (1994), pp. 195–213.
44. Held, *Democracy and the Global Order*, p. 275.
45. For a provocative critical discussion of this trend, see Maus, *Zur Aufklärung der Demokratie Theorie*, pp. 308–336.
46. Interestingly, Dworkin is only mentioned in passing here, for example, by Held, *Democracy and Global Order*, pp. 202, 217. For the most developed version of Dworkin's jurisprudence, see *Law's Empire* (Cambridge, USA: Harvard University Press, 1986).
47. Held, *Democracy and the Global Order*, pp. 205, 270–272; Archibugi, "From the United Nations to Cosmopolitan Democracy," pp. 143–148.
48. Held speculates that judicial bodies might consist of people "statistically representative of key social categories" rather than existing judicial personnel (Held, *Democracy and Global Order*, p. 206). This proposal also raises fundamental questions for the ideal of the rule of law, to the extent that distinct modes of legal reasoning typically generated by a specialized legal training and culture have long been associated with it. One might argue that this proposal minimizes some of the dangers of "judicial imperialism" that I hope to highlight here. However, discretionary rule exercised by members of statistically representative social groups may deserve to be described as democratic, but it cannot be considered consistent with the notion of the rule of law.
49. This, of course, is not the same thing as claiming that some measure of judicial discretion and the principle of the rule of law are mutually exclusive. Nor, for that matter, is a simultaneous commitment to constitutionally enshrined rights and the rule of law. But the relationship between these two features of liberal jurisprudence is more complex than Archibugi and Held seem to grasp.
50. Held, *Democracy and Global Order*, p. 279.
51. Held, "Democracy and the New International Order," in *Cosmopolitan Democracy*, pp. 115–116. This claim also seems questionable in light of the ambitious social-democratic, feminist, and environmental character of the rights they defend.
52. For a useful defense, see Jack Donnelly, *Universal Human Rights in Theory and Practice* (Ithaca: Cornell University Press, 1989), who provides some helpful remarks on the complex legal status of universal human rights (pp. 13–16).
53. Danilio Zolo, "The Lords of Peace: From the Holy Alliance to the New International Criminal Tribunals," in *Global Democracy*, pp. 79–80.
54. Held, *Democracy and Global Order*, p. 205.

55. Nearly twenty years ago, the human rights advocate Philip Alston perceptively warned of the dangers of proclaiming ambitious and poorly defined new rights beyond the basic civil, political, and social and economic rights based in the two International Human Rights Covenants, pointing out that many of the proposed new rights were typically characterized by enormous vagueness (for example, rights "to coexistence with nature," "not to be killed in war," or "to be free to experiment with alternative ways of life"). As Alston correctly observed, "a proliferation of new rights would be more likely to contribute to a serious devaluation of the human rights currency than to significantly enrich the overall coverage provided by existing rights" (Alston, "Conjuring Up New Human Rights: A Proposal for Quality Control" *American Journal of International Law* 78 [1984], p. 614). If I am not mistaken, Alston's anxieties take on special significance for the defenders of cosmopolitan democracy, as many of the proposed rights at the core of "cosmopolitan democratic law" seem remarkably reminiscent of those criticized by Alston.
56. Frederick Whelan, "Prologue: Democratic Theory and the Boundary Problem," in J. Roland Pennock and John W. Chapman (eds) *Liberal Democracy* (New York: New York University Press, 1983), pp. 18–19.
57. Michael Saward, "A Critique of Held," in *Global Democracy: Key Debates*, pp. 32–46, offers an enlightening discussion of this weakness of cosmopolitan democracy.
58. Whelan, "Prologue: Democratic Theory and the Boundary Problem," p. 19.
59. James Rosenau, "Governance and Democracy in a Globalizing World," in *Reimagining Political Community*, p. 31.
60. Held, *Democracy and the Global Order*, p. 236; "Democracy and the New International Order," pp. 113–114.
61. Held tends to refer in this context to a recent article on subsidiarity within the European Union by Karlheinz Neunreither in order to underscore the soundness of the tests of extensiveness, intensity, and comparative efficiency. But Neunreither's article in fact underlines the inadequacies of those tests within the European Union as devices for generating an adequate conception of subsidiarity, pointing out that they raise difficult questions for those committed to the "uniform enforcement of EC law" (Neunreither, "Subsidiarity as a Guiding Principle for European Community Activities," *Government and Opposition* 28 [1993], 217).
62. Richard Falk has thought hard about many of these possible reforms (*On Humane Governance* [University Park: Penn State Press, 1995]).
63. Schmitter, "The Future of Democracy: A Matter of Scale?" *Social Research* 66 (1999), 933–958.
64. Kelsen, *Peace Through Law*, p. ix.

CHAPTER 9

1. Jürgen Habermas, *Time of Transitions*, (ed and trans) Ciaran Cronin and Max Pensky (Cambridge, UK: Polity Press, 2006), p. 95.
2. Habermas, *Time of Transitions*, p. 96.
3. Habermas, *Time of Transitions*, p. 90.
4. See Maus, "From Nation-State to Global State, or the Decline of Democracy."
5. For a discussion of this issue, see Chapter 7.
6. Jürgen Habermas, *The Divided West*, (ed and trans) Ciaran Cronin (Cambridge, UK: Polity Press, 2006). Internal page references in this chapter refer to this text.
7. I use the term *global governance* in the sense introduced by James N. Rosenau, "Governance, Order, and Change in World Politics," in James N. Rosenau

and Ernst Otto-Czempiel (eds) *Governance Without Government: Order and Change in World Politics* (Cambridge, UK: Cambridge University Press, 1992), pp. 1–29.

8. See Jürgen Habermas, "Kant's Idea of Perpetual Peace, with the Benefit of Two Hundred Years' Hindsight," in *Perpetual Peace: Essays on Kant's Cosmopolitan Idea*, pp. 113–154.

9. Robert Dahl has updated these anxieties in his thoughtful "Can International Organizations be Democratic? A Skeptic's View," in *Democracy's Edges*, pp. 19–36.

10. Hauke Brunkhorst, *Solidarity: From Civic Friendship to Global Legal Community*.

11. His tendency to see the EU as a positive model for other supranational organizations generates problems. See the excellent essay by Adam Lupel, "Regionalism and Globalization: Post-Nation or Extended Nation?" *Polity* 36 (2004), 153–174.

12. I do not know what else to call a state that regularly disregards binding international and domestic prohibitions on torture, practices indefinite detention, and establishes secret offshore interrogation (and, probably, torture) camps.

13. Recall Neumann's argument that the dissolution of state sovereignty tended to go hand-in-hand with the disintegration of the rule of law (*Behemoth: The Structure and Practice of National Socialism*).

14. In his comments on global terrorism, a similar economism tends to creep in. See Michel Rosenfeld, "Habermas' Call for Cosmopolitan Constitutional Patriotism in an Age of Global Terror" *Constellations* 14 (2007), 159–181.

15. Think, for example, about recent global debates about international intervention in the former Yugoslavia, Rwanda, or Darfur.

16. See also Habermas, *Postnational Constellation*, pp. 89–112; *Time of Transitions*, pp. 73–109.

17. For a sample of the huge debate, see the essays collected in Michael Th. Greven and Louis W. Pauly (eds) *Democracy Beyond the Nation-State: The European Dilemma and the Emerging Global Order* (Lanham, MD: Rowman & Littlefield, 2000).

18. Habermas, *Time of Transitions*, p. 87.

19. Andrei Markovits, *Uncouth Nation: Why Europe Dislikes America* (Princeton, NJ: Princeton University Press, 2006).

20. See, for example, the *New Left Review* in recent years, where Schmitt often is cited favorably in critical discussions of U.S. foreign policy.

21. Glyn Morgan, *The Idea of a European Superstate: Public Justification and European Integration* (Princeton, NJ: Princeton University Press, 2005).

22. Realists like Morgenthau and Reinhold Niebuhr are vastly more nuanced thinkers than Habermas—or most present-day cosmopolitans—prefer to concede. See my *Hans J. Morgenthau: Realism and the Struggle for World Peace* (Cambridge, UK: Polity Press, forthcoming 2009).

23. Hans J. Morgenthau, *Politics Among Nations: The Struggle for Power and Peace* (New York: Alfred Knopf, 1954, 2nd ed.), pp. 93–154.

24. For a defense of this position, see Otfried Höffe, *Demokratie im Zeitalter der Globalisierung* (Munich: Beck, 1999).

25. Jürgen Habermas, "A Political Constitution for the Pluralist World Society?" (paper presented at University of Chicago Political Theory Workshop, October 10, 2005) .

26. To his credit, Habermas himself generally opposes this extreme view of what David Held and others have correctly criticized as the "hyper-globalization thesis" (Held, Anthony McGraw, David Goldblatt, and Jonathan Perraton, *Global Transformations: Politics, Economics, and Culture*).

Bibliography

Allen, Francis A. *The Habits of Legality: Criminal Justice and the Rule of Law* (New York: Oxford University Press, 1996).

Alston, Philip. "Conjuring Up New Human Rights: A Proposal for Quality Control" *American Journal of International Law* 78 (1984), 607–621.

———(ed). *The United Nations and Human Rights* (Oxford: Clarendon, 1992).

———. "Labor Rights Provisions in U.S. Trade Law: 'Aggressive Unilateralism'" *Human Rights Quarterly* 15 (1993), 1–35.

Arato, Andrew. "Procedural Law and Civil Society: Interpreting the Radical Democratic Paradigm" in Arato and Rosenfeld, Michel (eds) *Habermas on Law and Democracy* (Berkeley: University of California Press, 1998), 26–36.

Archibugi, Daniele. "Models of International Organization for Perpetual Peace Projects" *Review of International Studies* 78 (1984), 607–621.

———. "Cosmopolitical Democracy" *New Left Review* 4 (2000), 137–151.

———, and Held, David (eds). *Cosmopolitan Democracy: An Agenda for a New World Order* (Cambridge, UK: Polity Press, 1995).

———, and Held, David, and Koehler, Martin (eds). *Re-imagining Political Community: Studies in Cosmopolitan Democracy* (Stanford: Stanford University Press, 1998).

Arendt, Hannah. *On Violence* (New York: Harcourt Brace & Jovanovich, 1970).

Arthurs, Harry. "Labour Law without the State" *University of Toronto Law Journal* 46 (1996), 1–45.

———. "Private Ordering and Workers' Rights in the Global Economy: Corporate Codes of Conduct as a Regime of Labour Market Regulation" unpublished manuscript, York University (1999).

Barber, Benjamin. *Jihad vs. McWorld: How Globalism and Tribalism are Reshaping the World* (New York: Ballantine Books, 1996).

Bartholemew, Amy (ed). *Empire's Law: The American Imperial Project and the "War to Remake the World"* (London: Pluto, 2006).

Bast, Jürgen. *Totalitärer Pluralismus* (Tübingen: Mohr, 1999).

Bauman, Zygmunt. *Globalization: The Human Consequences* (Cambridge, UK: Polity, 1998).

Baynes, Kenneth. "Democracy and the *Rechtsstaat*: Habermas' *Faktizität und Geltung*" in Stephen K. White (ed) *The Cambridge Companion to Habermas* (Cambridge: Cambridge University Press, 1995), pp. 201–232.

Bellamy, Richard, and Castiglione, Dario. "Between Cosmopolis and Community: Three Models of Rights and Democracy within the European Union" in Daniele Archibugi, David Held, Martin Koehler (eds) *Reimagining Political Community*, pp. 152–178.

Benhabib, Seyla. *Critique, Norm, and Utopia: A Study of the Foundations of Critical Theory* (New York: Columbia University, 1986).

———. "In the Shadow of Aristotle and Hegel: Communicative Ethics and Current Controversies in Practical Philosophy" *The Philosophical Forum* 21 (1989–1990).

———. "Toward a Deliberative Model of Democratic Legitimacy" in Seyla Benhabib (ed) *Democracy and Difference: Contesting the Boundaries of the Political* (Princeton: Princeton University Press, 1996), pp. 67–94.

———. *The Claims of Culture: Equality and Diversity in the Global Era* (Princeton: Princeton University Press, 2002).

Blankenburg, Erhard. "The Poverty of Evolutionism: A Critique of Teubner's Case for 'Reflexive Law'" *Law and Society Review* 18 (1984), 273–290.

Bobbio, Norberto. *The Future of Democracy* (Minneapolis: University of Minnesota Press, 1987).

Bohman, James. "Complexity, Pluralism, and the Constitutional State: On Habermas' *Faktizität und Geltung*" *Law and Society Review* 28 (1994), 897–930.

———. *Public Deliberation: Pluralism, Complexity and Democracy* (Cambridge, USA: MIT Press, 1996).

———. "Globalization of the Public Sphere: Cosmopolitanism, Publicity, and Cultural Pluralism" *Modern Schoolman* LXXV (1998), 101–118.

———. "Citizenship and the Norms of Publicity: Wide Public Reason in Cosmopolitan Societies" *Political Theory* 27 (1999), 176–201.

———. "International Regimes and Democratic Governance: Political Equality and Influence in Global Institutions" *International Affairs* 75 (1999), 499–513.

Braithwaite, John, and Drahos, Peter. *Global Business Regulation* (Cambridge, U.K.: Cambridge University Press, 2000).

Bratton, William, McCahery, Joseph, and Picciotto, Sol (eds). *International Regulatory Competition and Coordination* (Oxford: Clarendon, 1996).

Brunkhorst, Hauke. "Globalizing Democracy Without a State: Weak Public, Strong Public, Global Constitutionalism" *Millennium* 31 (2002), 675–690.

———. *Solidarity: From Civic Friendship to a Global Legal Community* (Cambridge MIT Press, 2005).

Buchstein, Hubertus. "A Heroic Reconciliation of Freedom and Power: On the Tensions Between Democracy and Social Theory in the Late Work of Franz L. Neumann" *Constellations* 10 (2003), 228–240.

Calhoun, Craig (ed). *Habermas and the Public Sphere* (Cambridge, USA: MIT Press, 1992).

Carbonneau, Thomas (ed). *Lex Mercatoria and Arbitration* (Dobbs Ferry, NY: Transnational Juris Publications, 1990).

Cassese, Antonio. *International Law in a Divided World* (Oxford: Clarendon,1986).

Chambers, Simone. "Deliberative Democratic Theory" *Annual Review of Political Science 2003* (Washington, D.C.: APSA, 2003), 307–326.

Charnovitz, Steve. "Fair Labour Standards and International Trade" *Journal of World Trade Law* 20 (1986), 61–78.

———. "The Influence of International Labour Standards on the World Trading Regime" *International Labour Review* 126 (1987), 565–584.

Coates, Tony. "Neither Cosmopolitanism nor Realism" in Barry Holden (ed) *Global Democracy: Key Debates* (London: Routledge, 2000), pp. 87–102.

Cohen, Jean L. *Class and Civil Society: The Limits of Marxian Critical Theory* (Amherst: University of Massachusetts, 1982).

———. "Changing Paradigms of Citizenship and the Exclusiveness of the Demos" *International Sociology* 14 (1999), 245–268.

———. *Regulating Intimacy: A New Legal Paradigm* (Princeton: Princeton University Press, 2004).

———. "Whose Sovereignty? Empire vs. International Law" *Ethics & International Law* 18 (2004), 1–24.

————, and Arato, Andrew. *Civil Society and Political Theory* (Cambridge: MIT Press, 1997).

Cohen, Joshua. "Deliberation and Democratic Legitimacy" in A. Hamlin and B. Pettit (eds) *The Good Polity* (Oxford: 1989).

Collingsworth, Terry, Goold, W., and Harvey, J. "Time for a Global New Deal" *Foreign Affairs* 73 (1994), 8–14.

Compa, Lance, and Diamond, Stephen (eds). *Human Rights, Labor Rights, and International Trade* (Philadelphia: University of Pennsylvania Press, 1996).

Compa, Lance, and Hinchliffe-Darricarrere, T. "Enforcing Labor Rights Through Corporate Codes of Conduct" *Columbia Journal of Transnational Law* 33 (1995), 663–690.

Cotterell, Roger. *Law's Community: Legal Thought in Social Theory* (Oxford: Oxford University Press, 1997).

Cutler, Claire. "Global Capitalism and Liberal Myths: Dispute Settlement in Private International Trade Relations" *Millennium: Journal of International Studies* 24 (1995), 377–397.

————. "Public Meets Private: The International Unification and Harmonization of Private International Trade Law," *Global Society* 13 (1999), 25–48.

————. "Globalization, The Rule of Law, and the Modern Law Merchant: Medieval or Late Capitalist Associations?" *Constellations* 8 (2001), 480–502.

Dahl, Robert. "Can International Organizations Be Democratic? A Skeptic's View" in Ian Shapiro and Casiano Hacker-Cordon (eds), *Democracy's Edges*, pp. 19–36.

Dallmayr, Fred. "Hermeneutics and the Rule of Law" in Gregory Leyh (ed) *Legal Hermeneutics: History, Theory, and Practice* (Berkeley: University of California Press, 1992).

Denninger, Erhard. *Der gebändigte Leviathan* (Baden-Baden: Nomos, 1990).

Destler, I. M. *American Trade Politics*, 2nd ed. (New York; Twentieth Century Fund, 1992).

Dews, Peter. "Agreeing What's Right" *London Review of Books* (13 May 1993).

Donnelly, Jack. *Universal Human Rights in Theory and Practice* (Ithaca: Cornell University Press, 1989).

Dorman, P. "Worker Rights and International Trade: A Case for Intervention" *Review of Radical Political Economics* 20 (1988), 241–246.

Dryzek, John. *Deliberative Democracy and Beyond: Policy, Politics, and Political Science* (New York: Cambridge University Press, 1990).

Dworkin, Ronald. *Taking Rights Seriously* (Cambridge, USA: Harvard University Press, 1978).

————. *Law's Empire* (Cambridge, USA: Harvard University Press, 1986).

Edgren, G. "Fair Labour Standards and Liberalisation" *International Labour Review* 118 (1979), 523–536.

Eriksen, E. O., and Weigard, J. *Understanding Habermas: Communicating Action and Deliberating Democracy* (New York: Continuum, 2004).

Falk, Richard. *On Humane Governance* (University Park: Penn State Press, 1995).

Fine, Robert, and Smith, Will. "Jürgen Habermas' Theory of Cosmopolitanism" *Constellations* 10 (2003), 476–477.

Forst, Rainer. "The Rule of Reasons: Three Models of Deliberative Democracy" *Ratio Juris* 14 (2001), 469–487.

Franck, Thomas. *Political Questions/Judicial Answers: Does the Rule of Law Apply to Foreign Affairs?* (Princeton: Princeton University Press, 1992).

Fraser, Nancy. *Unruly Practices: Power, Discourse and Gender in Contemporary Social Theory* (Minneapolis: University of Minnesota, 1989).

————. "Rethinking the Public Sphere: A Contribution to a Critique of Actually Existing Democracy" in Craig Calhoun (ed) *Habermas and the Public Sphere*, pp. 109–142.

Fuller, Lon. *The Morality of Law* (New Haven: Yale University Press, 1964).

Gilpin, Robert. *The Political Economy of International Relations* (Princeton: Princeton University Press, 1987).

Görg, Christoph, and Hirsch, Joachim. "Is International Democracy Possible?" *Review of International Political Economy* 5 (1998), 585–616.

Gold, Joseph. "Strengthening the Soft International Law of Exchange Arrangements" *American Journal of International Law* 77 (1983), 443–489.

Golub, Stephen S. "Are International Labor Standards Needed to Prevent Social Dumping?" *Finance and Development* 34 (1997), 20–23.

Goode, Roy. *Commercial Law in the Next Millennium* (London: Sweet & Maxwell, 1998).

Gorz, Andre. *Critique of Economic Rationality* (New York: Verso, 1989).

Gowan, Peter. *The Global Gamble: Washington's Bid for Global Dominance* (New York: Verso, 1999).

Greven, Michael Th., and Pauly, Louis W. (eds). *Democracy Beyond the Nation-State: The European Dilemma and the Emerging Global Order* (Lanham, MD: Rowman & Littlefield, 2000).

Gross, Raphael. *Carl Schmitt und die Juden. Eine deutsche Rechtslehre* (Frankfurt: Suhrkamp, 2000).

Habermas, Jürgen. *The Structural Transformation of the Public Sphere* (Cambridge MIT Press, 1989)[1962].

———. *Legitimation Crisis* (Boston: Beacon, 1975).

———. "Überlegungen zum Evolutionaren Stellenwert des Modernen Rechts" in *Rekonstruktion des Historischen Materialismus* (Frankfurt: Suhrkamp, 1976).

———. "Zum Begriff der politischen Beteiligung" in Jürgen Habermas *Kultur and Kritik: Verstreute Aufsätze* (Frankfurt: Suhrkamp, 1977).

———. *Communication and the Evolution of Society* (Boston: Beacon Press, 1979).

———. "Hannah Arendt Begriff der Macht" in Habermas *Philosophisch-politische Profile* (Frankfurt: Suhrkamp, 1981).

———. *Theory of Communicative Action, Vols. I-II* (Boston: Beacon Press, 1981).

———. "The Tanner Lectures" in S. McMurrin (ed) *The Tanner Lectures on Human Values, VIII* (Salt Lake City: University of Utah, 1988).

———. "What does Socialism Mean Today? The Rectifying Revolution and the Need for New Thinking on the Left" *New Left Review* 183 (1990), 3–21.

———. "Further Reflections on the Public Sphere" in Craig Calhoun (ed) *Habermas and the Public Sphere* (Cambridge, USA: MIT Press, 1992), pp. 421–461.

———. *Between Facts and Norms: Towards a Discourse Theory of Law and Democracy* (Cambridge, USA: MIT Press, 1996) [1992].

———. "Kant's Idea of Perpetual Peace, with the Benefit of Two Hundred Years' Hindsight" in Matthias Lutz-Bachmann and James Bohman (eds) *Perpetual Peace: Essays on Kant's Cosmopolitan Idea* (Cambridge: MIT Press, 1997), pp. 113–154.

———. *The Postnational Constellation* (Cambridge, USA: MIT Press, 2001).

———. *The Divided West* (Cambridge, UK: Polity Press, 2006).

———. *Time of Transitions* (Cambridge, UK: Polity Press, 2006).

Hagen, Katherine. "Fundamentals of Labor Issues and NAFTA" *University of California at Davis Law Review* 27 (1994), 917–936.

Hansson, Goete. *Social Clauses and International Trade* (New York: St. Martin's, 1983).

Hauptmann, Emily. "Can Less Be More? Leftist Deliberative Democrats' Critique of Participatory Democracy" *Polity* 33 (2001), 397–421.

Hayek, Friedrich. *The Road to Serfdom* (Chicago: University of Chicago, 1944).

———. *Constitution of Liberty* (Chicago: University of Chicago Press, 1960).

————. *Law, Legislation, and Liberty, Vol. I-III* (London: Routledge & Kegan Paul, 1973).

Harvey, David. *The Condition of Postmodernity* (Oxford: Blackwell, 1990).

————. *Justice, Nature & the Geography of Difference* (Oxford: Blackwell, 1996).

Held, David. "Democracy, the Nation-State, and the Global System" in David Held (ed) *Political Theory Today* (Stanford: Stanford University Press, 1991).

————. "Democracy: From City-States to a Cosmopolitan Democratic Order?" *Political Studies* 40 (1992), 10–39.

————. *Democracy and the Global Order: From the Modern State to Cosmopolitan Governance* (Stanford: Stanford University Press, 1995).

————. "The Changing Contours of Political Community: Rethinking Democracy in the Context of Globalization" in Ian Shapiro and Casiano Hacker-Cordon (eds) *Democracy's Edges*, pp. 84–111.

————, and McGrew, Anthony. "Globalization and the Liberal Democratic State" *Government and Opposition* 28 (1993), 261–285.

————, and McGrew, Anthony, Goldblatt, David, and Perraton, Jonathan. *Global Transformations: Politics, Economics, and Culture* (Stanford: Stanford University Press, 1999).

Hirsch, Joachim. *Der nationale Wettbewerbsstaat. Staat, Demokratie und Politik im globalen Kapitalismus* (Berlin: Edition ID-Archiv, 1996).

Hirst, Paul, and Thompson, Graham. *Globalization in Question* (Cambridge: Polity, 1996).

Holden, Barry (ed). *Global Democracy: Key Debates* (London: Routledge, 2000).

International Labor Organization Working Party on the Social Dimensions of the Liberalization of International Trade Report (1998). Online. Accessed July 20, 2007. Available: www.ilo.org/public/english/20gb/docs/gb273/sdl-l.htm#

Iser, Matthias, and Strecker, David (eds). *Kritische Theorie der Politik—Eine Bilanz* (Baden-Baden: Nomos, 2003).

Jäger, Wolfgang. *Öffentlickeit und Parlamentarismus* (Stuttgart: Kohlhammer, 1973).

Kant, Immanuel. *Kant's Political Writings* (Cambridge: Cambridge University Press, 1970).

Kenen, Peter B. (ed). *Managing the World Economy: Fifty Years After Bretton Woods* (Washington, D.C.: Institute for International Economics, 1994).

Klare, Karl. "Judicial Deradicalization of the Wagner Act and the Origins of Modern Legal Consciousness, 1937–41" *University of Minnesota Law Review* 62 (1978).

Kline, Carol (ed). *International Regulation: New Rules for a Changing World Order* (San Francisco: Institute for Contemporary Studies, 1988).

Koskienniemi, Martti. *The Gentle Civilizer of Nations: The Rise and Fall of International Law 1870–1960* (Cambridge, UK: Cambridge University Press, 2001).

Kymlicka, Will. "Citizenship in an Era of Globalization: Commentary on Held" in Ian Shapiro and Casiano Hacker-Cordon (eds) *Democracy's Edges*, pp. 112–126.

Jay, Martin. *The Dialectical Imagination* (Berkeley: University of California, 1973).

Jackson, John H. *The World Trading System: Law and Policy of International Economic Relations* (Cambridge, MA: MIT Press, 1999).

James, Harold. *International Monetary Cooperation Since Bretton Woods* (Washington, D.C.: International Monetary Fund, 1996).

Jayasuriya, Kanishka (ed). *Law, Capitalism and Power in Asia: The Rule of Law and Legal Institutions* (London & New York: Routledge, 1999).

Kelly, Duncan. *The State of the Political: Conceptions of Politics and the State in the Thought of Max Weber, Carl Schmitt, and Franz Neumann* (Oxford: Oxford University Press, 2003).

Kelsen, Hans. *Peace Through Law* (Chapel Hill: University of North Carolina Press, 1944).

———. "Foundations of Democracy" *Ethics* LXVI (1955), 1–103.

Kennedy, David. "Turning to Market Democracy: A Tale of Two Architectures" *Harvard International Law Journal* 32 (1991).

Leary, Virginia. "The WTO and the Social Clause: Post-Singapore" *European Journal of International Law* 8 (1997), 118–122.

Lee, Eddy. "Globalization and Labor Standards: A Review of the Issues" *International Labour Review* 136 (1997), 173–191.

Lillich, R., and Brower, C. (eds). *International Arbitration in the 21ˢᵗ Century: Towards Judicialization and Uniformity?* (Irvington: Transnational Publishers, 1994).

Lowi, Theodore. *The End of Liberalism* (New York: Norton, 1979).

———. "The Welfare State, The New Regulation, and the Rule of Law" in A. Hutchinson and P. Monahan (eds) *The Rule of Law: Ideal or Ideology?* (Toronto: Carswell, 1987).

Adam Lupel. "Regionalism and Globalization: Post-Nation or Extended Nation?" *Polity* 36 (2004), 153–174.

Lutz-Bachmann, Matthias, and Bohman, Jim (eds). *Perpetual Peace: Essays on Kant's Cosmopolitan Ideal* (Cambridge, USA: MIT Press, 1997).

McCarthy, Thomas. *The Critical Theory of Jürgen Habermas* (Cambridge, USA: MIT Press, 1982).

———. *Ideals and Illusions: On Reconstruction and Deconstruction in Contemporary Critical Theory* (Cambridge: MIT Press, 1991).

McGrew, Anthony. *The Transformation of Democracy? Globalization and Territorial Democracy* (Cambridge: Polity Press, 1997).

———. "Realism vs. Cosmopolitanism" *Review of International Studies* 24 (1998), 387–398.

Mandel, H. "In Pursuit of the Missing Link: International Worker Rights" *Columbia Journal of Transnational Law* 27 (1989), 465–481.

Marshall, T. H. *Citizenship and Social Class* (London: Pluto, 1992).

Mason, Tim. *Nazism, Fascism and the Working Classes* (Cambridge: Cambridge University Press, 1990).

Maus, Ingeborg. *Bürgerliche Rechtstheorie und Fascismus. Zur sozialen Funktion and aktuellen Wirkung der Theorie Carl Schmitts* (Munich: Wilhelm Fink, 1976).

———. "Perspektiven 'reflexiven Rechts' im Kontext gengenwärtige Deregulierungstendenzen" *Kritische Justiz* 19 (1986), 390–405.

———. *Zur Aufklärung der Demokratietheorie* (Frankfurt: Suhrkamp, 1992).

———. "Liberties and Popular Sovereignty: On Habermas' Reconstruction of the System of Rights" *Cardozo Law Review* 17 (1996), 825–882.

———. "Volkssouveranität und das Prinzip der Nichtintervention in der Friedensphilosophie Immanuel Kants" in Hauke Brunkhorst (ed) *Einmischung Erwünscht? Menschenrechte und Bewaffnete Intervention* (Frankfurt: Suhrkamp, 1998).

———. "From Nation-State to Global State or the Decline of Democracy" *Constellations* 13 (2006), 465–484.

Mittelman, James H. (ed). *Globalization: Critical Reflections* (Boulder: Lynne Rienner, 1996).

Morgan, Glyn. *The Idea of a European Superstate: Public Justification and European Integration* (Princeton, NJ: Princeton University Press, 2005).

Morgenthau, Hans J. *Politics Among Nations: The Struggle for Power and Peace* (New York: Alfred Knopf, 1954, 2ⁿᵈ ed).

Mustill, Lord Justice. "The New *Lex Mercatoria*: The First Twenty-Five Years" *Arbitration International* 4 (1988).

Neumann, Franz L. *The Rule of Law: Political Theory and the Legal System in Modern Society* (Leamington Spa, UK: 1986 [1936]).

———. *Behemoth: The Structure and Practice of National Socialism, 1933–1944* (New York: Oxford University Press, 1944).

———. *The Democratic and Authoritarian State* (New York: Free Press, 1957).

———. *The Rule of Law Under Siege: Selected Essays of Franz L. Neumann and Otto Kirchheimer* (Berkeley: University of California Press, 1996).

Neunreither, Karlheinz. "Subsidiarity as a Guiding Principle for European Community Activities" *Government and Opposition* 28 [1993], 206–220.

Niesen, Peter, and Herberoth, Benjamin (eds). *Anarchie der kommunikativen Freiheit. Jürgen Habermas und die Theorie der internationalen Politik* (Frankfurt: Suhrkamp, 2007).

Nonet, Philippe, and Selznick, Philip. *Law and Society in Transition: Toward Responsive Law* (New York: Harper & Row, 1978).

Offe, Claus. *Contradictions of the Welfare State* (Cambridge: MIT Press, 1987).

Passerin d'Entreves, Maurizio. *The Political Philosophy of Hannah Arendt* (New York: Routledge, 1994).

Pease, Donald, and Goold, William. "The New GSP: Fair Trade with the Third World" *World Policy Journal* 2 (1985), 351–366.

Pensky, Max (ed). *Globalizing Critical Theory* (Lanham: Rowman & Littlefield, 2005).

Peters, Bernhard. *Die Integration moderner Gesellschaften* (Frankfurt: Suhrkamp, 1993).

Picciotto, Sol. "The Control of Transnational Capital and the Democratisation of the International State" *Journal of Law & Society* 15 (1988), 58–76.

———. *International Business Taxation: A Study in the Internationalization of Business Regulation* (London: Weidenfeld and Nicolson, 1992).

Preeg, Ernest. *Traders in a Brave New World* (Chicago: University of Chicago Press, 1995).

Purvis, Nigel. "Critical Legal Studies in Public International Law," *Harvard International Law Journal* 32 (1991).

Raynauld, A., and Vidal, J. *Labor Standards and International Competitiveness: A Comparative Analysis of Developing and Industrialized Countries* (Cheltenham: Edward Elgar, 1998).

Raz, Joseph. "The Rule of Law and Its Virtue" in Jospeh Raz *The Authority of Law* (Oxford: Clarendon, 1979), pp. 210–229.

Reinicke, Wolfgang. *Global Public Policy: Governing Without Government?* (Washington, D.C.: Brookings Institute, 1998).

Rosenau, James. "Governance, Order, and Change in World Politics" in James Rosenau and Ernst-Otto Czempiel *Governance Without Government: Order and Change in World Politics* (Cambridge: Cambridge University Press, 1992), pp. 1–29.

Rosenfeld, Michel. "Law as Discourse: Bridging the Gap Between Democracy and Rights" *Harvard Law Review* 108 (1995).

———. "Habermas' Call for Cosmopolitan Constitutional Patriotism in an Age of Global Terror" *Constellations* 14 (2007), 159–181.

Rosett, Arthur. "Unification, Restatement, Codification and Reform in International Commercial Law" *American Journal of Comparative Law* 39 (1992), 403–416.

Rothstein, R. "The Global Hiring Wall" *American Prospect* 17 (1994), 55–61.

Sassen, Saskia. *Losing Control?: Sovereignty in an Age of Globalization* (New York: Columbia University Press, 1996).

Scheuerman, William E. *Between the Norm and the Exception: The Frankfurt School and the Rule of Law* (Cambridge, USA: MIT Press, 1994).

———. "The Rule of Law and the Welfare State: Towards a New Synthesis" *Politics and Society* 22 (1994), 195–213.

————. *Carl Schmitt: The End of Law* (Lanham, MD: Rowman & Littlefield, 1999).

————. *Liberal Democracy and the Social Acceleration of Time* (Baltimore: Johns Hopkins University Press, 2004).

Schlechtriem, Peter. *Uniform Sales Law: The UN Convention on Contracts for the International Sale of Goods* (Vienna: Manzsche Verlags und Universitätsbibliothek, 1986).

Schmalz-Bruns, Rainer. "Deliberativer Supranationalismus; demokratisches Regieren jenseits des Nationalstaats" *Zeitschrift für Internationale Beziehungen* 6 (1999), 184–244.

Schmid, Thomas (ed). *Befreiung von falscher Arbeit: Thesen zum garantierenten Mindesteinkommen* (Berlin: Wagenbach, 1986).

Schmitt, Carl. *Völkerrechtliche Grossraumordnung mit Interventionsverbot für raumfremde Mächte* (Berlin: Deutscher Rechtsverlag, 1939).

————. "Die Raumrevolution" *Das Reich* (29 September 1940), 3.

————. "Reich und Raum. Elemente eines neuen Völkerrechts" *Zeitschrift der Akademie fuer Deutsches Recht* 7 (1940), 201–202.

————. "Das Meer gegen das Land" *Das Reich* (9 March 1941), 17–18.

————. "Raum and Grossraum im Völkerrecht" *Zeitschrift fuer Völkerrecht* 24 (1941), 145–149.

————. *Verfassungsrechtliche Aufsätze aus den Jahren 1924–1954* (Berlin: Duncker & Humblot, 1973).

Schmitter, Phillip. "The Future of Democracy: A Matter of Scale?" *Social Research* 66 (1999), 933–958.

Schneiderman, David. "Investment Rules and the Rule of Law" *Constellations* 8 (2001), 521–537.

Shapiro, Ian, and Hacker-Cordon, Casiano (eds). *Democracy's Edges* (Cambridge: Cambridge University Press, 2000).

Shklar, Judith N. *Legalism: Law, Morals, and Political Trials* (Cambridge, MA: Harvard University Press, 1986).

Sinclair, Timothy. "Passing Judgment: Credit Rating Processes as Regulatory Mechanisms of Governance in the Emerging World Order" *Review of International Political Economy* 1 (1994), 514–538.

de Sousa Santos, Boaventura. "The Postmodern Transition: Law and Politics" in Austin Sarat and Thomas Kearns (eds) *The Fate of Law* (Ann Arbor: University of Michigan, 1993).

Stirk, Peter. *Critical Theory, Politics and Society: An Introduction* (London: Pinter, 2000).

Stopford, John, and Strange, Susan. *Rival States, Rival Firms: Competition for World Market Shares* (Cambridge: Cambridge University Press, 1991).

Strange, Susan. *Casino Capitalism* (New York: Blackwell, 1980).

————. *The Retreat of the State: The Diffusion of Power in the World Economy* (Cambridge: Cambridge University Press, 1996).

Suleiman, E. N. (ed). *Parliaments and Parliamentarians in Democratic Politics* (New York: Holmes and Meier, 1986).

Tamanaha, Brian Z. *On the Rule of Law: History, Politics, Theory* (Cambridge: Cambridge University Press, 2004).

Tapiola, K. "The Importance of Standards and Corporate Responsibilities: The Role of Voluntary Corporate Codes of Conduct" *OECD Conference on the Role of International Investments in Development: Corporate Responsibilities and the OECD Guidelines for Multinational Enterprises* (Paris: OECD, 1995).

Teubner, Gunther. *Standards und Direktiven in Generalklauseln* (Frankfurt: Athenaeum, 1971).

————(ed). *Law Without a State* (Aldershot, UK: Dartmouth, 1997).

Turley, J. " 'When in Rome': Multinational Misconduct and the Presumption Against Territoriality" *Northwestern University Law Review* 84 (1999), 598–664.

Unger, Roberto M. *Law in Modern Society* (New York: Free Press, 1976).

van den Berg, Albert. *International Dispute Resolution: Towards an International Arbitration Culture* (Hague: Kluwer, 1998).

Van Wezel Stone, Katherine. "Labour in the Global Economy" in William Bratton, Joseph McCahery, and Sol Picciotto (eds) *International Regulatory Competition and Coordination* (Oxford: Clarendon, 1996), pp. 443–476.

von Schomberg, Rene and Baynes, Kenneth (eds). *Discourse and Democracy: Essays on Habermas' Between Facts and Norms* (Albany, NY: SUNY Press, 2002).

Wallach, Lori, and Sforza, Michelle. *Whose Trade Organization? Corporate Globalization and the Erosion of Democracy* (Washington, D.C.: Public Citizen, 1999).

Waters, Malcolm. *Globalization* (New York: Routledge, 1995).

Weber, Max. *Economy and Society, Vols. I-II* (Berkeley: University of California, 1979).

Whelan, Frederick. "Prologue: Democratic Theory and the Boundary Problem" in J. Roland Pennock and John W. Chapman (eds) *Liberal Democracy* (New York: New York University Press, 1983).

White, Stephen K. *The Recent Work of Jürgen Habermas: Reason, Justice, & Modernity* (Cambridge: Cambridge University Press, 1988).

Wiener, Jarrod. *Globalization and the Harmonization of Law* (London: Pinter, 1999).

Wiggershaus, Rolf. *The Frankfurt School: Its History, Theories and Political Significance* (Cambridge, USA: MIT Press, 1998).

Williams, Heather. "Mobile Capital and Transborder Labor Rights Mobilization" *Politics & Society* 27 (1999) 139–166.

Young, Iris Marion. *Justice and the Politics of Difference* (Princeton: Princeton University, 1990).

———. *Inclusion and Democracy* (Oxford: Oxford University Press, 2000).

———. "Modest Reflections on Hegemony and Global Democracy" *Theoria* 103 (2004), 1–14.

Zacher, Mark W. *Governing Global Networks* (Cambridge: Cambridge University Press, 1995).

Zolo, Danilio. *Cosmopolis: Prospects for World Community* (Cambridge: Polity Press, 1997).

Zürn, Michael. *Regieren jenseits des Nationalstaates* (Frankfurt: Suhrkamp, 1998).

Index